Neil Bracht
editor

Health
Promotion
at the
Community
Level

SAGE SOURCEBOOKS FOR THE HUMAN SERVICES SERIES 15

SAGE PUBLICATIONS
The International Professional Publishers
Newbury Park   London   New Delhi

For information address:

SAGE Publications, Inc.
2455 Teller Road
Newbury Park, California 91320

SAGE Publications Ltd.
6 Bonhill Street
London EC2A 4PU
United Kingdom

SAGE Publications India Pvt. Ltd.
M-32 Market
Greater Kailash I
New Delhi 110 048 India

Printed in the United States of America

Library of Congress Cataloging-in-Publication Data

Main entry under title:

Health promotion at the community level / edited by Neil Bracht.
    p. cm. — (Sage sourcebooks for the human services ; vol. 15)
    Includes bibliographical references.
    ISBN 0-8039-3858-6 (C). — ISBN 0-8039-3859-4 (P)
    1. Health promotion.   2. Community health services—Citizen
participation. I. Bracht, Neil F. II. Series: Sage sourcebooks
for the human services series ; v. 15.
RA427.8H494   1990
362.1'0425—dc20   90-39607
                                                 CIP

FIRST PRINTING, 1990

Sage Production Editor: Diane S. Foster

CONTENTS

Unnecessary death and disability can be prevented—and better health can be maintained—only through a partnership that involves the serious commitment of individual citizens, the communities in which they live, the employers for whom they work, voluntary agencies, and health professionals. Government agencies at all levels must encourage and bolster their efforts. (U.S. Department of Health and Human Services, *Healthy People: Report of the Surgeon General*, 1974)

FOREWORD

LESTER BRESLOW

A modern movement termed *health promotion* has emerged out of the historical need for a fundamental change in strategy to achieve and maintain health. During the initial era of public health, concern about communicable diseases appropriately dominated thinking. That led to the "cleanup" campaigns of the nineteenth century, and later to the discovery of microbiologic agents of disease and development of means for their control. Breaking the chain of infection became the focus of attention, later supplemented by strengthening people's resistance to the effects of microbes. Environmental measures were clearly of great importance: sewage disposal, water treatment, pasteurization of milk, food protection, and avoidance of crowding. These actions, directed at preventing the spread of infectious agents and bolstered by immunizations against specific diseases, proved remarkably effective against the major health problems of the day.

But another day has brought new health problems, a new system responsible for their origin, and a new set of requirements for their control. The current major problems, mainly the chronic diseases of middle and later life, arise out of conditions to which people are exposed when they enter modern industrialized life and their response to those conditions: plenty of calories, especially in the form of fats; lessened demands for physical exertion but heightened demands on the psyche; easy access to tobacco and excessive amounts of alcohol; and motor vehicle transport. Interaction of people with that new milieu constitutes the system that has generated present-day epidemics such as cardiovascular disease, cancer, chronic respiratory disease, cirrhosis, trauma, and diabetes.

Again, scientific progress has disclosed enough about the nature of the current human-environment-disease system for the social organization of health advance. Breaking the chain of infection and building human resistance to it will no longer suffice. It has become necessary to establish health-protective social policies concerning those aspects of life in industrialized societies that seriously jeopardize health, and to help people cope with such conditions of life so long as they exist.

In former times, social action against principal health problems consisted largely of erecting physical barriers to the transmission of disease agents and providing immunizations. It also included attention to the medical needs of mothers and children. Education of people concerning personal hygiene, such as hand washing and sputum control, and other aspects of health played some role. The situation, however, induced action mainly toward environmental protection.

Now recognition has grown that people's behavior in their present milieu and the conditions of life that influence behavior, rather than direct physical exposure to biological disease agents, constitute the major health issue. The social environment—especially access and encouragement to indulge in tobacco, excessive alcohol and calories, and too little physical exercise—has become more significant for health nowadays than physical environmental hazards. That is the reason for the profound shift in health strategy.

Progress in the new situation has been under way for some time. Tobacco and hard liquor use is declining, exercise is trendy in some circles, seat-belt use is up. Not all signs are favorable, however. Obesity continues at a high level and even appears to be increasing. Some segments of the population lag seriously in overcoming behavior that is adverse to health. For example, people with low educational levels continue smoking cigarettes, and their children also become addicted to nicotine. Corresponding to the generally positive behavior changes, along with some medical advances, coronary heart disease mortality has fallen sharply and the lung cancer epidemic has reached its peak among men. People have started learning, as individuals, to cope with the conditions of life that induce these and other principal diseases. More important for the long term, they have initiated social changes to create a more healthful milieu in which to live. Thus television advertising of cigarettes has been banned nationally, smoking is curtailed on airplanes and prohibited in many places, and some states have increased taxes on tobacco products as a measure against their use.

Health promotion is thus advancing. This book is designed to guide professionals in both the health and community organization fields as well as interested citizens in their actions to improve community health. Its significance lies in its potential to accelerate favorable trends and open additional ones. A far cry from earlier efforts aimed directly at influencing individuals to adopt healthier behavior patterns, the emphasis here is on the community. As editor, Neil Bracht has sought deliberately to bring together what has been learned in recent years about community organization process and community intervention strategies, and to demonstrate the applicability of this knowledge to the health field.

In so doing, he gives recognition to the fact that while individuals act in ways that affect health, the community largely determines their actions. Hence the focus here is on communitywide health promotion. Norms are established at the community level and transmitted to individuals as strong guidance. Realization of that relationship, and building health promotion strategy clearly geared to it, should help overcome the lingering resistance to health promotion as "blaming the victim." Social action is needed for health promotion. It must be directed principally at the social situations that influence people's health-related behavior rather than at the physical environment that impinges on health without the intermediary of individual behavior. While the task of perfecting the physical environment for health is by no means complete, the new health environment requires greater attention to such social forces as the extensive advertising of alcohol, widespread portrayal of alcohol use in films and television as "the thing to do," inadequate constraint of driving while intoxicated, and low taxes on alcoholic beverages. These circumstances exert a profound effect on health.

This volume offers substantial help to those interested in the community approach to health promotion. It reflects the considerable knowledge gained in the Stanford Five City Project, the Minnesota Heart Health Program, and the Pawtucket and North Karelia experiences in which several of the authors sharpened their expertise. It outlines principles and practical advice concerning important aspects of organizing for communitywide health promotion, such as how to use local media while operating within budget constraints, patterns of academic-community relationships, participation of local health professionals, implications of work-site health promotion experience for other organized groups, involving people in evaluation, and institutionalization of efforts initiated from outside the community. These and other issues addressed here immediately confront those who undertake health promotion in the community. Three programs in underserved communities are insightfully described to indicate the special problems in those segments of the population.

This timely book makes a valuable contribution to the field.

ACKNOWLEDGMENTS

The community health promotion concepts and experiences reported in this volume owe much to the research and demonstration support provided by the National Institutes of Health. The National Heart, Lung and Blood Institute's funding of the three heart disease prevention projects in the United States (Minnesota, Pawtucket, and Stanford) yielded more than 10 years of collaborative effort in community implementation by investigators associated with the projects. Dr. Elaine Stone (NHLBI) facilitated many scientific exchanges. This foundation of collective work provided the motivation to develop this book.

While researchers associated with the three community demonstrations mentioned above have made major contributions to the content of this volume, more than half of the contributing authors bring research and community implementation experience from non-heart health projects. The book draws upon and reports on the larger arena of health promotion that is expanding nationally and internationally.

Work on the manuscript began in the fall of 1987 during a single-quarter research leave from the University of Minnesota. In northern and western Europe, I was able to begin to analyze and compare experiences in Minnesota and related U.S. projects with several European health demonstrations. I was fortunate to be able to collaborate on the implementation of the Cancer Prevention Project in Stockholm, Sweden, with faculty of the Karolinska Institute. Additional visits and consultations at Lund University's Community Health Sciences Department at Malmo, the Nordic School of Public Health, Gotenborg, and Heartbeat Wales in Cardiff helped me to learn more about cross-cultural implementation experiences. A visit to the North Karelia Project in Finland, now in its seventeenth year of operation, reinforced the importance of lay and community involvement, as did participation in the European Healthy Cities Symposium in Pecs, Hungary. Work with staff of the WHO Health Promotion Office in Copenhagen, including attendance at the Second International Conference on Health Promotion in Adelaide, Australia, broadened my appreciation of the social and policy context for health promotion. While there are differences in the social and political structures of European, Western Pacific, and North American societies, the processes of community analysis, community activation, implementation, and diffusion show many similarities.

In the Division of Epidemiology at the University of Minnesota School of Public Health, I have been able to work with and learn from a stimulating interdisciplinary group of faculty and community staff. To my home department in the Graduate School of Social Work, I am grateful for the released time that enabled me to serve as director of community organization for the Minnesota Heart Health Program during the last 10 years.

Collaborative opportunities with the Minnesota Department of Health, especially staff in the Division of Health Promotion and Education, deepened my understanding of the adaptations required to develop health promotion programs in small towns and rural areas. Informal discussions with staff of the Kaiser Community Studies Program were helpful as well.

A critical contribution to this book, mostly unknown to those who gave it, has come from the input of numerous citizens' health boards and groups in communities where I have been involved directly or have visited. Their perspectives have been invaluable to me in formulating successful citizen participation strategies, including work with special populations and ethnic minority groups.

As the design for the book was taking shape, it was fortuitous that progress on the manuscript coincided with intensive planning for the Community Intervention Trial for Smoking Cessation (COMMIT), an 11-community study in the United States and Canada funded by the National Cancer Institute (NCI). The director of the project's 22-member investigator group, Dr. Terry Pechacek, was interested in having a guide available to local staff in these cities. This interest prompted a further collaboration among NCI, myself, and the contributing authors to produce this volume more quickly. Many of the concepts, analyses, protocols, and training materials produced by this experienced NCI investigator group have found their way into this book. Several members of this project's Steering Committee contributed to chapters. The discussions and "debates" of the COMMIT Steering Committee meetings challenged and sharpened my ideas.

I wish to express my gratitude for the many editorial and secretarial support services that made the completion of this text possible, especially the editorial revisions of Mary Alice Schumaker. I am also indebted to the contributing authors, without whose assistance this book could never have been produced.

I would like to acknowledge the many contributions to this book by the researchers involved in the Community Intervention Trial for Smoking Cessation. First, at the National Cancer Institute:

Joseph W. Cullen, Ph.D., STCP Coordinator
Terry F. Pechacek, Ph.D., Project Officer
Margaret E. Mattson, Ph.D., Evaluation Director
Marc Manley, M.D., M.P.H., Medical Officer, STCP
William R. Lynn, Public Health Adviser
Lamar F. Neville, M.S.W., Assistant to the Project Officer
David P. Byar, M.D., Biometry Branch, DCPC
Mitchell Gail, M.D., Ph.D., Biostatistics Branch, DCE
Sylvan Green, M.D., Biometry Branch, DCPC
Donald Corle, M.S., Biometry Branch, DCPC
Laurence S. Freeman, Biometry Branch, DCPC

At the Coordinating Center:
Information Management Services, Inc.
Janis Beach, Principal Investigator
Carol Giffen, D.V.M., Co-Principal Investigator

Thanks to the research institutions involved and their principal investigators:

Kaiser Foundation Research Institute (Berkeley, California):
    Lawrence Wallack, Dr.P.H.
Waterloo Research Institute (Waterloo, Ontario, Canada)
    Allen Best, Ph.D.
University of Iowa (Iowa City, Iowa): Paul Pomrehn, M.D.
University of Massachusetts Medical School (Worcester, Massachusetts):
    Judith K. Ockene, Ph.D.

University of Medicine and Dentistry of New Jersey (Newark, New Jersey):
Norman Hymowitz, Ph.D.

Lovelace Medical Foundation (Albuquerque, New Mexico):
Neill F. Piland, Dr.P.H.

American Health Foundation (New York, New York):
Mario A. Orlandi, Ph.D., M.P.H.

Roswell Park Memorial Institute (Buffalo, New York):
Michael Cummings, Ph.D., M.P.H.

Research Triangle Institute (Research Triangle Park, North Carolina):
Tyler D. Hartwell, Ph.D.

Oregon Research Institute (Eugene, Oregon):
Edward Lichtenstein, Ph.D.

Fred Hutchinson Cancer Research Center (Seattle, Washington):
Maureen M. Henderson, M.D.

Thanks also to the COMMIT Steering Committee chairperson, Erwin Bettinghaus, Ph.D., of Michigan State University, and to these other coinvestigators and/or project directors:

Kathy Corbett, Ph.D.
Paul Pomrehn, M.D.
Lawrence A. Meinert, M.D.
Alfred McAlister, Ph.D.
Robert H. Shipley, Ph.D.
Beti Thompson, Ph.D.
Martin S. Taylor, Ph.D.
Glorian Sorensen, Ph.D., M.P.H.
Lawrence Berger, M.D., M.P.H.
Russell Sciandra, M.A.
Russell E. Glasgow, Ph.D.

Neil Bracht
Minneapolis, Minnesota

INTRODUCTION

NEIL BRACHT

This book has been developed to assist a wide range of professional and lay leaders as they undertake efforts to mobilize community resources and citizen energy for communitywide health promotion, environmental protection, and disease prevention programs. The reported experiences from numerous community health demonstrations are intended to contribute to an understanding of what is required to implement community-based prevention programs successfully. One key message emanating from these demonstrations is that new cooperative partnerships that include representatives from government, industry, labor, education, religion, media, and medicine are necessary to realize community goals.

While most of what has been published about recent community demonstrations focuses on risk-factor intervention results and channels of effective delivery and diffusion (e.g., schools), the health promotion literature also reflects an increasing recognition that the success of population-based intervention depends, in large part, on the effective application of community organization theory and principles. Most of the North American, European, and Western Pacific community intervention studies use elements of the community organization process in order to facilitate community analysis and citizen activation, engage organizational resources, and increase community ownership and control. The active involvement of the community, its leaders, and its organizations is generally assumed to be a necessary ingredient for successful populationwide strategies.

Comprehensive community health approaches typically combine community organization and citizen involvement principles with tested behavioral strategies of life-style and/or policy intervention. Contributors to this volume have expertise in both *community organization process* and *community intervention strategies*. An important motivation in the development of this edited volume was to illustrate the necessary integration between these.

The overall rationale for the community approach as presented in this book has roots not only in public health practice but in a number of other disciplines. Community-based approaches arise from the "pooling" of theory from many disciplines, ranging from biomedicine to communications. Developing disciplines such as social marketing, for example, borrow concepts, strategies, and techniques from their commercial counterparts for the promotion of ideas and behavior rather than products. Contributions from the emerging science of behavioral epidemiology when combined with the techniques of community analysis provide a substantial foundation for accurate community diagnosis. Other biomedical and epidemiological studies contribute an understanding of disease development and distribution in total populations. Application of community and behavioral change theories to health and disease areas are key to designing effective life-style change programs. Strategies derived from diffusion theory, including the uses of media, are central to a comprehensive strategy of health promotion. Community development and community organization methods add the perspective of "empowering" communities and building local capacity for social and health improvements.

Three themes unify these several disciplinary views about the process of community-based social and behavioral change. These themes are repeated throughout the chapters of this book. First is the emphasis on powerful social forces influencing individuals' behavior—the idea that behavior is formed and influenced by the dominant culture as experienced in myriad social relations in the context of the community. Communities shape individuals' behavior both symbolically and tangibly, transmitting values and norms. As systems of exchange and influence, communities establish opportunities for people to behave in some ways but not in others.

A second common theme is that communities themselves may be mobilized to act as change agents to achieve social and behavioral outcomes. Conceptually, mobilizing communities to act as change agents means that they both give legitimacy to values and norms for desirable behavior and make the social and physical environment more conducive for individuals to act. Practically, mobilizing means engaging multiple community networks of public and private organizations and special interest groups to channel and coordinate their resources (personnel, time, money, goods, services) in a broad range of interpersonal, group, and mass communication strategies. While each community is unique, the processes to be followed in the analysis, design, organizing, implementation, and diffusion of programs are similar.

The third theme is that early and sustained participation by community members and leaders is necessary for the realization of community ownership and program maintenance. Special sensitivities and applications are required in adapting health promotion technology to ethnic minority communities and special population groups. In Part V of the book, selected special population case studies are presented to provide the reader with concrete illustrations of how such programs can be designed and carried out.

The community health promotion approach, when combined with supplementary clinical and/or individual approaches (such as smoking cessation clinics), has a number of advantages over other approaches:

- The burden of chronic or environmentally induced disease cuts across most sectors of the community. The causes of these diseases are complex and rooted for the most part in cultural phenomena.
- Community approaches affect the social milieu of individuals and are oriented toward changing the norms, values, and policies surrounding behavior.
- Community approaches are better integrated into the total community, since interventions are built into existing community structures.
- Community approaches better ensure longevity of change because the social context of behavior proscribes certain activities and local ownership generates continuing responsibility.
- Community approaches are generally more comprehensive and ensure better allocation and coordination of scarce health resources.
- Community approaches reflect shared responsibility for health and move away from individual strategies only or victim blaming. Community approaches actually augment individuals' capacity for change.

Do all health problems or social issues require a communitywide, comprehensive approach? Easy answers to this question are not readily available. Community representatives in concert with public health, social, medical, and legislative leaders and others are probably best able to make such a determination. The current AIDS situation illustrates the importance of mobilizing communitywide concern and energies to reduce the spread of disease. Like AIDS, health promotion and lifestyle change programs are not immune from ethical considerations or questions of values and social equity. Increasingly, these questions are receiving attention and discussion in the literature, but they lie outside the more limited purpose of this volume.

Even when communitywide strategies are recommended as a result of community analysis and diagnosis, variations in community resources and readiness may inhibit a more comprehensive approach. Circumstances may require modifications and compromises to "ideal" elements of a communitywide approach. This, of course, is already happening in smaller communities with restricted resources. Health promotion as a relatively new scientific field will undoubtedly undergo many transformations in both theory and practice.

Proponents of a community approach emphasize how local values and norms shape individual attitudes and behaviors. Despite the lip service paid to the importance of changes within the social milieu, community health demonstrations, for the most part, continue to measure individual behavior change. This is partially due to the lack of empirically tested theories that explain the mechanisms of broad social and cultural change. The literature that does exist is scattered and therefore not familiar to many in the field. It seemed appropriate, then, that a synthesis and conceptual framework for community change be presented early in this book. Thus Part I, following an introduction to contemporary health promotion issues by Lawrence Green and John Raeburn, focuses on communitywide health change. In Chapter 2, Beti Thompson and Susan Kinne review and synthesize the theoretical underpinnings of social change and the mechanisms employed to influence change in both social systems and individuals. Various levels of change and interactions among these levels are identified.

Following the explication of the theoretical framework for social change, the next chapter is more pragmatic. How can health professionals and community organizers help make change happen in a community? In short, what are the guiding principles for stimulating community change? In Chapter 3, Neil Bracht and Lee Kingsbury adapt the generally accepted principles and techniques of community organization to program-specific health promotion projects. These authors develop a five-stage model applicable to most health projects. Lee Kingsbury as a contributing author adds a state public health department perspective to her extensive experience in applied urban and rural community projects.

This application of the community organization approach (sometimes referred to as community development) to public health education efforts is not new. As mentioned above, organized community effort is basic to public health philosophy and practice and was included in Winslow's classic definition of public health. An extensive literature search confirms that organizing citizen groups for planned social change is a widely used approach in communitywide improvement efforts. Results from reported case studies, along with the plethora of current communitywide intervention projects in North America, Western Europe, and elsewhere, are providing evidence of the feasibility of combining traditional community organization and citizen participation strategies with the new technologies associated with social marketing, social learning, and diffusion theories.

In Part II, community analysis and activation processes are presented. Steps in assessing and monitoring community services, leadership, and readiness are presented in Chapter 4. Bo Haglund brings to this multiauthored chapter his extensive experience in Sweden, where the first large urban cancer prevention project is under way in Stockholm County. Rita Weisbrod and Neil Bracht add their experience in community research studies. The results of an extensive literature review on citizen participation are presented by Neil Bracht and Julie Gleason in Chapter 5, including tested strategies of citizen involvement drawn primarily from the ten-year Minnesota Heart Health Program. This content builds on the principles of community organization as outlined in Chapter 3. In Chapter 6, Maurice Mittelmark provides perspective on the practical aspects of balancing research and evaluation requirements with the needs of the community and the kind of partnership arrangements required. Many demonstrations with complex evaluation components are generated by university-based researchers. Special problems arise in these joint relationships, and Mittelmark offers insights from his extensive background in applied research. Basic questions and approaches to specific evaluation strategies are discussed in a later chapter by Phyllis Pirie.

Part III focuses on commonly used and validated communitywide intervention strategies. Contributing authors in this section have considerable experience in community applications. June Flora and Diana Cassady, associated with the Stanford Heart Disease Prevention Project, explain the roles and functions of media in Chapter 7. Media involvement is placed here as a logical extension of the community activation process presented in Part II.

Glorian Sorensen, Russell Glasgow, and Kitty Corbett are associated with the National Cancer Institute's 11-community heavy smoking project, COMMIT. Their rich background in promoting health programs in work sites and other community organizations is reflected in Chapter 8. Russell Luepker and Lennart Råstam, two physicians, combine to discuss in Chapter 9 some strategies that have proven effective in work with medical and related health practitioners in both the United States and Sweden.

Several important principles enunciated in the early sections of the book are developed further in Part IV, which focuses on evaluation approaches, long-term maintenance, and wider diffusion of community health programs. Chapter 10, by Phyllis Pirie, addresses evaluation issues, with emphasis on asking the "right" questions. She draws on ten years of education evaluation in the Minnesota study. In Chapter 11, Craig Lefebvre reviews strategies to maintain programs. His work builds on the Pawtucket Heart Health Project in Rhode Island, which comprises special efforts to reach low-income and minority populations that reside there. Guy Parcel, Cheryl Perry, and Wendell Taylor collaborate in Chapter 12 to discuss new strategies for wider geographic and program dissemination. They have been associated with projects that have large school-based education and behavioral change goals. Local community efforts can help shape regional and national policy adaptations. Here, diffusion theory is integrated with examples from a school-based program.

Several applied community demonstrations (case studies) emphasizing multi-intervention strategies adapted to minority communities and/or special populations are presented in Part V. The case studies were specifically written for this book and emphasize the processes involved in adapting approaches, messages, and interventions. These studies reinforce principles discussed in the preceding chapters. Also, various guides and sample plans to assist organizers in program design, implementation, and evaluation may be found in several of the chapters of this book.

The plethora of community health interventions now under way (the Health Promotion Institute, Wales, now lists an information base for 135 programs in 30 countries) suggests widely differing goals, values, and community-based strategies. While no single text or guide can possibly meet all the expectations of such a diverse field of interest, an effort has been made to avoid program exclusiveness and theoretical parochialism by using multiple authors who can incorporate the experiences of several different projects, both national and international.

Community health approaches are not new. What is new is what has been learned from numerous demonstrations in the last 15-20 years. This volume reports on the progress of these recent years. We hope that it advances the development of broad-based community health programs and the larger "health for all" goals envisioned by the World Health Organization.

Part I

COMMUNITYWIDE CHANGE: THEORY AND PRACTICE

Chapter 1

CONTEMPORARY DEVELOPMENTS IN HEALTH PROMOTION
Definitions and Challenges

LAWRENCE W. GREEN
JOHN RAEBURN

Until quite recently there had been little effort to seek consensus on a definition of health promotion. A U.S. federal definition was first presented for comment at the Ninth International Conference on Health Education (Green, 1979). A European working group for the World Health Organization (WHO) produced a discussion document on health promotion concepts and principles (WHO Regional Office for Europe, 1984). Nutbeam's (1986) glossary of health promotion terms contributed to the consensus effort. The First International Conference on Health Promotion in Ottawa concisely captured the essence of the earlier definitions by defining health promotion as "the process of enabling people to increase control over and to improve their health" (WHO, 1986, p. iii).

Reports and discussions on health education and health promotion policies in Third World countries differ from some of the health promotion views in industrialized nations (Green, 1986b; Ottawa Working Group, 1986). The relationship of "healthy public policy" to health promotion was further analyzed and elaborated at the Second International Conference on Health Promotion in Adelaide (WHO, 1988).

AUTHORS' NOTE: This chapter is based on Green and Raeburn, "Health Promotion: What Is It?" *Health Promotion: An International Journal*, 1988, adapted with permission of Oxford University Press, and on a presentation given at the XIII World Conference on Health Education, Houston, TX, August 1988.

From the above meetings and reports, two theoretical and sometimes ideological perspectives on health promotion can be contrasted. The first emphasizes political and sociological or "system" factors in health. The second emphasizes personal and small group decision making, psychological factors, and health education methods. An integration of these viewpoints appears to prevail in actual policies and practice, though some advocates and practitioners continue to defend or to push for one of the more polar views on the health promotion spectrum. Because diverse interests and constituencies cohabit the world of health promotion, there is a need for concepts that transcend and integrate the wide variety of viewpoints. This chapter suggests a set of such concepts. We begin by considering why definitions of health promotion are important and why they evoke controversy.

THE CONTROVERSY OVER DEFINITIONS

Some of the answers to these questions must come from the fact that health promotion is one of the first and few (along with public health) truly interdisciplinary enterprises (not to say professions) in health that feels genuinely emancipated from the domination of medicine. While medicine has its part to play in health promotion, it represents but one aspect of something larger. Health promotion does not take its primary impetus from medicine or the medical model. This departure from the security and hegemony of medicine has left an ideological vacuum, and nature abhors a vacuum. Ideologues, professionals, interest groups, and representatives of numerous disciplines have attempted to appropriate the field for themselves. Health and education professionals, behavioral and social scientists, public administrators, town planners, futurists, holistic health and self-care advocates, liberals, conservatives, voluntary associations, funding agencies, governments, community groups, and many others all want something from health promotion, all want to contribute something, and all bring their own orientation to bear on it. No wonder those engaged in this developmental venture have differing opinions and all become uneasy when definitions seem to prescribe the future of health promotion.

Besides the variety of professional, scientific, and commercial views produced by these multiple groups, a theoretical and sometimes ideological division—or, more accurately, spectrum—cuts across the field. Broadly, this can be characterized as the "individual versus the system" debate. On one side, stereotypes of the individual school associate it with a history of educational, mass media, interpersonal communications, group dynamics, community development, and intraorganizational change strategies. At the extreme end of this side of the continuum are cognitive psychologists, behaviorists, and those insisting on a highly individualist concept of life-style. This approach has recently ascended, with its strong identification with research in the behavioral sciences and its general political appeal to governments concerned with containing medical care costs and to commercial marketing of health promotion services and products. Most governments adopting a health promotion policy have based their approach on the identification of a finite number of life-style areas—such as smoking, alcohol abuse, diet, and exercise—shown to account for the major causes of disease and disability in their societies. These behavioral risk factors can be quantified and specifically targeted for strategic planning.

Some critics of this approach advocate a system view, where *system* stands for the social, economic, political, institutional, cultural, legislative, industrial, and physical-environmental milieus in which behavior takes place (e.g., Minkler, 1989). The advocates of the system view argue that interventions aimed at changing the behavior of individuals are inadequate because the system is a more powerful and pervasive determinant of behavior and of health than decisions made by individuals operating in a supposed free-choice situation. Also, say the system advocates, a focus on individual behavior is too appealing to conservative governments; it allows them to evade their responsibility for social change. It also tends to lead to a brand of health promotion most suitable for the middle class and to charges of victim blaming, wherein ill health resulting from faulty life-styles (such as smoking) is seen as the responsibility of the individual rather than the result of the social pressures under which individuals live. As with the other side of the continuum, the systems side has its shades and variations of theory, philosophy, ideology, and strategy.

Critics of the system view argue that the life-styles of people implicated by epidemiological and medical research as responsible for a large proportion of the leading causes of death and disability are undeniably under at least some control by those at risk. To deprive them of access to the information and skills needed to take some action would be unethical. Furthermore, the system changes some seek to make unilaterally affect other aspects of life besides health, so the public will insist on having a role in the decision making about their social systems and environments. Thus we will be required to educate or persuade individuals in order to make changes in systems.

In their pure forms, the system and behavioral models represent quite different perspectives that would lead to quite different action. But we fail to find any pure cases in practice or even fully developed in policy or program plans. It seems that some of those who write or speak most passionately on behalf of either of the pure forms are not active in the real world of practice, politics, or policy. The pure forms are largely academic contrasts that have tended to create more heat than light. Though it might have seemed otherwise, few health educators or behavioral scientists in health promotion ever advocated ignoring system forces in behavior or health; few system advocates ever asserted outright that behavior was irrelevant or that individuals had no role in health promotion. The more experienced practitioners and politicians in health seek to merge these two perspectives into an integrated, total person-environment approach to health promotion, where responsibility for health is shared between individuals and systems (Green, 1986a).

Some of the debate over the definition of health promotion and the contrasting of these polar views has portrayed the American policy in health promotion as the premier example of a policy that is highly individualistic in its orientation. This characterization has face validity in the context of the American tradition of rugged individualism, suspicion of centralized government, and a consumer-driven market economy. But on closer inspection of the federal documents themselves (*Healthy People,* U.S. Department of Health and Human Services, 1974; *Objectives for the Nation,* U.S. Department of Health and Human Services, 1980; *Strategies for Promoting Health for Specific Populations,* U.S. Department of Health and Human Services, 1981/1987), one finds that the U.S. policy could be characterized as balanced, if not more systems oriented than individual change oriented. Of the 15 priorities for disease prevention and health promotion, one-third are addressed to the environment, one-third to health care systems, and one-third to behavior. Of the 226 objectives for the nation in disease prevention and health promotion, a much larger proportion are addressed to environmental and health care systems changes than to behavioral changes. Even within the behavioral risk factors identified as priorities for health promotion, a substantial number of the objectives for the nation address changes in policies, organizations, environments, and economic support for behavior.

When the argument turns to the broader conception of health promotion and the Ottawa Charter, which encompasses environment as it relates directly to health, as distinct from environment as it relates to behavior, the American policies in health promotion must be viewed in the context of the overall national strategy for disease prevention and health promotion. The number of priorities and objectives set for the physical environment under the rubric "health protection" is equal to the number for health behavior under the rubric "health promotion." Another equal number of priorities are set for preventive health services. Thus it is true that health promotion has been more narrowly defined to encompass the behavioral risk factors in U.S. policy, but this policy is inseparable from the parallel objectives in health protection and preventive health services addressing environmental and system factors in health.

HEALTH, HEALTH BEHAVIOR, AND SOCIAL CONTEXT

How we look at health promotion depends in part on the way we define *health*, at least on how the word is used in the term *health promotion*. What are we trying to promote?

The 1946 WHO definition of health as "a state of complete physical, mental and social well-being and not merely the absence of disease or infirmity" has had its share of critics, but they have largely been concerned with the notion of *complete*. The real significance of this definition came with its recognition that health is more than its physical aspects, and more than just the absence of disease. The definition viewed health as a multidimensional (holistic) phenomenon, with multiple determinants, one that can be defined by its positive (well-being) rather than negative aspects. Such a definition has difficulty finding a place in government health systems with most of their resources invested in approaches to health defined by morbidity and mortality. Holistic and positive aspects have long been integral to concepts of health in many cultures, but with the financial and knowledge control of the health systems in Western societies largely in the hands of organizations, professionals, and technological medicine, these aspects get lost in systems. No wonder one view of health promotion seeks to circumvent systems and another seeks to overhaul them.

WHO (1978) affirmed the principles behind this holistic definition of health in the Alma Ata declaration on primary health care, which especially emphasized the social dimensions of health. This declaration was made against a background of evidence that health care resources are too concentrated in centralized, professionally dominated, high-technology institutions, especially hospitals, at the expense of access to less institutional primary health care at the local, community level. According to its report, "the [Alma Ata] conference emphasized the importance of full and organized community participation and ultimate self-reliance with individuals, families and communities assuming more responsibility for their own health." This conference also has had its critics, but, again, the principal sentiments of self-reliance and fuller community participation in health matters have filtered into new policies, although to a lesser extent in practice (Green, 1986c).

The Alma Ata declaration and some of the newer policies in health promotion can be seen as a reaction against traditional Western health systems ministering to individual sick patients in clinical settings, where the professional rules supreme. Increasingly, health policy initiatives seek to work with people in the context of their everyday environments—their homes, schools, and work sites—many aspects of which condition their behavior and their health. This in turn leads to more of a bird's-eye view of environments and systems within which people live, so that social and political factors receive more emphasis and public health and policy views of health emerge as complements to the biomedical view. Along with this is a self-help trend seeking to equalize the power balance between "the people" and "professionals." Of course, what the bland repetition of these concepts and words does not convey is the power of the feeling behind many of them. These are more than sociological concepts for many people. They invoke ideologies related to people's rights, professional privilege, distribution of resources, and inequality. People who are associated with "old" or "reactionary" views have considerable feeling registered against them. We would argue, however, that any realistic view of the determinants of health and of appropriate health promotion requires a balance of individual, institutional, community, societal, and political perspectives.

The Alma Ata and Ottawa declarations insist that neither people nor health should be seen in isolation. Each is nested in systems that profoundly affect behavior and health. Health promotion must take this ecological fact into account. Such an ecological view represents a move away from the reductionist tendency of biomedical science and some applications of health education in the service of centralized, categorical, and vertical programs, to a broader systems view. This view recognizes the interaction of life-style and environment when health is being considered. In this view, the individual *and* the context are of equal account. It legitimates *both* a life-style *and* a systems approach to health promotion.

An ecological model of health promotion says that health is the product of the individual's continuous interaction and interdependence with his or her ecosphere—this is, the family, the community, the culture, the societal structure, and the physical environment. Characteristic modes of interacting over time constitute a life-style, as distinct from discrete acts or behavior. The determinants of a life-style must be seen as a combination of intrapersonal and external environmental forces, continuously interacting. In some instances, health promotion programs need to emphasize the individual or behavioral side; in others, the environmental side needs emphasis as the point of intervention. If the individual has a sense of harmony with, or a degree of mastery over, the everyday environment, then his or her health is likely to be good. But with oppression, poverty, limited opportunity, and lack of mastery, health will suffer.

Health, in the Ottawa Charter, is still given the original WHO definition of a state of complete physical, mental, and social well-being, to reach which "an individual or group must be able to identify and to realize aspirations, to satisfy needs, and to change or cope with the environment" (WHO, 1986). Such health is viewed as "a resource for everyday life," which seems to imply that it is equivalent to having sufficient energy, stamina, and physical capacity to meet the demands of daily living. Significantly, the terms *life-style* and *health education* seem to have been replaced in the charter with the concept of "developing personal and social skills through providing information, education for health and enhancing life skills." How this is similar to, or different from, what has been understood by concepts of health behavior and life-style change in the past is not clear. But, certainly, it appears that the intention of the charter is to broaden the base of health promotion beyond a personal life-style approach to a more political approach, so that policy, rather than behavior, now becomes the center of gravity. Our plea is to include *all* the dimensions relevant to health promotion, and to build on the past as well as expand into the future.

THE ROOTS OF HEALTH PROMOTION IN EARLIER DEVELOPMENTS

In looking at the past, we are aware that many threads have been woven into the pattern for health promotion as it now appears. Here, we examine these briefly to remind ourselves of past issues that will continue to exist to some extent in the future.

Besides the foregoing declarations and charters, the notable threads of development that converged to produce contemporary policies in health promotion include (a) the long-standing reliance of public health programs and agencies on health education to gain the cooperation of the public; (b) the community development and mass communications movements and technologies of the 1950s and 1960s, which converted top-down recruitment of public cooperation into grass-roots initiatives reflecting the public's enlightened self-interests; (c) the self-care, civil rights, and women's movements of the 1960s, which demanded a transfer of authority and resources to people previously beholden to others; (d) the worldwide inflation and cost containment concerns of the 1970s, which led to cutbacks in social programs and caps on expenditures for high-tech medical care; (e) the growing recognition of diminishing returns on investments in medical care and communicable disease control, at least in Western countries, and of increasing chronic diseases attributable to life-style; (f) the strengthening scientific base of social, behavioral, and educational research applied to health; and (g) the growing disillusionment and impatience of the public with conventional medical approaches to health, supplanted by more imaginative (and sometimes ephemeral) concepts encompassing social, mental, and spiritual qualities of life.

THE PURPOSES AND GOALS
OF HEALTH PROMOTION

The foregoing concepts, influences, and trends have converged in charting where health promotion is currently going. In the enthusiasm of moving rapidly beyond the past, there is a danger of needless rejection of good ideas, and of polarization into ideological camps. To achieve a synthesis of potentially conflicting elements in the "new public health," we need concepts that transcend these elements. We suggest that such a concept is at hand in the principle of *enabling*. This is a key word in the Ottawa Charter's definition of health promotion: "Health promotion is the process of enabling people to increase control over and to improve their health" (WHO, 1986). *Enabling* derives from the verb *to enable*, defined in *Webster's Ninth New Collegiate Dictionary* as "to provide with the means or opportunity . . . to make possible, practical, or easy" and "to give legal power, capacity, or sanction to." This signifies possibly the most important trend of the late 1980s, that of *people* holding power in health matters, not just institutions, officials, professionals, or technology. A potential battleground takes shape because although many administrators and professionals in the health field pay lip service to the concept of passing increased power to the community, in practice very few can actually bring themselves to do it. "We know best" is the covert, if not overt, philosophy of most health professionals. The principal purpose or raison d'être of the health promotion of the future could be seen to be the increasing transfer of control of important resources in health, notably knowledge, skills, authority, and money, to the community. What are some of the theoretical and philosophical underpinnings of the concept of enabling?

Since the Industrial Revolution in the West, sociologists and others have been writing about the destruction of natural community and the replacement of traditional social structure and cultural patterns by a "new order," one based on the values and technological advances of industrialized society (Raeburn, 1986). For most societies, viewed from an ecological perspective, their long-established traditions and structures represented an optimal person-environment adaptation, since they evolved in those settings over millennia. In these settings, many people-based systems of health care and health enhancement existed and, although by modern standards their results may not always have equaled those of Western medicine, they often worked for, and had value for, those people. In addition to community doctors, shamans, and other healers, much that pertained to health was passed from generation to generation through the medium of the family and other social and educational systems at the heart of the person's own cultural context, and many aspects of life, such as one's relationship to the land or the spirit world, would be seen as relevant to health.

Industrial societies have placed their management of health and human welfare issues into the hands of "experts," who in turn are typically associated with large, centralized bureaucracies. Thus a relatively impersonal service takes over some of the most intimate and important human concerns—birth, death, sickness, health, education, care of the elderly and disabled, to mention just a few. This is not to lay the blame at anyone's feet for this state of affairs—most of us in industrial societies have been only too willing for this process to happen, and, in many ways, the service systems approach has had impressive results. But strong sentiments and evidence that originated with the self-help movement of the 1960s hold that this process has reached, and in some cases exceeded, its limits. In those countries still coming to terms with the industrial way, there is a mounting diffidence about accepting it in its entirety.

The pendulum now seems to be swinging from a technology- and institution-based approach to health to a more people-based approach. There could hardly be a total rejection of high-technology medicine and health services—these clearly have many benefits in such areas as infectious disease control and treatment—but the search is now on for those areas in the health and human welfare domain that can be handed back to the people. It is in this context that a new era of health promotion seems to be emerging, one that uses the expertise and resources available from professionals and technicians but also involves people at the community level in a fuller and more participatory way. A potential source of tension here is the question, Who will ultimately have *control* over health promotion? On the one hand, many feel this control should go to the community; on the other, many administrators, professionals, and funding bodies may be reluctant to let this happen. But regardless of this issue, at the heart of the enabling approach to health promotion is the concept of returning power, knowledge, skills, and other resources in a range of health areas to the community—to individuals, families, and whole populations.

If this approach is accepted, three important questions arise. First, What health areas can people deal with most effectively in the context of their everyday lives? Second, What is the best way for this to happen? Third, How can public policy support the concept of enabling? These questions are obviously relative to the cultural and societal situation of each nation and community. Here, we do no more than suggest a few principles in broad terms.

To the first question, concerning what aspects of health lend themselves most readily to the enabling process, a broad lead is given by the five action areas of the Ottawa Charter—that is, health promotion action involves building healthful public policy, creating supportive environments, strengthening community action, developing personal skills, and reorienting health service.

To develop policy, widespread public awareness and consultation are necessary, together with setting up mechanisms for advocacy. For environmental change (such as town planning or protecting the environment) people can undertake their own projects or be a significant part of the planning process.

Community action probably holds the greatest potential for an enabling approach, with its emphasis on self-help groups, community projects, and neighborhood and community development, all of which can be under the control of the communities themselves, rather than under centralized direction and control.

For personal skills to develop, information, training, and resources are needed. People can manage and control their own activities. Finally, the health services are probably the principal vehicle through which resources can be routed to make an enabling approach possible, and most agree that health services generally need to be more open to input from the community.

The overriding principle in all five action areas is the provision of appropriate resources and avenues for people individually and collectively to have an active role in all aspects of health, and whenever possible to have significant control over what is undertaken. Obviously, with the broad canvas suggested by the Ottawa Charter, there is almost the whole of life to tackle to improve health. So who decides the priorities? At a central level, considerations of social equity would govern decisions about allocation of resources. The decisions as to which health-related issues should be addressed first should be largely left up to local populations. This requires, most probably, a systematic approach to gathering information about needs and wishes through local surveys and other formal means. Professionals will be required to assist with these processes and to provide information and backup for most aspects of what is being outlined here.

The second question raised above, that of the best way to go about health promotion from an enabling perspective, gives rise to a second level of definition. Health promotion can be defined from an operational standpoint as the combination of educational, organizational, economic, and environmental supports for action conducive to health. So that people *can* deal effectively with their own health promotion needs and activities, they need information and skills, together with the financial, professional, and organizational resources to put such knowledge and skills to use. It might be thought that the approach to health promotion being outlined here would diminish the role of professionals, but this is not the case. However, the professional will undoubtedly have a different role, that of consultant, advocate, mediator, and supporter, rather than being the one who always controls the situation. This puts professionals and "the people" on a more equal footing—as partners rather than in a hierarchical relationship with the professional on top. A good example in practice of the kind of health promotion methodology that could arise from the adopting of an enabling perspective is that provided by the Canadians in their new health promotion policy framework (Epp, 1986). Here, two of the three main health promotion mechanisms are labeled "self-care" and "mutual aid" (the third is "healthy environments"), the idea being that resources would be made directly available to individuals and citizen groups to work on their own health promotion activities.

The third question, concerning how an enabling approach would relate to healthful public policy, has already been partly answered above, in that any such approach requires policy at all levels to assure active involvement of people in formulating public policies and programs. Policies to return control of programs to local groups raise questions of evaluation, for if governments provide public money directly to citizen groups, they should want assurance that the resources are being appropriately used and are having good effects. But in addition, in the wider arena of intersectional policy, public awareness, consultation, and participatory planning are essential. There is a danger that an overly policy-led approach to health promotion would largely be a case of "experts planning for people." When making policy for whole populations, through broad legislative and regulatory initiatives directed at health resources such as alcohol control or food policy, it is sometimes too easy to decide what is in the nation's or the people's interests, often under the influence of powerful economic interest groups, without actually consulting those involved. This centralized approach may not work well if people are unmotivated to comply with the policy or legislative moves being made. The fundamental principle for policy planning here is to start where people are and involve them throughout the policy development process.

How does an enabling approach to health promotion apply to behavior change? This is more than an academic question. Many countries already have vertical health promotion offices set up on a behavioral risk factor model (e.g., smoking programs, alcohol and drug programs, nutrition programs). It is of considerable interest to people working in those programs to know how their futures may be affected by the decentralization and enabling policies currently afoot. We believe that the majority of life-style programs would be best conducted in an enabling way. That is, rather than set up treatment or education programs run by experts, people can set up their own groups and activities according to their own inclinations and needs. To do this, however, they will need resources. For example, if a local group of people want to run their own smoking cessation or weight control program, they will need appropriate knowledge and skills to do this. This is where the professional life-style-oriented health education specialist comes in—as a consultant and backup to this process and, in many cases, as someone who can help initiate the self-help process and develop appropriate resources for this kind of activity. The evidence indicates that self-help groups run by nonprofessionals do as well as, if not better than, equivalent groups run by professionals, so that efficacy is typically not an issue here. Rather, it is a matter of how professionals see themselves operating, and of overall philosophy. An added bonus of the self-help approach is that the local group gets the benefit of social support from peers, and also gains a sense of control over their own lives—both factors that are demonstrably health enhancing.

COMMUNITY ACTION: A NEW CENTER OF GRAVITY?

Rather than taking sides in a polarized debate over whether the system or the individual should be the center of gravity for health promotion, the appropriate focus could well be the community. Without getting deeply into definitions of *community*, we refer here either to geographical or interest communities, consisting of relatively small, noninstitutional aggregations of people linked together for common goals or other purposes. We believe that the most effective vehicle for health promotion activity, whether it be directed at policy, environmental change, institutional change, or personal skills development, is the human group, a coalition with all its aspects of social support and organizational power. Community groups can exist to set priorities in health promotion, to run programs, to advise public officials, and to help each other in a wide variety of ways. These groups are perfect vehicles for an enabling approach. As the Ottawa Charter says, "Health promotion works through concrete and effective community action in setting priorities, making decisions, planning strategies and implementing them to achieve better health. At the heart of this process is the empowerment of communities, their ownership and control of their own endeavors and destinies" (WHO, 1986). This puts the enabling approach in a nutshell. In addition, there has developed over the last 20 years or so in some parts of the world a strong tradition of community development work that incorporates many of the principles espoused here. Some of the most interesting health initiatives in developing countries come out of a community development model. Community development puts the control over the determinants of health where it belongs—with the people—and is perhaps the best antidote to that most pernicious of modern political ills, the fragmentation, disempowerment, and alienation of the ordinary citizen.

SUMMARY

The definitional and operational challenges of practical health promotion seem to be torn between ideological and theoretical perspectives on health promotion between policy-oriented sociological or system models and more professional service-oriented individual or social psychological models sometimes associated with the terms *health education, behavior change,* and *life-style.* An integration of these viewpoints appears to prevail in actual policies and in practice, though some advocates continue to debate the terms and to defend the polar models. Some of the historical and conceptual roots of health promotion have been discussed. Some concepts seem to be more divisive than others. The diverse interests and constituencies involved need concepts that transcend and integrate the wide variety of viewpoints. We suggest that the concept of *enabling* be the focal integrative concept, capturing as it does the essence of the "new public health's" intended shift in power base from a dominance by bureaucracies to more control by the community. In terms of action, we suggest *community* as the optimal point of intervention, situated as it is at a point of balance between the system and the individual. With *enabling* and *community* accepted as pivotal concepts for an integrated approach to health promotion, all other action and policy can flow with less rancor and the greater cooperation essential to the intersecting needs of health promotion.

Other issues will resolve themselves more effectively when the fundamental issue of participation has been addressed. For example, the complex relationship of health promotion to health protection and preventive medical services will be sorted out locally according to local needs. National policies will still be required to address the important question of equity, and the marshaling of centralized resources for research on such matters as appropriate measures of positive health and for professional training in an enabling model. Some of these issues are debated in other chapters of this volume.

The principal points we have attempted to make can be summarized as follows:

(1) There is a danger that a misreading of the Ottawa Charter for Health Promotion will lead to a disregard of the history of health promotion to date, and to a splintering into ideological camps. An integrated approach is possible.

(2) First and foremost, the primary consideration in health promotion is not policy or education, but the ordinary people whose health is at stake. They should not just be "consulted" or "educated," they should be brought actively into the health enterprise in a significant way through the processes encompassed by the term *enabling*. Enabling is a matter of power, resources, control, and who sets the priorities. It is the key concept for an integrated approach that spans the various components and ideologies of health promotion.

(3) The road to enabling is through direct channeling of resources of knowledge, skills, and finance to the community, a process involving education with appropriate organizational, economic, and policy supports.

(4) The action areas of the Ottawa Charter are of importance for health promotion, but as a totality they are extremely broad and diffuse. We suggest that the appropriate center of gravity for these diverse areas is community action, following an overall philosophy of community development and participation.

Health promotion requires intervention and action. We hope that this chapter will stimulate further progress toward a broad consensus on what form this action should take at a practical level in the community.

REFERENCES

Epp, J. (1986). Achieving health for all: A framework for health promotion. *Health Promotion, 1*(4), 419-428.

Green, L. W. (1979). National policy in the promotion of health. *International Journal of Health Education, 22*, 161-168.

Green, L. W. (1986a). Individuals versus systems: An artificial distinction that divides and distorts. *Health Link, 2*(3), 29-30.

Green, L. W. (1986b). *New policies for health education in primary health care.* Geneva: World Health Organization.

Green, L. W. (1986c). The theory of participation: A qualitative analysis of its expression in national and international health policies. *Advances in Health Education and Promotion, 1*(Part A), 211-236.

Minkler, M. (1989). Health education, health promotion and the open society: An historical perspective. *Health Education Quarterly, 16*, 17-30.

Nutbeam, D. (1986). Health promotion glossary. *Health Promotion, 1*(1), 113-127.

Ottawa Working Group on Health Promotion in Developing Countries. (1986). Health promotion in developing countries: The report of a workshop. *Health Promotion, 1*(4), 461-462.

Raeburn, J. M. (1986). Toward a sense of community: Comprehensive community projects and community houses. *Journal of Community Psychology, 14*, 391-398.

U.S. Department of Health and Human Services. (1974). *Healthy people: Report of the surgeon general.* Washington, DC: Government Printing Office.

U.S. Department of Health and Human Services. (1980). *Public health service—promoting health/preventing disease: Objectives for the nation.* Washington, DC: Government Printing Office.

U.S. Department of Health and Human Services. (1987). Strategies for promoting health for specific populations. *Journal of Public Health Policy, 8,* 369-423. (Original work published 1981)

World Health Organization. (1978). *Alma Ata 1978: Primary health care.* Geneva: Author.

World Health Organization. (1986). The Ottawa charter for health promotion. *Health Promotion, 1,* iii-v.

World Health Organization. (1988). *Report on the Adelaide Healthy Public Policy Conference.* Denmark: Author.

World Health Organization Regional Office for Europe. (1984). *Health promotion: Concepts and principles* (ICP/HSR602). Copenhagen: Author.

Chapter 2

SOCIAL CHANGE THEORY
Applications to Community Health

BETI THOMPSON
SUSAN KINNE

The increasing focus on "community" in health promotion is due, at least in part, to growing recognition that behavior is greatly influenced by the environment in which people live. Proponents of community approaches to behavioral change recognize that local values, norms, and behavior patterns have a significant effect on shaping an individual's attitudes and behaviors (Abrams, Elder, Carleton, Lasater, & Artz, 1986; Carlaw, Mittelmark, Bracht, & Luepker, 1984; Farquhar et al., 1977; McAlister, Puska, Salonen, Tuomilehto, & Koskela, 1982; Puska et al., 1985). This recognition has been paralleled by a call for new ways to achieve behavioral change. Rather than emphasizing change made by individuals, this new "community" approach argues that permanent, large-scale behavioral change is best achieved by changing the standards of acceptable behavior in a community; that is, by changing community norms about health-related behavior (Abrams et al., 1986; Farquhar, 1978; Farquhar, Maccoby, & Wood, 1985; Stunkard, Felix, Yopp, & Cohen, 1985; Syme & Alcalay, 1982; Van Parijs & Eckhardt, 1984).

Since publication of the 1970 World Health Organization report on community initiatives, increasing attention has been paid to community organization as a means of achieving large-scale change in both primary prevention and treatment of chronic health problems (Blackburn, 1983; Farquhar, 1978; Green, 1986). The authors of the report agreed that community organization could change the community setting to support healthier life-styles. That change would be translated to reductions in individuals' health risk behavior, which would, in turn, lead to decreases in chronic disease morbidity and mortality.

Community organization is based on the "principle of participation" (Green, 1986; Green & McAlister, 1984), which states that large-scale behavioral change requires the people heavily affected by a problem to be involved in defining the problem, planning and instituting steps to resolve the problem, and establishing structures to ensure that the desired change is maintained (Green, 1986; Vandevelde, 1983). The "principle of ownership" is closely related to the principle of participation. *Ownership* means that local people must have a sense of responsibility for and control over programs promoting change, so that they will continue to support them after the initial organizing effort (Kahn, 1982; Kettner, Daley, & Nichols, 1985; Rothman, 1979). Both principles follow from the same basic premise: Change is more likely to be successful and permanent when the people it affects are involved in initiating and promoting it.

In the last 15 years, a number of major health promotion initiatives have used a community approach to change behavior (Abrams et al., 1986; Carlaw et al., 1984; Cohen, Stunkard, & Felix, 1986; Elder et al., 1986; Farquhar, Fortmann, et al., 1985; McAlister et al., 1982; Mittelmark et al., 1986; Puska et al., 1985; Tarlov et al., 1987). Most of these efforts addressed multiple risk factors related to cardiovascular disease, with goals of changing smoking, dietary, and screening behavior. All of them described themselves as "community projects" and used different community institutions, organizations, groups, and individuals in the delivery of the interventions. Most emphasized public education through mass media, schools, and other organizations.

The majority of these projects recognized the need to change the social context of their communities, arguing that the environment has a significant influence on facilitating or inhibiting the adoption of new behaviors (Carlaw et al., 1984; Farquhar et al., 1977; Farquhar, Maccoby, & Wood, 1985; McAlister et al., 1982; Puska et al., 1985). Some researchers discussed the importance of changing community norms; documentation of such changes could be used as measures of the success of their projects. Community organization was seen as a means to achieve social context changes and normative changes.

Despite this emphasis on the community and community organization, in practice, the existing community projects pay little attention to norm and value change and seldom measure such change, relying instead on measuring individual change (Farquhar, Fortmann, et al.,

1985; Leventhal, Cleary, Safer, & Gutmann, 1980). In the area of smoking, for example, traditional approaches have been focused on the individual, with little or no attention given to the broad social context in which the individual acts. A great deal has been accomplished at that level; smoking cessation programs have proliferated so that no smoker need look very far for help in quitting. The smoker, however, functions in a social context that contains many cues to continue the smoking habit. Tobacco use is surrounded by a context that lures people into smoking (Mausner, 1973). Few, if any, smoking control efforts have systematically addressed that context (Feinhandler, 1986).

The dearth of empirical attention paid to changing community norms and values can be partially attributed to the lack of comprehensive theories explaining how such change occurs. Change programs tend to be primarily driven by "middle-range" theories that address the process of changing behavior among individuals or some component of the community (Elder et al., 1986; Farquhar et al., 1977; Green & McAlister, 1984; Maccoby & Alexander, 1980). There are, however, sound theoretical underpinnings that can be used to develop a more comprehensive conceptual framework for component change.

In this chapter, the process of change in social context and community norms is tied to a broad theoretical framework. The chapter is organized into the following parts: (a) the general principles of systems and communities, (b) general sociological perspectives of change, (c) middle-range or process theories concerned with changing components of the community, (d) a synthesis and application to community change, and (e) measuring community change.

GENERAL PRINCIPLES
OF COMMUNITIES AND SYSTEMS

For well over a hundred years, social scientists have been engaged in the systematic study of communities. From this work, at least two important principles can be identified. The first relates to definitions of *community,* and the second applies a "systems" perspective to communities.

Community. Many definitions of *community* have been devised (Bell & Newby, 1971), and Warren (1958) provides a succinct yet broad definition that forms the basis for the one given here. We look upon the community as a group of people sharing values and institutions. Community components include locality, an interdependent social group, interpersonal relationships, and a culture that includes values, norms, and attachments to the community as a whole as well as to its parts (Bell & Newby, 1971). This definition is important in that it distinguishes communities from mere aggregates of people, who tend not to share common goals. An underlying principle of this definition is that communities form a whole greater than the assemblage of individuals within them.

Systems. The second principle can be found in a systems view of the world; simply, communities can be viewed as systems. An inherent assumption of views of general social structure and change is that societal structures are systems that are long lasting, functionally interdependent, and relatively stable (Ashby, 1958; Boulding, 1978; von Bertalanffy, 1962). The system is based on some degree of cooperation and consensus on societal goals, norms, and values. The system is made up of various subsystems or sectors, individuals, and the interrelationships among them (see Figure 2.1). The system, however, is not a simple aggregation of its component parts; rather, it is a unique structure that includes all the parts and the relations that connect them. The system provides the context for all activities, including making choices about behaviors. Thinking of a community from a systems perspective allows a better understanding of the interconnections of the various community levels, sectors, relationships, and members.

The community system includes individuals, subsystems, and the interrelationships among the subsystems. At least a century of anthropological work has identified important subsystems of any community system. These are the political sector, economic sector, health sector, education sector, communication sector, religious sector, recreational sector, and social welfare sector. In addition, community organization studies have identified two additional sectors as being important for achieving changes in the community system. These include voluntary and civic groups, such as health-related agencies, political action groups, and other grass-roots groups, and other groups that may be specific to particular communities. A schematic of the community system and its various parts and relationships is presented in Figure 2.1.

The view of the community as a system provides some insights into community organization for change. From a systems perspective, change in one sector usually implies that adjustments or responses will eventually occur in other parts of the system. Thus it is clear that community change may begin at any level of the community. Change that begins with one sector, however, may take a long time to affect the entire system. In addition, many factors may interrupt or divert the

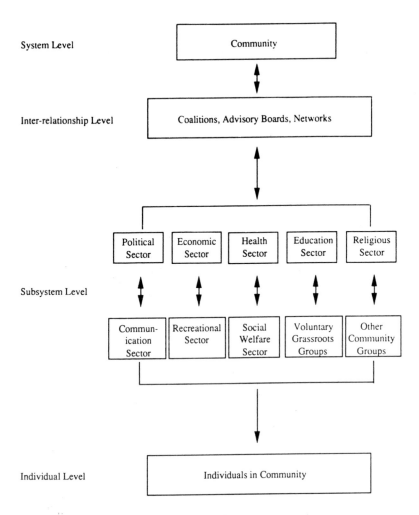

Figure 2.1. Schematic of Community as System

change effort. Typical examples of such factors include changing community agendas, changes in resources available, and changes in organizations that have taken a leadership role in addressing a specific issue.

From a community organization perspective, the target of change is generally the entire system—the community itself. Making changes at the system level will maximize the rapid dissemination of those changes throughout the various sectors of the system. For such change to occur, new rules for appropriate behavior must become a part of the total system or community. From this perspective, it is not enough to change only a sector or part of the community, although changes in the sectors or subsystems, especially the political and economic spheres, may contribute to overall system change.

Since change is the goal of most community intervention studies, it is important to understand how and why such change is likely to occur. Many theorists have presented views on this topic, and these are reviewed in the next section.

GENERAL SOCIOLOGICAL
PERSPECTIVES OF CHANGE

Social change is regarded as "the significant alteration of social structures (that is, patterns of social action and integration), including consequences and manifestations of such structures embodied in norms (rules of conduct), values, and cultural products and symbols" (Moore, 1963, p. 34). Social change is generally regarded as change in large social structures, and such change is generally preceded or followed by changes in the normative structure of a system. Norms are the shared rules and expectations that govern everyday life (Robertson, 1977), and they produce the regularity of behavior that allows individuals to be part of a larger social group. Normative change takes place when a shift occurs in the rules that govern behavior. The shift does not apply only to specific individuals, but also to expectations governing behavior for the entire system or subsystem within which it occurs.

Two major perspectives have been used to explain social change: functionalist and conflict views. In general, functionalist theories emphasize patterns and processes that maintain a system (Cancian, 1960; Hempel, 1959; Nisbet, 1973; Parsons, 1951), while conflict theories see imbalance as a constant part of any system, resulting in ongoing adjustments (Dahrendorf, 1959; Domhoff, 1969; Frank, 1967; Mills, 1959). Proponents of the two perspectives hold correspondingly different views on social change.

Proponents of the functionalist view see social change as a gradual, adaptive process oriented toward system reform. Systems, from this perspective, are based on cooperation and consensus, especially in the areas of societal goals, norms, and values (Robertson, 1977). Social norms are viewed as the links that help hold the system together. Social change occurs when parts of the system break down and are no longer able to contribute to system maintenance or when external or environmental changes overwhelm the system. Social norms change along with the system to provide new rules of conduct to help maintain the reformed system. An example of this can be seen in emerging norms surrounding tobacco use. Technical changes—recognition of the dangers of smoking and of inhaling secondhand smoke—are leading to restrictions in public smoking. As this secular trend accelerates, smokers find it is no longer appropriate to light up in all settings, and new rules for smoking must be developed.

Social change theories based on the conflict view see social change as occurring when one of several interests in a system gains ascendancy (Domhoff, 1969). Social norms, as in the functionalist view, help maintain a system, but in a coercive, rather than consensual, sense. Those who control important parts of a system, especially the economic and political sectors, establish the social norms, and attempts to change norms are likely to be met with resistance by them. Again, the norms regarding tobacco use can be used to illustrate this perspective. The tobacco industry, with its significant economic resources and strong lobby, helps to maintain government price supports and advertising privileges. In addition, it has managed to define smoking as an individual choice or problem—a social norm recently upheld in civil cases against tobacco companies (e.g., the 1988 New Jersey case, *Cipollone v. Liggett et al.*). A change in social norms, from this perspective, will result when an opposing interest group, such as a nonsmokers' rights group or the surgeon general, is able to exert more influence over the parts of the system now controlled by the tobacco industry. A different set of norms, such as a view of tobacco as an addictive substance, may then prevail.

In these two system-level or "macro" theories, different aspects of society are seen as the causes of change. Both views confirm that impetus for change originates both within and outside of the system, although functionalists usually emphasize extrasystemic factors while conflict theorists look for internal explanations. And although functionalist and conflict perspectives provide a framework for describing systems, their parts, their interactions, and change, they do not specifically address the processes of change. To understand those processes, an examination of specific theories is required.

MIDDLE-RANGE AND PROCESS THEORIES OF CHANGE

The general principles of the social change theorists are supplemented with more than half a century of work in communities. From that background, as well as some other contexts, a set of process theories that addresses community change has been developed. These include theories at the individual, organizational, community, and environmental levels.

Individual-Level Change Theories

Bandura's social learning approach is one of the most familiar models of change used in the health field (see, e.g., Bandura, 1969; Elder et al., 1986). In brief, the individual is regarded as a self-determining organism who acts on and reacts to environmental stimuli, and acquires new ideas and behaviors by modeling them on focal others. In practice, this type of change is promoted by exposure to these role models. This is accomplished by mass media that increase access to the new ideas and behaviors, by use of prominent people as change initiators, and by exploitation of existing social networks that maximize interpersonal contact (Bandura, 1969; Lasater et al., 1984). Creation of social networks or linkages among people ("networking") is another ancillary technique to improve the likelihood that a target individual will learn and adopt a new behavior from those around him or her.

Explaining the interplay of knowledge, attitudes, and behavior has always been a challenge for psychology. The social learning approach recognizes that simple cognitive acquaintance with new material is not sufficient to motivate individual change (Bandura, 1969). Social norms and values, often implicit in this approach's description of behavioral acquisition, set limits on what will be considered and how easily it will be accepted. This suggests that a change in norms, however accomplished, will contribute to a change in people's learning and in their eventual behaviors.

The influence of norms is recognized also by community psychology, a field that subscribes to the opinion that one can change the individual by altering the environment (Kelly, 1979; Kelly, Snowden, & Munoz, 1977). However, the specific causal elements of the environment are not distinguished. Instead, theoretical statements of community psychology take the general form of reporting that *this* kind of community environment produces individuals with *these* particular characteristics and/or difficulties, while *that* alternative community is peopled with individuals with quite different traits. Convert the first environment to resemble the second, and the individuals in the first community will more closely approximate those in the second community. In this holistic view of community, the importance of beliefs, values, and specific behavioral norms is clear, though the mechanism whereby they can be changed is not.

Theories of collective action, especially those that emphasize rational choice, can be applied to individual-level change; they presume that national calculation of individual interest is the basis for decisions to participate in or abstain from particular activities (Heath, 1976; Olson, 1965). Critics of this approach argue that the theory is not an explanation of behavior, but a description of behavior based in exchange theories—people usually act as if they were rational. Proponents reply that what is important is the accuracy of the prediction, not the realism of its assumptions about behavior. This suggests that changes in the incentive structures of an individual will alter his or her behavior. For some behaviors, this approach works well (Becker, 1977). People may be convinced to perform well in their jobs in return for higher pay. In other situations, the role of the incentive structure is less clear. People may continue to drink or smoke even though there are penalties or deterrents attached to those behaviors. While such views may not be particularly helpful in understanding how widespread behavior change can be achieved, they may be useful for understanding community mobilization—that is, how people can be motivated to work toward community change.

Organizational-Level Change Theories

Clearly, the individual cannot be the only source of system change. The systems perspective recognizes that changes in subsystems and their interrelationships can also influence the system. The subsystems of a community consist primarily of organizations and individuals who work toward a common goal. The political sector, for example, may include organizations that promote certain political positions, groups responsible for governance, and individuals who hold political office. Organizational theories are useful in understanding how key organizations within a subsystem can contribute to subsystem change.

Organizations and institutions can be altered in ways that are distinct from change in their membership (Grusky & Miller, 1981; Scott, 1981). Organizations are systems in themselves and espouse their own norms and values; thus they are also capable of change (Ermann & Lundman, 1978; Zey-Ferrell & Aiken, 1981). As Rogers and Shoemaker (1971) make clear, organizations learn and change through a process of diffusion. Networks between organizations facilitate diffusion of ideas and practices. The leadership structure of an organization may support change in response to changing external or internal conditions, and this is likely to have an effect on individuals within the organization. Good examples can be found in the area of organizational deviance, where individuals within an organization may find themselves following "company orders" that contradict social norms (Ermann & Lundman, 1978; Grusky & Miller, 1981). The classic heavy electrical equipment antitrust cases of the 1960s revealed that company officials repeatedly and willfully violated antitrust laws; yet these officials, to a person, stated that they were only following company policy (Geis, 1978).

The extensive literature on organizational change details the many forms such change may take. Organizational change may result from collective action or social movements (Gusfield, 1962; Olson, 1965; Zey-Ferrell & Aiken, 1981). Many occupational health and safety regulations have their roots in such movements. External changes may lead to shifts in the internal power of groups; new leadership may then pursue its own interests within the organization. A good example is the appointment of Surgeon General C. Everett Koop, whose agenda for his organization included an emphasis on the dangers of tobacco use.

Another approach with relevance for community change is that of organizational development (Grusky & Miller, 1981; Lippett, 1982), which links individual and organizational change by advocating manipulation of organizational norms of behavior. Changing organizational norms affects both the way members behave with each other and the methods the organization may use to pursue its goals. Examples of this are especially prevalent in work-site studies of democratic decision making as a management technique (Zey-Ferrell & Aiken, 1981).

Interorganizational linkages may also change the structure of organizations. A variation of the social network approach has been applied to this kind of change (Cook, 1977). In this view, mobilization and involvement of key community organizations will provide the impetus for total community participation in a change program (Cohen et al., 1986). The key organizations network with each other and, in a manner congruent with diffusion theory, the "change" spreads throughout the community. For many proponents of this view, community change is nothing more than the aggregated activities of the organizations.

Community-Level Change Theories

At the level of the community as a whole, some practical approaches for change have been formalized. The most familiar is that of community organization. Rothman (1979) has described three general ways to intervene in the community: locality development, social planning, and social action. The first maximizes local participation (ownership), the second emphasizes rational planning and problem solving, and the third uses mobilization and activation of disadvantaged groups, who then demand redistribution of resources. These draw implicitly on different theoretical bases and reflect the awareness that different situations and objectives call for very different methods of change. Since the models are not "pure," in that much overlapping occurs when social change is attempted, usually a mix of methods is advocated for any single situation.

The social work tradition of community organization, combined with anthropological insight about cultural differences, has given rise to the field of community development (van Willigen, 1976). (This is not to be confused with what Rothman and others refer to as "community development," which is a broader field of social and economic improvement and has much more in common with what Rothman refers to as "locality development.") In the anthropological version of community development, local participation may be encouraged, but the emphasis is on economic development that is harmonious with the native culture. The outcome is community change, but the concern is less with process than with efficient achievement of this economic aim. Its normative consequences are of secondary interest. Nevertheless, this approach has some useful ideas for community change efforts; for example, providing resources to the community can help expedite the achievement of desired individual behavior changes.

Another view of community change relies heavily on organizational relationships. Previously, we saw how some theorists viewed community change as the aggregated activities of organizations. In another version of this view, proponents identify organizations and their linkages as "the community" (Elder et al., 1986). The approach is a tempting one because it is empirically manageable. A sizable literature details how this organizational network may be conceptualized and measured (Burt & Minor, 1983; Mulford, 1984). Because of its sophisticated methodological development, it can provide useful indicators of change in community structure and function. For example, changes in decision making, power, and influence can be tracked to ascertain what groups are having the primary impact on a community (Galaskiewicz, 1979).

Environmental-Level Change Theories

When we speak of community change, we rely implicitly on our ability to distinguish "community" from its environment. This ability may be analytical rather than practical, but it does allow us to think about external sources of community change. Environmental-level theories of social change are important because external stimuli can influence the system. Secular trends in national norms, for example, may have an impact on the community system, just as at the organizational level, exogenous shifts can change the balance of power at the community level.

Economic theories of supply and demand provide one framework for describing this process of adjustment (Becker, 1977). Entire communities, for example, have declined because industries have moved out of town when demand for their products decreased. In many cases this kind of change requires the community to make significant adjustments to maintain its system—schools, jobs, services, and so on. Social movements can also affect the larger environment, thus constraining or changing the options open to particular systems (Gusfield, 1962; Troyer & Markle, 1983). The civil rights movement of the 1960s required new formal and informal norms about relationships among people in a variety of settings. There may also be policy changes at a higher level—state laws or regulations, for instance—that affect a community in a completely exogenous manner. Hiring laws, tobacco restrictions, and increases in taxes are all good examples of such externally imposed constraints on behavior.

In summary, a number of theories at various levels have been used to explain how communities or other systems can change. Most of the views suggest strategies that could be used as part of an effort for community change. In the next section, these views are synthesized and applied to a specific issue.

SYNTHESIS AND APPLICATION
TO COMMUNITY CHANGE

The general principles and discrete theories discussed above have been applied in a variety of settings, and have achieved some level of empirical support. They have not yet been integrated into a larger theoretical framework of community change; nevertheless, we can use them to present a synthesis that draws from theories at each of the levels discussed above. Schematically, this integrated approach is represented in Figure 2.2. Communities can be considered systems. General sociological theories can help explain how the system is held together as a whole, while the middle-range or process theories can be used to explain how change occurs within the components of the system.

As depicted, the system is stable (functionalist view), with most of the system components (e.g., individuals and subsystems) in consensus on societal goals, norms, and values. Within the system, however, there are vested interests that act to preserve the status quo, while collective action or social movements may arise to counter those vested interests (conflict view). The system also interacts with the environment. External stimuli, in the form of laws, policies, and critical events, may influence norms and values within the system. The external stimuli may lead to social movements or collective actions to change community behaviors. Change within the community may be planned either internally or externally. External forces often use social planning or locality development theories to orchestrate change. "Partnership" arrangements between internal and external resources are more common. The Minnesota Heart Health Program illustrates the effects of a 10 year cooperative project that is now locally owned (N. Bracht, personal communication, 1988; Mittelmark et al., 1986).

At the subsystem level, various important organizations work together to achieve change in the community. Social network theory and interorganizational theory explain how such connections are initiated and sustained. As various groups become involved, the change is diffused to other groups in the community. Theories that explain this process include diffusion, community development, and organizational development. Some organizations may take on leadership roles and thus become more important than other subsystems as change agents. Especially critical are the political and economic subsystems, since they frequently are able to move a change in norms from the organizational level to the community level.

Individuals, because they interact with the subsystems, are subjected to changing norms and practices at the subsystem level. New norms may be reinforced by role models who make the appropriate behavior change. Social learning theory explains how individual change may occur in response to such role models. Eventually, because of

External Environment

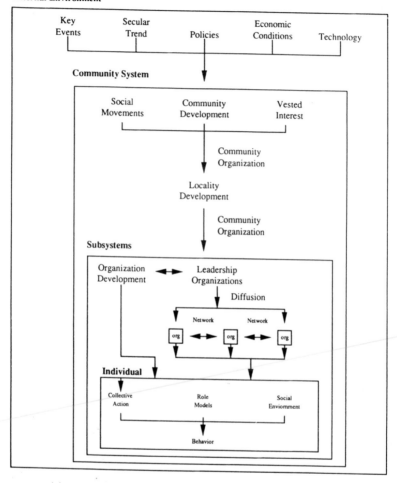

Figure 2.2. A Synthesis of Change Theories

organizational change and change in subsystems and their interrelationships, new norms prevail and widespread individual change is likely to
occur.

This synthesis provides a theoretical explanation for activities that
have been used singly or in varying combinations in community projects. It can be applied to a variety of community projects attempting

to achieve community change. As an illustration, consider the example of an externally initiated community project targeting smoking cessation and prevention. On the environmental level, the project itself may be regarded as an external stimulus to the community. Another external stimulus is the growing secular trend to treat smoking as an activity that affects the entire public, not merely the smoker who practices the habit (system theory). As a result, some collective actions (employee agitation for smoke-free work areas) and small social movements (Doctors Ought to Care, Americans for Nonsmokers' Rights) address the issue. In addition, changes in smoking policy at the national, state, and local levels have some impact on the local community.

At the community level, project investigators use community organizations to unite organizations and individuals in defining smoking as an issue (interorganizational approach, social networking). By providing some resources (community development, economic theory) and establishing a base of expertise from which the community can draw (community development), the investigators seek to integrate themselves with community leaders and groups (interorganizational approach). Through the social networking process, subsystems within the community system link together to address the issue. Influential community members are identified and serve as spokespersons and role models for others (social learning).

As the project continues, ideas, methods, and goals are diffused throughout the community (diffusion theory). Community subsystems (e.g., workplaces, schools) make policy changes that are congruent with the goals of the project. Other normative changes also occur. Examples include a community policy enforcing restriction of sales of tobacco products to minors, community funding designated to promote smoking prevention activities in schools, community restrictions on places where smoking is allowed, and a special local tax on tobacco products, with the proceeds earmarked for smoking cessation activities. These examples indicate changes in the rules and expectations for the whole system, not merely for some individuals within it, and thus indicate that smoking norms have changed. These changes are accompanied by behavioral changes in smoking prevalence and cessation rates.

The theoretical synthesis could just as easily be applied to other types of community projects. Health promotion projects, substance abuse projects, adolescent pregnancy prevention projects, and movements to empower deprived groups can also be understood and guided by this analytic approach.

A final topic relevant to the theoretical synthesis is the task of measuring community change. Past community projects have tended to measure change in individuals and to generalize those results to the community (Jacobs et al., 1986; Leventhal et al., 1980). In the perspective discussed here, community change requires a change in the whole system; thus it is important to look at other kinds of measures. These are reviewed in the next section.

MEASURING COMMUNITY CHANGE

The application of this conceptual framework suggests a number of measures of community change. Measurement should be undertaken at each analytical level. To assess change at the individual level, it is important to know how much individuals are influenced by a community project. Appropriate measures might include surveys to determine individual (a) awareness of the project, (b) knowledge about the problem being addressed, (c) participation in the project, and (d) appropriate changes in behavior.

To assess change at the subsystem level, changes within community organizations and groups are good indicators. Some areas of change are (a) policies that address the problem of concern, (b) support for the project, (c) participation in the project, and (d) any other activities that indicate involvement in the problem being addressed.

We must also measure changes in interrelationships among the various subsystems. These changes can be detected by considering the importance of "social connectedness" in the community and looking for shifts in the extent to which organizations and groups are involved with each other. Indicators of change in social connectedness include (a) coalition development, (b) subsystem participation in community boards and task forces, and (c) subsystem involvement in community-wide activities.

Finally, we must look at the whole system and assess changes in community norms and values. This can be done by looking for changes in (a) community policy on the issue, (b) community enforcement procedures, and (c) public perceptions of shifts in norms, which can be assessed on both individual and subsystem levels. Another important factor lies outside the system: the impact of the external environment. Environmental changes can be compared with local changes to assess the impact of external stimuli on the community. For example, secular trends and national and state laws are external stimuli that are likely to affect community change.

SUMMARY

The community approaches discussed in this book use a wide variety of tactics and techniques to achieve reductions in health risk behavior. Most studies acknowledge that their goal is to replace the norms that lead to high-risk behavior with norms that support healthier life-styles. Unfortunately, very few projects have been able to find or develop a comprehensive theoretical basis for directing their activities, and even fewer have been able to document any change in the norms surrounding health behaviors. Without a sound theoretical explanation of community normative change, it is impossible to develop good measures to document such change.

Despite the lack of an integrated theoretical explanation of community change, many theoretical premises and principles can be applied to this area. In this chapter, we have examined a number of those principles and premises and have combined them into a theoretical synthesis that can be useful for community projects. The synthesis takes well-established practices and provides a theoretical explanation for their utility. It also suggests other directions in which to move to achieve comprehensive community change. In addition, the synthesis can be used to develop a variety of measures of change at all levels of analysis, including that of the community itself.

This synthesis can help guide the activities of community projects by providing a framework for action. It is a holistic approach based on a systems perspective with the potential to address all aspects of the community system. As such, it recognizes the total environment within which individuals act.

With the increasing attention given to chronic diseases such as cancer and heart disease, it has become obvious that traditional interventions designed to change the behavior of high-risk individuals have too little impact to lower chronic disease rates. Community intervention is one strategy that emerged in response to that recognition in the early 1970s. Based on the idea that behavior is heavily influenced by environment, this approach seeks to change community norms and values regarding behaviors that contribute to chronic diseases. Over the last 15 years, community health promotion has proven to be one of the most exciting and promising newer approaches. By strengthening its theoretical base and developing better tools to measure results, we can test its effectiveness and establish its utility for the future.

REFERENCES

Abrams, D. B., Elder, J. P., Carleton, R. A., Lasater, T. M., & Artz, L. M. (1986). Social learning principles for organizational health promotion: An integrated approach. In M. F. Cataldo & T. J. Coates (Eds.), *Health and industry: A behavioral medicine perspective* (pp. 28-51). New York: John Wiley.

Ashby, W. R. (1958). General systems theory as a new discipline. *General Systems, 3,* 1-6.

Bandura, A. (1969). *Principles of behavior modification.* New York: Holt.

Becker, G. S. (1977). *The economic approach to human behavior.* Chicago: University of Chicago Press.

Bell, C., & Newby, H. (1971). *Community studies: An introduction to the sociology of the local community.* New York: Praeger.

Blackburn, H. (1983). Research and demonstration projects in community cardiovascular disease prevention. *Journal of Public Health Policy, 4,* 398-421.

Boulding, K. E. (1978). General systems theory: The skeleton of science. In J. Shafritz & P. Whitbeck (Eds.), *Classics of organization theory* (pp. 121-131). Oak Park, IL: Moore.

Burt, R. S., & Minor, M. J. (1983). *Applied network analysis: A methodological introduction.* Beverly Hills, CA: Sage.

Cancian, F. M. (1960). Functional analysis of change. *American Sociological Review, 25,* 818-827.

Carlaw, R. W., Mittelmark, M. B., Bracht, N., & Luepker, R. (1984). Organization for a community cardiovascular health program: Experiences from the Minnesota Heart Health Program. *Health Education Quarterly, 11,* 243-252.

Cohen, R. Y., Stunkard, A., & Felix, M. R. J. (1986). Measuring community change in disease prevention and health promotion. *Preventive Medicine, 15,* 411-421.

Cook, K. S. (1977). Interorganizational relations. *Sociological Quarterly, 18,* 62-82.

Dahrendorf, R. (1959). *Class and class conflict in industrial society.* Stanford, CA: Stanford University Press.

Domhoff, W. D. (1969). Where a pluralist goes wrong. *Berkeley Journal of Sociology, 14,* 35-57.

Elder, J. P., McGraw, S. A., Abrams, D. B., Ferreira, A., Lasater, T. M., Longpre, H., Peterson, G. S., Schwertfeger, R., & Carleton, R. A. (1986). Organizational and community approaches to community-wide prevention of heart disease: The first two years of the Pawtucket Heart Health Program. *Preventive Medicine, 15,* 107-117.

Ermann, M. D., & R. J. Lundman (Eds.). (1978). *Corporate and governmental deviance: Problems of organizational behavior in contemporary society.* New York: Oxford University Press.

Farquhar, J. (1978). The community-based model of life style intervention trials. *American Journal of Epidemiology, 108,* 103-111.

Farquhar, J. W., Fortmann, S. P., Maccoby, N., Haskell, W. L., Williams, P. T., Flora, J. A., Taylor, C. B., Brown, B. W., Solomon, D. S., & Hulley, S. B. (1985). The Stanford

Five-City Project: Design and methods. *American Journal of Epidemiology, 122,* 323-334.

Farquhar, J. W., Maccoby, N., & Wood, P. D. (1985). Education and communication studies. In W. W. Holland, R. Detels, & G. Knox (Eds.), *Oxford textbook of public health* (Vol. 3, pp. 207-221). Oxford: Oxford University Press.

Farquhar, J. W., Wood, P. D., Breitrose, H., Haskell, W. L., Meyer, A. J., Maccoby, N., Alexander, J. K., Brown, B. W., McAlister, A. L., Nash, J. D., & Stern, M. P. (1977). Community education for cardiovascular health. *Lancet, 1,* 1192-1195.

Feinhandler, S. J. (1986). The social role of smoking. In R. D. Tollinson (Ed.), *Smoking and society* (pp. 167-187). Lexington, MA: Lexington.

Frank, A. G. (1967). Sociology of development. *Catalyst, 3,* 28-42.

Galaskiewicz, J. (1979). *Exchange networks and community politics.* Beverly Hills, CA: Sage.

Geis, G. (1978). White collar crime: The heavy electrical equipment antitrust cases of 1961. In M. D. Ermann & R. J. Lundman (Eds.), *Corporate and governmental deviance: Problems of organizational behavior in contemporary society.* New York: Oxford University Press.

Green, L. W. (1986). The theory of participation: A qualitative analysis of its expression in national and international health politics. *Advances in Health Education and Promotion* (Vol. 1, pp. 211-236). Greenwich, CT: JAI.

Green, L. W., & McAlister, A. L. (1984). Macro-intervention to support health behavior: Some theoretical perspectives and practical reflections. *Health Education Quarterly, 11,* 322-339.

Grusky, O., & Miller, G. A. (Eds.). (1981). *The sociology of organizations: Basic studies* (2nd ed.). New York: Free Press.

Gusfield, J. R. (1962). Mass society and extremist politics. *American Sociological Review, 27,* 19-30.

Heath, A. (1976). *Rational choice and social exchange.* Cambridge: Cambridge University Press.

Hempel, C. G. (1959). The logic of functional analysis. In E. Gross (Ed.), *Symposium on sociological theory.* New York: Harper.

Jacobs, D. R., Luepker, R. V., Mittelmark, M. B., Folsom, A. R., Pirie, P. L., Mascioli, S. R., Hannan, P. J., Pechacek, T. F., Bracht, N. F., Carlaw, R. W., Kline, F. G., & Blackburn, H. (1986). Community-wide strategies: Evaluation design of the Minnesota Heart Health Project. *Journal of Chronic Diseases, 39,* 775-788.

Kahn, S. (1982). *A guide for grassroots leaders: Organizing.* New York: McGraw-Hill.

Kelly, J. G. (1979). Tain't what you do, it's the way that you do it. *American Journal of Community Psychology, 7,* 239-261.

Kelly, J. G., Snowden, L. R., & Munoz, R. F. (1977). Social and community interventions. *Annual Review of Psychology, 28,* 323-361.

Kettner, P., Daley, J. M., & Nichols, A. W. (1985). *Initiating change in organizations and communities: A macro practice model.* Monterey, CA: Brooks/Cole.

Lasater, T., Abrams, D., Artz, L., Beaudin, P., Cabrera, L., Elder, J., Ferreira, A., Knisley, P., Peterson, G., Rodrigues, A., Rosenberg, P., Snow, R., & Carleton, R. (1984). Lay volunteer delivery of a community-based cardiovascular risk factor change program: The Pawtucket experiment. In J. D. Matarazzo, S. H. Weiss, J. A. Herd, N. E. Miller, & S. W. Weiss (Eds.), *Behavioral health: A handbook of health enhancement and disease prevention* (pp. 1166-1170). New York: John Wiley.

Leventhal, H., Cleary, P. D., Safer, M. A., & Gutmann, M. (1980). Cardiovascular risk modification by community-based programs for life-style change: Comments on the Stanford study. *Journal of Consulting and Clinical Psychology, 48,* 150-158.

Lippett, G. L. (1982). *Organization renewal* (2nd ed.). Englewood Cliffs, NJ: Prentice-Hall.

Maccoby, N., & Alexander, J. (1980). Use of media in lifestyle programs. In P. O. Davidson & S. M. Davidson (Eds.), *Behavioral medicine: Changing health lifestyles* (pp. 351-370). New York: Brunner/Mazel.

Mausner, B. (1973). An ecological view of cigarette smoking. *Journal Abnormal Psychology, 81*, 115-126.

McAlister, A., Puska, P., Salonen, J. T., Tuomilehto, J., & Koskela, K. (1982). Theory and action for health promotion: Illustrations from the North Karelia Project. *American Journal of Public Health, 72*, 43-50.

Mills, C. W. (1959). *The sociological imagination*. New York: Grove.

Mittelmark, M., Luepker, R. V., Jacobs, D., Bracht, N. F., Carlaw, R. W., Crow, R. S., Finnegan, J., Kline, F. G., Mullis, R. H., Murray, D. M., Pechacek, T. F., Perry, C. L., Pirie, P. L., & Blackburn, H. (1986). Education strategies of the MHHP. *Preventive Medicine, 15*, 1-17.

Moore, W. E. (1963). *Social change*. Englewood Cliffs, NJ: Prentice-Hall.

Mulford, C. L. (1984). *Interorganizational relations: Implications for community development*. New York: Human Sciences.

Nisbet, R. (1973). *The social philosophers*. New York: Crowell.

Olson, M. (1965). *The logic of collective action*. Cambridge, MA: Harvard University Press.

Parsons, T. (1951). *The social system*. New York: Free Press.

Puska, P., Nissinen, A., Tuomilehto, J., Salonen, J. T., Koskela, K., McAlister, A., Kottke, T. E., Maccoby, N., & Farquhar, J. W. (1985). The community-based strategy to prevent coronary heart disease: Conclusions from the ten years of the North Karelia Project. *Annual Review of Public Health, 6*, 147-193.

Robertson, I. (1977). *Sociology*. New York: Worth.

Rogers, E. M., & Shoemaker, F. F. (1971). *Communication of innovations: A cross-cultural approach* (2nd ed.). New York: Free Press.

Rothman, J. (1979). Three models of community organization practice. In F. M. Cox, J. L. Erlich, J. Rothman, & J. E. Tropman (Eds.), *Strategies of community organization: A book of readings* (pp. 86-102). Itasca, IL: Peacock.

Scott, W. R. (1981). *Organizations*. Englewood Cliffs, NJ: Prentice-Hall.

Stunkard, A. J., Felix, M. R. J., Yopp, P., & Cohen, R. Y. (1985). Mobilizing a community to promote health: The Pennsylvania County Health Improvement Program (CHIP). In J. C. Rosen & L. J. Solomon (Eds.), *Prevention in health psychology* (pp. 143-190). Hanover, NH: University Press of New England.

Syme, L. S., & Alcalay, R. (1982). Control of cigarette smoking from a social perspective. *Annual Review of Public Health, 3*, 179-199.

Tarlov, A. R., Kehrer, B. H., Hall, D. P., Samuels, S. E., Brown, G. S., Felix, M. R., & Ross, J. A. (1987). Foundation work: The health promotion program of the Henry J. Kaiser Family Foundation. *American Journal of Health Promotion, 2*(2), 74-80.

Troyer, R. J., & Markle, G. E. (1983). *The battle over smoking*. New Brunswick, NJ: Rutgers University Press.

Vandevelde, M. (1983). The semantics of participation. In R. M. Kramer & H. Specht (Eds.), *Readings in community organization practice* (3rd ed., pp. 95-105). Englewood Cliffs, NJ: Prentice-Hall.

Van Parijs, L. G., & Eckhardt, S. (1984). Public education in primary and secondary cancer prevention. *Hygie, 3*(3), 16-28.

van Willigen, J. (1976). Applied anthropology and community development administration: A critical assessment. In M. V. Angrosino (Ed.), Do applied anthropologists apply anthropology? *Southern Anthropological Society Proceedings, 10*, 81-91.

von Bertalanffy, L. (1962). General systems theory: A critical review. *General Systems, 7*, 1-20.

Warren, R. L. (1958). Toward a reformulation of community theory. *Community Development Review, 9*, 41-48.

Zey-Ferrell, M., & Aiken, M. (Eds.). (1981). *Complex organizations: Critical perspectives*. Glenview, IL: Scott/Foresman.

Chapter 3

COMMUNITY ORGANIZATION PRINCIPLES IN HEALTH PROMOTION
A Five-Stage Model

NEIL BRACHT
LEE KINGSBURY

In Chapter 2, the theoretical foundations for understanding social change at the community level are presented. The focus of this chapter is the process of purposefully stimulating conditions for change and mobilizing citizens and communities for health action, often referred to as *community organization.* Mobilizing communities means channeling resources (people, goods and services, time, money). Organizers engage networks of government, voluntary, and special interest groups in coordinated efforts to activate a broad range of resources and new program interventions. In short, the community organization process seeks to stimulate and coalesce community energies, interests, and resources in a collective response.

This organizing process is a critical aspect of health action and is a kind of "glue" that maintains citizen interest, nourishes participation in programs, and encourages support for long-term maintenance of successful intervention efforts. Because the term *community organization* has several meanings and definitions, we will, for purposes of consistency and clarity, use the following definition:

Community organization is a planned process to activate a community to use its own social structures and any available resources (internal or external) to accomplish community goals, decided primarily by community representatives and consistent with local values. Purposive social change interventions are organized by individuals, groups, or organizations from within the community to attain and then sustain community improvements and/or new opportunities.

An important outcome of this ongoing process of community and citizen involvement is community ownership. Communities must shape their own program directions and emerge with the necessary skills and resources to manage continued efforts. To do this, effective partnership strategies, as discussed in Chapter 5, must be established. Community analysis methods, as outlined in Chapter 4, support the process of community self-determination. In research-oriented demonstrations with predetermined interventions and goals, the degree of community involvement can be restricted. Mittelmark discusses how to balance research and community interests in Chapter 6.

Community representatives clearly have a choice in whether to participate in health demonstrations that originate outside the community. Experiences from the Minnesota and Pawtucket Heart Health programs and the National Cancer Institute's COMMIT (Heavy Smokers) project suggest that even when externally predetermined goals and interventions are decided upon by university researchers, a community can exercise local influence in shaping the implementation of intervention strategies to be tested. Professionals may design programs and facilitate the change process, but they seldom can direct or control all facets of the community intervention and implementation process.

This chapter presents a five-stage model of organizing for health promotion that builds on principles developed through years of field experience and research in many fields. In addition to the reported experiences of several recent community demonstrations, some of the more important influences that shaped the model's development include (a) the historical and theoretical contributions of applied community organization work, (b) general principles of social and community change, and (c) elements of organizational development and community decision making. We briefly discuss each of these prior to presenting the five-stage process.

COMMUNITY ORGANIZATION

History

The evolution of community organization practice and methods covers a period of some 75 years. Its history is documented by several writers, particularly from the social work field, where community organization has been taught and researched as an area of professional practice since the 1940s (Cox, Erlich, Rothman, & Tropman, 1979; Kramer & Specht, 1975). Principles of community organization draw from national and international experience in a wide range of disciplines. Prominent among these are urban and rural sociology, social work, political science, health education, anthropology, international community development, consumer advocacy, and university extension services. Documents produced by the United Nations began referring to the field of community development in the 1950s. Numerous community organization efforts in the United States were undertaken in the 1960s and 1970s as a result of a plethora of federal comprehensive projects (model cities, neighborhood community health centers, and so on).

The community organization approach is not new to public health. Public health issues were early targets for community organization and social reform (Miller, 1976). The work of charity organization societies and settlement houses, for example, included health and environmental protection efforts. Block committees of local mothers (e.g., Hull House in Chicago) were organized in support of early maternal and child health clinics. The National Citizens' Committee on Prevention of Tuberculosis worked closely with public health professionals to combat infectious diseases during this period. The National Mental Hygiene movement of the 1930s was a citizen-based group that also supported the work of professional associations. Rosen (1974), a noted public health historian, has written about the early interrelationship between social welfare and public health services:

> To a large extent the history of social medicine is also the history of social policy (welfare). . . . The roots of social medicine are to be found in organized social work. It was here that medicine and social science found a common ground for action in the prevention of tuberculosis, securing better housing and work conditions. (p. 112)

More recently, Simmons (1975) and Cleary, Kichen, and Ensor (1985) have documented many successful health education programs (including programs for minority populations) that have utilized community organization strategies.

Theoretical Considerations

Researchers have noted that key elements of the community may be activated to induce or support social and behavioral change (Rogers, 1962; Rogers & Shoemaker, 1971; Twain, 1983; Zaltman & Duncan, 1977). These have included technology strategies and techniques, social organization (relationships, structures, resources), ideology (knowledge, beliefs, attitudes), and social and behavioral change agents. Change agents attempt to increase citizen participation and mobilize for social action (Alinsky, 1946; Beal & Hobbs, 1964; Bennis, Benne, & Chin, 1969; Cobb & Elder, 1972; Milbrath & Goel, 1977). Community activists often describe this process as "empowering" communities, or building capacity for future action based on ideologies of localism, coalition building, and mass participation (Adrian, Rossi, Dahl, & Lloyd, 1960; Biddle & Biddle, 1965; Dunham, 1963; Goodenough, 1963; Mayer, 1972; Rothman, 1970; Smith, Macaulay, & Associates, 1980; Voth & Jackson, 1981). Wandersman (1984) has used organizational development principles to assess self-help organizations and factors associated with their longevity. A common theme unifying these various views about the process of social and behavioral change is the emphasis on how community social forces influence individual behavior—the belief that behavior is formed and influenced by the dominant culture, including social relationships (Aiken & Mott, 1970; Blum, 1981; Brown, 1984; Warren, 1963).

While most disciplinary perspectives emphasize that planning for change needs to be systematic and data based, there are, of course, many forms of change that are spontaneous or unplanned. Anecdotal evidence attests to the success of such efforts (e.g., early civil rights sit-ins). In this chapter, we focus on systematic or planned change, but we recognize the importance of grass-roots citizen responses to community issues.

In reviewing the theory base for community organization, Kramer and Specht (1975) offer this sobering perspective:

> Theoreticians are only beginning to define and test basic concepts such as organization, power and participation. There are few, if any, theories about community work in the sense of logically, interrelated propositions that enable prediction. . . . There are numerous topologies, taxonomies, hypotheses, metaphors, conceptual frameworks and other substitutes for

theory. On the other hand, as practitioners and researchers struggle to codify practice wisdom, an applied social science will develop that will be useful for practice. (p. 4)

Recent Applications

For many years, Rothman's (1970) three models of community organization practice have provided some of the most useful conceptualizations for understanding various approaches to organizing (see Table 3.1). One drawback to this three-model concept was recognized by Rothman himself:

> Having isolated and set off each of these models or three types, it would be well to point out that we are speaking of analytical extremes and that in actual practice these orientations are overlapping rather than discrete. Practice in any of these orientations may require techniques and approaches that are salient in another. (p. 23)

These observations ring true to organizers and researchers involved in communitywide health promotion projects of the last 10-15 years in the United States and abroad. Comprehensive approaches require strategies of *locality development* with broad community participation and citizen ownership. Considerable *social planning* technology is used in community needs assessment and analysis work. Professional planners are frequently involved in assisting communities and citizens to determine needs and intervention strategies. Increasingly, social policy, legislation, and advocacy initiatives (such as in campaigns for nonsmokers' rights) are being used in *social action* orientations. The WHO Healthy Cities Project reflects growing interest in policy change at the community intersectoral level and, again, combines elements from all three models. The National Cancer Institute's heavy smoking prevention project in 11 cities uses approaches from all three models.

Several major public health demonstrations have successfully employed community strategies (Carlaw, Mittelmark, Bracht, & Luepker, 1984; Elder, Hovell, Lasater, Wells, & Carleton, 1985; Farquhar, Fortmann, et al., 1985; McAlister, Puska, Koskela, Salonen, & Maccoby, 1980; Maccoby & Solomon, 1981; Puska, Salonen, Tuomilehto, Nissinen, & Kottke, 1983; Stunkard, Felix, Yopp, & Cohen, 1985). Community organization components can be identified in all of these projects and are described in some detail in reports from the North Karelia, Pawtucket, and Minnesota projects (Carlaw et al., 1984; Lefebvre, Lasater, Carleton, & Peterson, 1987; McAlister et al., 1980).

Table 3.1

Three Models of Community Organization Practice According to Selected
Practice Variables

	Model A (Locality Development)	Model B (Social Planning)	Model C (Social Action)
Categories of community action	self-help; community capacity and integration (process goals)	problem solving with regard to substantive community problems (task goals)	shifting of power relationships and resources; basic institutional change (task or process goals)

SOURCE: Adapted from Rothman's (1970) comprehensive table of variables.

These experiences, along with many other community-based programs in North America, Europe, Australia, and New Zealand, more specifically apply community organization theory and practice to health promotion.

STIMULATING COMMUNITY CHANGE FOR HEALTH PROMOTION

Stimulation or activation of the community is a process whereby the community (a) becomes aware of a condition or problem that exists within the community, (b) identifies that condition as a priority for community action, (c) institutes steps to change the condition, and (d) establishes structures to implement and maintain program solutions. Community activation requires not only the creation or presence of an issue, but also the identification and activation of community groups and individuals to deal with the issue. Guiding principles for community health promotion organizing are shown in Table 3.2.

COMMUNITY DECISION-MAKING BEHAVIOR

Communities differ in how they set about the process of health promotion. A number of decision-making characteristics or traditions may inhibit or facilitate a community's activation. Wandersman (1984)

Table 3.2

Guiding Principles for Health Promotion Organizing

- Planning must be based on a historical understanding of the community. Conditions that inhibit or facilitate interventions must be assessed.

- Because the issue or problem is usually one of multiple (rather than single) causality, a comprehensive effort using multiple interventions is required.

- It is important to focus on community context and work primarily through existing structures and values.

- Active community participation, not mere token representation, is desired.

- For the project to be effective, intersectoral components of the community must work together to address the problem in a comprehensive effort.

- The focus must be on both long-term and short-term problem solving if the longevity of the change is to endure beyond the project's demonstration period.

- Finally, and most important, the community must share responsibility for the problem and for its solution.

---

discusses some of these. Two important variables to be considered are the complexity of the social structures and the demographic components of the community (homogeneity versus heterogeneity). The degree of social acceptability and trust of the change agent or group propelling the change are especially important in minority communities (see the case studies presented in Part V of this volume). Since a basic premise of community organization is that the community "owns" the project and hence the community (through a representative community group) must set its own goals and objectives for changing the condition, the organizer or change agent only facilitates this process.

In *Initiating Change in Organizations and Communities*, Kettner, Daley, and Nichols (1985) describe a process of organizational and community change that begins with the identification of the change opportunity and concludes with a reassessment of the situation in the final step. This book can be useful as an additional resource in the preliminary stage of program planning. Kettner et al. point out that community organizing steps and processes do not always proceed in orderly fashion. While the book is helpful in setting forth an idealized model, the authors' generic model, like other community organization models, often lacks the specification required of newer community-based health projects. Experiences from former disease prevention programs in North America, as well as recent comprehensive/intersectoral community-based health promotion efforts in Europe, suggest at least five specific stages within which citizen involvement and organizing occurs.

FIVE STAGES OF ORGANIZING:
A COMMUNITY HEALTH PROMOTION MODEL

What follows is a description of a five-stage community organizing process (see Figure 3.1). Each stage has several key elements. Citizen involvement is possible and recommended in all stages. As mentioned earlier, organizing work is a dynamic process. The overlapping of these stages is common, and some of the tasks or key elements may need to be repeated. For example, planning for maintenance must begin early in the analysis and design phase and then must be reassessed during both the maintenance and reassessment stages. Reassessment and dissemination activities also occur in earlier stages—they do not suddenly appear in the final stage.

Stage 1: Community Analysis

Successful implementation of communitywide health promotion and intervention programs depends, in large part, on two interrelated sets of activities: first, accurate analysis and understanding of a community's needs, resources, social structure, and values; and second, early citizen leader and organizational involvement to build collaborative partnerships and facilitate broad community participation. This latter activity ensures that programs are designed to reflect community values and encourage community ownership. Assessing *community capacity to support a project, potential barriers that exist,* and *community readiness for involvement* are key areas of the community analysis. The methodology for community analysis or assessment is described in detail in Chapter 4.

Key Elements

(1) Define the community. One of the first tasks should be to determine the geographic focus and/or community boundaries of the project. Will the project focus on a neighborhood, a city, a county, or a region? Historical or economic issues may influence the choice of community boundaries. Typically, organizers will want to decide on the community target area after consulting with representatives from major social institutions or sectors, such as education, health, recreation, business,

Figure 3.1. Community Organization Stages

religious, media, and civic organizations, and government. It is helpful to solicit information on past community organization efforts, their successes, failures, and decision-making processes. If more than one community is involved, the patterns of social interaction and cooperative decision making should be discerned. Past studies completed in the community may assist in this process. Focus groups can be a helpful survey strategy in developing this information (see Krueger, 1988). Small groups of people can provide "focused" insights and perceptions about alternative directions. Krueger (1988) discusses this technique in detail.

(2) Collect data. Community analysis involves the collection and analysis of a variety of data (see a summary in Chapter 4, Table 4.1). The compilation of a comprehensive community profile of health and demographic information is quite helpful. This "community profile" includes information on community resources, history, and readiness for action. For a detailed description of the community profile, see Chapter 4. Sample community analysis profiles are presented in the case studies in Part V of this volume.

Organizers must determine what citizens perceive as community needs and must identify who can get things done, who is ready to provide resources, who needs to be involved in decision making, and who may be opposed to health promotion efforts. Gathering the variety of data necessary takes considerable time, but in the process the groundwork for the informed mobilization of selected citizens begins.

(3) Assess community capacity. In discussing community capacity, Brager and Halloway (1978, p. 127) describe *driving forces* as those capacities that support change and *restraining forces* as potential or existing barriers that hinder or create resistance to change. These authors offer helpful suggestions in making such a "force field" analysis. What are the forces that will support change? As mentioned earlier, the current level of health promotion activity in the community and the potential for increasing activity need to be assessed and summarized. This summary should provide concise information on current programs, identify key leaders or influentials within each of the various community sectors, and describe organizational structure(s), available skilled personnel, programmatic and financial resources, and the general feasibility of increasing the community's interest in a particular health agenda. Based on this assessment of potential, the types of resources needed to develop an adequate community program are defined for each community sector, as are the types of actions needed to increase capacity. Identification of potential collaborating organizations, programs, and individuals is emphasized.

(4) Assess community barriers. An analysis of potential barriers or restraining forces is crucial to good planning. Organizers should look for unique local characteristics and customs that could enhance or inhibit interventions. Ethnic dietary patterns, for example, may need to be understood if interventions are to be designed successfully. Will voluntary organizations cooperate with a new program effort? Do people doubt they can make changes? What is the extent of grass-roots citizen involvement in decision making? Historically, has this community been resistant to other changes?

The initiation of a change process can be viewed as creating its own barriers. As Nix (1978) states, resistance to change is a normal human reaction. He defines five kinds of changes people frequently resist:

(1) changes not clearly understood
(2) changes they or their representatives had no part in bringing about
(3) changes that threaten their vested interest and security
(4) changes advocated by those they do not like or trust
(5) changes that do not fit into the cultural values of the community

After conditions that might inhibit interventions are identified, strategies or alternative ways of handling resistance and barriers must be developed. Community organizers need to be proactive, to provide alternative methods and strategies, and to match their actions with any identified levels of resistance.

(5) Assess readiness for change. How ready a community may be for change will influence program planning. Information previously collected during assessment of community capacity and barriers will help here. The organizing group will want to assess the intensity of community interest, the urgency of the problem as perceived by key influentials, and the general awareness levels of community members. How receptive are top decision makers? How has the community reacted to similar issues or past community organizing efforts?

(6) Synthesize data and set priorities. Once data have been gathered from all the above sources, summary reports must be compiled. Typically these include the health data collected, community needs, current levels of activity, barriers, potential resources, and readiness for health promotion. An overall community profile of these needs, resources, and readiness emerges. Researchers must analyze the data carefully in order to make appropriate plans and choices. Community members review the profile, thoroughly discuss all of the information and ideas, and set priorities. A consensus decision-making process involving key community leaders is most often used for synthesizing ideas and setting priorities.

Stage 2: Design and Initiation

Following community analysis, the first design aspects for a community intervention begin to emerge. Concurrently, formal activities to mobilize citizens begin with the establishment of a structure to elicit and/or coordinate broad citizen support and involvement (informal mobilization of selected citizens began during the analysis stage). As decisions are being made about design and organizational structure, other actions are under way, including identifying individuals to participate in a community board or similar structure, contacting individuals to serve on the board or solicit interest, asking other community individuals and groups to assist or supplement the board in the project, developing working relationships between the project and various collaborating groups, and legitimating the board's activities within the community.

Key Elements

(1) Establish a core planning group and select a local organizer/coordinator. Green and McAlister (1984) have described the extensive planning and coordination efforts that communitywide health promotion programs require. A core group is usually responsible for long-term planning. This group consists of five to eight interested members who make a commitment to plan and participate in the administration of the project. The group's responsibilities usually include calling public attention to the data analysis and identified needs, writing a mission statement, choosing the organization's structure, selecting a coordinator, and identifying and recruiting board members.

The experience and skill of the lead coordinator or organizer is extremely important to program success. The person employed for this purpose must understand how change occurs in communities and must be knowledgeable about local history and values. A local person is preferred. Past experience in facilitating organizational collaboration, including good management skills, is critical. At the interpersonal level, one looks for a highly energetic person with good listening and conflict-resolution skills.

(2) Choose an organizational structure. There are several alternative structures for organizing community involvement and participation, including advisory board, council or panel, coalition, lead agency, informal network, and grass-roots or advocacy movements. These alternative structures are discussed in detail in Chapter 5. The type chosen depends on the community culture, history, and past decision-making style, but successful programs are likely to use parts from several models. An important lesson to be learned from earlier demonstration projects is that these citizen structures are dynamic. Often they evolve into new or modified arrangements. Organizing structures can be combined. New structures can emerge.

Table 3.3

Community Institutional Sectors Represented on a Typical Community Board*

city/regional government
local newspaper/media
public schools
business/work sites
labor unions
ethnic minority groups
community college
medical/health professionals
hospitals
churchs
health voluntary agencies
social/human services agencies
public health agencies
chamber of commerce
grass-roots/advocacy groups

*For purposes of illustration we will frequently use the *Citizen Board* as our structural model.

Project sponsors, particularly if from outside the community, must depend on citizen groups to exercise decision-making authority. Citizens do not want to rubber-stamp prior decisions. Local organizations have the right to make changes and sometimes even mistakes in organizing and planning.

(3) Identify, select, and recruit organization members. The citizen board (or other chosen structure) should have members representing all major community institutions and groups, including commercial, volunteer, political, minority, religious, recreational, medical, public health, and media. Generally, these representatives should be people who can speak and make decisions for the organizations or people they represent. An example of the composition of a board is presented in Table 3.3. In addition to appropriate representation, enlisting people from differing backgrounds and interests provides creative thinking and fresh approaches to community change. Citizen boards need members who are positive thinkers—enthusiastic people who believe in the mission of the project and who enjoy a challenge.

(4) Define the organization's mission and goals. A mission statement provides the organization with its purpose and vision. It should concisely and briefly communicate what is to be achieved. (An example of a mission statement is presented in Table 3.4; this statement was developed by a citizen board in Bloomington, Minnesota.) In addition

Table 3.4

Citizen Board Mission (1987)

Bloomington Heart and Health Program, Inc. is a community health education program aimed at reducing levels of heart disease and promoting health.

The program will

- provide opportunities for people to adopt healthy life-styles in eating patterns, smoking cessation, physical activity, and weight control.
- advocate changes in the physical and social environment.
- coordinate with and support efforts of other community groups.

---

to the mission statement, reasonable and measurable goals and objectives are essential. They are the measurements for success and will help staff and volunteers assess their progress. In Chapter 10, a guide to developing an evaluation plan is presented. Consultation with academic or research personnel may also be helpful at this time. An example of a reasonable, measurable goal is as follows: "to enable 20% of interested pregnant women smokers in Bloom County to stop smoking for at least one year." This example specifies the nature of the situation or goal to be attained (what), the quantity or amount of the situation or goal to be attained (extent), the community group or target portion of the population or environment in which attainment is desired (who), the geographic boundaries where the intervention will be implemented (where), and the time frame within which the desired situation or goal will be reached (when).

(5) Clarify roles and responsibilities of board members, staff, and volunteers. Defining roles and responsibilities for individual board and task force members, organizations, volunteers, and staff will help establish smooth working relationships. Roles can be clarified and assigned in keeping with individual abilities, interests, and expectations. Written or verbal job descriptions or agreements are often used by both volunteers and organizational staff to specify the length of the commitment, training opportunities available, specific tasks and functions, support from staff, personal expectations, and organizational commitment, if any.

The citizen board's overall responsibility is to plan and coordinate the communitywide program activities. Typical tasks of a board include the following: electing officers; approving budgets; selecting program office site; reviewing data; writing, approving, and prioritizing goals and objectives; developing annual action plans and disseminating information about them; assisting in coordinating programs; conducting public awareness campaigns; and recruiting additional volunteers to serve on task forces and to review evaluation plans. Issues of the board's legal liability may surface. State laws and practices should be reviewed and legal guidance solicited.

(6) Provide training and recognition. Since active citizen involvement in decision making, planning, and implementation is desired, skills-oriented training is often essential. Training helps members increase confidence about their abilities and contributions to community projects and builds understanding of the extent of the health problem being addressed, the consequences of that problem, and alternative solutions. Orientation and training may take many forms (e.g., weekend retreats, training sessions during board meetings). Ongoing education yields long-term benefits, including the development of new leadership to incorporate and sustain program efforts in the community.

Successful community organization efforts offer specific rewards, benefits, and recognition to volunteers and staff as well as to program participants. Recognition of program successes and associated personal accomplishments builds pride, raises morale, boosts the awareness of the organization, and maintains better understanding, interest, and commitment. Project or professional staff need to recognize the small successes of each program component and continually create different ways to reinforce and reward people.

Stage 3: Implementation

Implementation turns theory and ideas into action, translating design into effectively operating programs. Professionals and citizens are mobilized and involved in the planning of a sequential set of activities to accomplish their mission. Implementation plans should maximize the use of available resources and existing institutions and adapt to local constraints and values. Cost estimates should be included, along with time frames. Chapters 7, 8, and 9 provide information on the implementation of various broad-based health promotion interventions. The case studies presented in Part V can also be useful to the reader.

Key Elements

(1) Generate broad citizen participation. Throughout the implementation process, continuing to reach out to people and encourage their

involvement is important. There are many ways to bring people into the process as active and productive participants; Lofquist (1983) gives several examples. Organizing task forces or work groups is one way to broaden the base of community support and ownership in the project. Task forces address specific components of the project. Members of the target population should be included on task forces or involved in choosing the most promising strategies.

Professional organizers sometimes fear loss of control in turning over some intervention work to task forces, but this is a critical step. With appropriate information and guidance, citizens can successfully form partnerships with health professionals to plan and conduct programs for their community. In the process of learning new skills themselves, citizens gain motivation, and their community ownership is enhanced.

Community task forces usually require staff support. Typically, a citizen board member will chair a task force, but, with few exceptions, paid staff are necessary to attend to details and to provide technical support and consultation. This needs to be anticipated in the design stage.

(2) Develop a sequential work plan. Developing a practical plan of work will include both short-term problem solving and long-term planning. Community members may want to rush the process. The tendency can be to want to jump in with both feet. Organizers will need to channel enthusiasm, helping task forces and work groups to select, evaluate, and modify implementation steps according to community needs, perceptions, and overall program protocols. The sequential steps for implementation listed below are adapted from the planning steps outlined by the Planned Approach to Community Health (PATCH), a Centers for Disease Control (1987) community health program, and have been helpful in focusing an enthusiastic community group in a practical planning process. These steps assume that the priority health problem/need and target audience have been selected and that a task force/ work group has been appointed.

- *Determine priority intervention activities.* Review existing services and policies and identify gaps. Choose areas that need strengthening. Thoroughly analyze the pros and cons of each possible activity. What will be acceptable to the community and target group?
- *Plan the intervention.* Set the goal and determine specific knowledge, attitude, and behavior or skill change objectives. Develop a timetable for each activity. A master timetable listing all activities will ensure

coordination. Determine incentives that will encourage program participation and develop a media plan. Consider the target group and carefully design media events and advertising around its interests. Social marketing and media campaigns can be sophisticated and may need technical/professional experts (see Chapter 7 for more detailed information on mass media planning).

- *Obtain resource support.* This task entails identifying and involving all the appropriate people whose endorsement or collaboration is needed to ensure success. Engage staff and volunteers who are willing to spend concentrated time on all the details that need attention in carrying out the activity. Adequate financial and material resources, such as instructors, facilities, equipment, and education materials, need to be determined. Each cost associated with the intervention activity must be estimated. Develop a budget, consider funding options, and locate potential sources of support, both in kind and financial.

- *Design the evaluation.* Select criteria to measure intervention effectiveness. Develop data collection methods and protocols (see Chapter 10).

- *Provide feedback.* Determine how participants, supporting organizations, and the community at large will be informed of the project's accomplishments (newsletters, public forums, and so on).

(3) Use comprehensive, integrated strategies. To change community health behavior, more than periodic or "one-shot" program interventions are required. A comprehensive and coordinated effort using multiple strategies that has the potential to influence community norms widely is necessary (Farquhar, Flora, & Good, 1985). Activities must provide people with health information and opportunities to make and practice healthful choices as well as to develop community support for these choices in the form of economic incentives and policies that promote healthy choices. Whether the choice is to develop new activities where gaps exist or to strengthen existing activities, combining multiple strategies in a community has a synergistic effect; each component complements and reinforces the others.

(4) Integrate community values into the programs, materials, and messages. No matter how good an intervention seems on paper, when it is implemented in a community it must speak that community's language (Vincent, Clearle, Johnson, & Sharpe, 1988). The approaches and messages must be acceptable to the community. Community leaders can be encouraged to incorporate local values and symbols into the programs. Two case studies presented in Part V of this volume discuss the development of materials and messages that are responsive to local norms (see Chapters 13 and 14).

Stage 4: Program Maintenance-Consolidation

During this stage, community members and staff gain experience and success with the programs. Problems in implementation have been encountered, but have been dealt with successfully. The organization is developing a solid foundation in the community, and the programs are gaining acceptance. Program elements are being more fully incorporated into the established structures of the community, and community ownership is taking place. Task forces now reassess their past efforts and determine new tasks. In Chapter 11, Lefebvre discusses in detail strategies for maintaining and institutionalizing programs. Bracht and Gleason outline techniques for increasing local board ownership and incorporation of programs in Chapter 5.

Key Elements

(1) Integrate intervention activities into community networks. Integrating intervention activities into established community structures creates a broad context for the adoption and maintenance of health-promoting behaviors and norms. This integration can take place early in the implementation phase or can occur later, as organizations gain confidence in program operation. Key influentials can assist in program adoption and organizational maintenance. The local community board must be active in this process.

(2) Establish a positive organizational culture. Elements of a positive organizational culture have been described by Allen and Allen (1987). This positive climate is a critical factor in promoting and maintaining successful change projects. A positive environment fosters cooperation, improves retention of staff and volunteers, and sets the stage for the development of community ownership of the project. It is the result of good group process and is developed and nurtured through an attitude of trust and openness. Staff must demonstrate trust-earning behaviors, including respect and discretion. In a positive organizational environment, people look for opportunities rather than obstacles and for strengths rather than weaknesses in one another. Mistakes are used as training opportunities, and conflicts are resolved quickly and openly.

(3) Establish an ongoing recruitment plan. Turnover of volunteers and even of paid staff is to be expected in long-term projects. This requires establishment of a plan to identify, recruit, and involve new people in the project on an ongoing basis. Updating the community organization profile helps in seeking out and enlisting new members.

(4) Disseminate results. Disseminating information on project activities and early results of their evaluation increases visibility, communitywide acceptance, and involvement. Communities and citizens will respond to repeated, clear messages describing what has been done and what continuing effort is required to solve the problem. Messages are reinforcing when community influentials and decision makers are involved in their presentation. Dissemination of information, of course, occurs in all phases of community health promotion. Maintaining high visibility is essential to project maintenance.

Stage 5: Dissemination-Reassessment

Reassessment of activities occurs continuously throughout the various phases of the community organizing effort. Process or formative evaluations assist the project group in reassessing strategies that have worked and those that have experienced difficulty. Steps are retraced, programs are modified, expanded, and/or abandoned. At some point, usually near the end of the project, the organization formally assesses what has been learned and determines future directions. Results from the various types of evaluations outlined in Chapter 10 will be helpful in this reassessment period.

Key Elements

(1) Update the community analysis. Updating the community analysis involves looking for changes in leadership, resources, and organizational relationships in the community. Key community members, opinion leaders, and organizations in a community will change over time. Reviewing these changes may point to a need for new collaborators and for efforts to recruit new board and task force members. Additional organizations may need representation if programs are to be continued. For example, the City Parks and Recreation Office in one community became more active at the end of a demonstration project as it took on responsibility to incorporate more physical activity campaigns into its regularly scheduled agenda of events.

(2) Assess effectiveness of interventions/programs. The board will most likely be using some type of formal evaluation plan as the basis for examining the success of its intervention efforts. An evaluation plan that includes ongoing monitoring of programs and activities can make possible periodic reviews of the status and progress of each activity. Monitoring involves establishing appropriate record-keeping systems that collect data for analysis and summary. Community groups may

need to contract for research expertise in conducting evaluations; local universities and colleges may be willing to assist in such efforts.

A variety of quantitative and qualitative indicators of success can be evaluated. Awareness, participation, support, attendance, and behavior change are examples of quantitative indicators. Qualitative indicators include retention of staff and volunteers, levels of decision making by citizen groups, and feedback and involvement from participants and sponsoring agencies.

Programs are intended to change behaviors and norms and to become institutionalized in the community. Existing organizations may become sponsors or "owners" of specific programs. Some programs may need new sponsors, which will require a longer development period. Some programs will be evaluated as ineffective and will be discarded or modified.

(3) Chart future directions and modifications. The process of planning future directions is often a formal one that includes revising and rewriting goals and objectives to reflect the updated community analysis and program evaluations. Some community boards may consider the need for a marketing survey or analysis to determine directions further. Developing a strategy for continued collaboration and networking should be emphasized. Seeking new sources of funding may be required as part of the continuation effort.

(4) Summarize and disseminate results. Project continuation is partially dependent on maintaining high visibility in the community through effective communication with and further diffusion among key groups within the community. These include leaders, program participants, media representatives, potential support sources, and other influential organizations. Murray (1986) has described a successful dissemination strategy in one Minnesota community.

Oral and written reports can provide information to the community. Simple, concise charts and graphs can communicate results effectively. These visual communication tools should cover program availability, user acceptability and preferences, barriers, and so on. Evidence of program impact can be shared with other communities, and local and statewide networks can be developed. Information on successful or unsuccessful programs and activities can be an impetus for other communities to initiate or expand health promotion programs. For example, a 4-H group in a small rural town (Green Isle) in Minnesota adapted successful projects from the Minnesota Heart Health Program and implemented school cafeteria and physical exercise projects that affected hundreds of people in its area. The town was recognized by the secretary of the U.S. Department of Health and Human Services for its grass-roots health promotion effort.

CONCLUSION

As community health promotion programs have proliferated and expanded nationally and internationally, a common set of essential tasks has emerged from their community mobilization and implementation experiences. Programs in dissimilar locales and with different goals encounter common issues that must be anticipated and resolved. Based on the experiences of many community health demonstration projects, we have identified the most common issues that arise: community representativeness and partnership; mission clarity and program boundaries; type of evaluation and tracking; identification of resistance and facilitating forces; volunteer involvement; training and reinforcement; staff recruitment and competencies; resources for maintenance and local ownership; and dissemination of results.

The five-stage model presented in this chapter addresses these issues and identifies the key elements to be dealt with in each stage. The model attempts to bring more systematic approaches to the applied science of community organization for health promotion.

REFERENCES

Adrian, C. R., Rossi, P. H., Dahl, R. A., & Lloyd, R. (1960). *Social science and community action*. East Lansing: Michigan State University, Board of Trustees.

Aiken, M., & Mott, P. E. (Eds.). (1970). *The structure of community power*. New York: Random House.

Alinsky, S. D. (1946). *Reveille for radicals*. Chicago: University of Chicago Press.

Allen, R. F., & Allen, J. (1987, Winter). A sense of community, a shared vision and a positive culture: Core enabling factors in successful culture based health promotion. *American Journal of Health Promotion*, pp. 40-47.

Beal, G. M., & Hobbs, D. (1964). *The process of social action in community and area development*. Ames: Iowa State University, Cooperative Extension Service.

Bennis, W., Benne, K., & Chin, R. (1969). *The planning of change*. New York: Holt, Rinehart & Winston.

Biddle, W. W., & Biddle, L. (1965). *The community development process: The rediscovery of local initiative*. New York: Holt, Rinehart & Winston.

Blum, H. L. (1981). Planning as a preferred instrument for achieving social change. In H. L. Blum, *Planning for health: Generics for the eighties* (pp. 39-85). New York: Human Sciences.

Brager, G., & Halloway, S. (1978). *Changing human service organizations: Politics and practice.* New York: Macmillan.

Brown, E. R. (1984). Community organization influence on local public health care policy: A general research model and comparative case study. *Health Education Quarterly, 10*(3/4), 205-233.

Carlaw, R. W., Mittelmark, M. B., Bracht, N., & Luepker, R. (1984). Organization for a community cardiovascular health program: Experiences from the Minnesota Heart Health Program. *Health Education Quarterly, 11*, 243-252.

Centers for Disease Control. (1987, April). *The community, state and CDC: Partners in a planned approach to community health.* Atlanta, GA: Center for Health Promotion and Education, Division of Health Education.

Cleary, H., Kichen, J., & Ensor, P. (1985). *Advancing health through education: A case study approach.* Palo Alto, CA: Mayfield.

Cobb, R., & Elder, C. (1972). *Participation in American politics: The dynamics of agenda building.* Baltimore: Johns Hopkins University Press.

Cox, F. M., Erlich, J. L., Rothman, J., & Tropman, J. E. (Eds.). (1979). *Strategies of community organization: A book of readings* (3rd ed.). Itasca, IL: Peacock.

Dunham, A. (1963). Some principles of community development. *International Review of Community Development, 11*, 141-151.

Elder, J. P., Hovell, M. F., Lasater, T. M., Wells, B. L., & Carleton, R. A. (1985). Applications of behavior modification to community health education: The case of heart disease prevention. *Health Education Quarterly, 12*, 151-168.

Farquhar, J., Flora, J., & Good, L. (1985). *Integrated comprehensive health promotion programs.* Monograph prepared for the Kaiser Family Foundation, Palo Alto, CA.

Farquhar, J., Fortmann, S., Maccoby, N., Haskell, W. I., Williams, P., Flora, J., Taylor, C. B., Brown, B. W., Solomon, D. D., & Hulley, S. (1985). The Stanford Five-City Project: Design and methods. *American Journal of Epidemiology, 122*, 323-334.

Goodenough, W. A. (1963). *Cooperation in change.* New York: Russell Sage Foundation.

Green, L. W., & McAlister, A. L. (1984). Macro-intervention to support health behavior: Some theoretical perspectives and practical reflections. *Health Education Quarterly, 11*, 322-339.

Kettner, P., Daley, J., & Nichols, A. (1985). *Initiating change in organizations and communities.* Monterey, CA: Brooks/Cole.

Kramer, R., & Specht, H. (Eds.). (1975). *Readings in community organization practice* (2nd ed.). Englewood Cliffs, NJ: Prentice-Hall.

Krueger, R. (1988). *Focus groups: A practical guide for applied research.* Newbury Park, CA: Sage.

Lefebvre, B. C., Lasater, T., Carleton, R. A., & Peterson, G. (1987). Theory and delivery of health programming in the community. *Preventive Medicine, 16*(6), 890-895.

Lofquist, W. A. (1983). *Discovering the meaning of prevention: A practical approach to positive change.* Tucson, AZ: Ayd.

Maccoby, N., & Solomon, D. S. (1981). Heart disease prevention: Community studies. In R. E. Rice & W. Paisley (Eds.), *Public communication campaigns* (pp. 105-126). Beverly Hills, CA: Sage.

Mayer, R. R. (1972). *Social planning and social change.* Englewood Cliffs, NJ: Prentice-Hall.

McAlister, A., Puska, P., Koskela, K., Salonen, J. T., & Maccoby, N. (1980). Psychology in action: Mass communication and community organization for public health education. *American Psychologist, 35*(4), 375-379.

Milbrath, W., & Goel, M. L. (1977). *Political participation: How and why do people get involved in politics?* (2nd ed.). Chicago: Rand McNally.

Miller, C. (1976). Social change and public health: A rediscovery. *American Journal of Public Health, 66*(1), 54-60.

Minnesota Department of Health. (1988, January). *A guide for promoting health in Minnesota: A community approach.* Minneapolis: Author.

Mittelmark, M., Luepker, R. V., Jacobs, D., Bracht, N., Carlaw, R., Crow, R., Finnegan, J. R., Grimm, R. H., Jeffrey, R. W., Kline, F. G., Mullis, R. M., Murray, D. M., Pechacek, T., Perry, C. P., Pirie, P. L., & Blackburn, H. B. (1986). Community-wide prevention of cardiovascular disease: Education strategies of the Minnesota Heart Health Program. *Preventive Medicine, 15,* 1-17.

Murray, D. M. (1986). Dissemination of community health promotion programs: The Fargo-Moorhead Heart Health Program. *Journal of School Health 56*(9), 375-381.

Nix, H. L. (1978). *The community and its involvement in the study planning action process* (HEW Publication No. CDC 78-8355). Washington, DC: Government Printing Office.

Puska, P., Salonen, J. T., Tuomilehto, J., Nissinen, A., & Kottke, T. E. (1983). Evaluating community-based preventive cardiovascular programs: Problems and experiences from the North Karelia Project. *Journal of Community Health, 9*(1), 49-63.

Rogers, E. N. (1962). *Diffusion of innovations.* New York: Free Press.

Rogers, E. M., & Shoemaker, F. F. (1971). *Communication of innovations: A cross-cultural approach* (2nd ed.). New York: Free Press.

Rosen, G. (1974). *Medical police to social medicine.* New York: Science History Publications.

Rothman, J. (1970). Three models of community organization practice. In F. M. Cox, J. L. Erlich, J. Rothman, & J. E. Tropman (Eds.), *Strategies of community organization* (pp. 20-36). Itasca, IL: Peacock.

Rothman, J., Erlich, J., & Teresa, J. (1981). *Changing organizations and community programs.* Beverly Hills, CA: Sage.

Simmons, J. (Ed.). (1975). Making health education work. *American Journal of Public Health, 65*(Suppl.), 13.

Smith, D. H., Macaulay, J., & Associates. (1980). *Participation in social and political activities: A comprehensive analysis of political involvement, expressive leisure time and helping behavior.* San Francisco: Jossey-Bass.

Stunkard, A. J., Felix, M. R. J., Yopp, P., & Cohen, R. Y. (1985). Mobilizing a community to promote health: The Pennsylvania County Health Improvement Program (CHIP). In J. C. Rosen & L. J. Solomon (Eds.), *Prevention in health psychology* (pp. 143-190). Hanover, NH: University Press of New England.

Twain, D. (1983). *Creating change in social settings: Planned program development.* New York: Praeger.

Vincent, M. I., Clearle, A. F., Johnson, C. G., & Sharpe, P. A. (1988). *Reducing unintended adolescent pregnancy, through school/community educational interventions: A South Carolina case study.* Atlanta, GA: U.S. Department of Health and Human Services, Public Health Service, Centers for Disease Control.

Voth, D. E., & Jackson, V. N. (1981). *Evaluating citizen participation: Rural and urban community development* (Working Paper). Washington, DC: Center for Responsive Governance.

Wandersman, A. (1984). Psychology and community change. In K. Heller (Ed.), *Psychology and community change: Challenges of the future* (pp. 337-339). Homewood, IL: Dorsey.

Warren, R. L. (1963). *The community in America.* Chicago: Rand McNally.

Zaltman, G., & Duncan, R. (1977). *Strategies for planned change.* New York: John Wiley.

Part II

COMMUNITY ANALYSIS
AND CITIZEN ACTIVATION

Chapter 4

ASSESSING THE COMMUNITY
Its Services, Needs,
Leadership, and Readiness

BO HAGLUND
RITA R. WEISBROD
NEIL BRACHT

Community analysis is the process of assessing and defining needs, opportunities, and resources involved in initiating community health action programs. This process is variously referred to in the literature as "community diagnosis," "community needs assessment," "health education planning," and "mapping." Analysis is a critical first step not only in shaping the design of project interventions but also in adapting implementation plans to unique community characteristics. The product of community analysis is a dynamic community profile, blending quantitative health and illness statistics and demographic indicators with qualitative information on political and sociocultural factors. The profile includes a community's image of itself and its goals, its past history and recent civic changes, and its current resources, readiness, and capacity for health promotion activities. Finally, a community analysis specifies directions for action.

The process of completing a comprehensive analysis of the community often provides the first opportunity for citizen involvement in a community health project. Analysis is not done *on* the community but *with* the community. Citizens and organizations are involved in the study process to increase awareness and "ownership" of the program and to build commitment to local action. Studies of the community can rarely be completed if local citizens do not cooperate. Level of cooperation is, in itself, a factor in assessing community readiness. Thus, in addition to its planning function, the process of conducting a community study is intended to lead to citizen activation and participation in a designated health intervention. In this chapter we begin with a brief note on the meaning of community and then review the traditions and approaches that have influenced current community assessment and diagnostic models. This is followed by the presentation of methods for both quantitative and qualitative data collection, including suggestions for special studies to increase information about selected social groups in a community.

WHAT IS COMMUNITY?

In beginning a community analysis, one of the first questions asked is, What is a community? How is it defined? No single definition or concept of community serves all fields of investigation or professional intervention. *Community* has multiple meanings and has been studied from varying perspectives by sociologists, geographers, medical specialists, anthropologists, urbanologists, and social workers. Some define community as a psychological bond or relationship that unites individuals in a common goal or experience. Others use the term in the geographic or physical sense, as a space with political or economic boundaries. Yet space alone does not tell us all we need to know about community membership. Residents of a small farming town may consider "distant" farmers to be active members of their town or service area.

Many characteristics of community structure and interaction have been identified in the writings of sociologists, including such useful concepts as community complexity, horizontal and vertical linkage among institutions, centralization of authority, regional autonomy, community identification, and social integration of the population. We rely principally in this chapter on Warren's (1969) social systems view of the community, which focuses assessment on four important features: space or boundaries, social institutions, social interaction, and social control. The type of problem or intervention being planned will determine the nature and level of analysis required in any of these four areas.

In any analysis of a community, the geographical boundaries must be specified and should approximate the view held by most local residents. Once this is determined, an assessment of social institutions (education, health, recreation, business/labor, religious, communications/media, government, and so on) is undertaken in order to understand which organizations currently take responsibility for providing programs and services. This assessment also allows for the estimation of the possibilities for coordinating communitywide programs of health action. Social interaction patterns should also be studied for what they can reveal about community cleavages, coalitions and influence networks, and sources of social support for individuals and groups (Hansson, 1988). An examination of social control mechanisms and norms is also useful. Social control is a function of many community institutions (church, school, police, and so on) and is based on values, norms, and customs. Local regulations and enforcement policies (e.g., concerning the sale of cigarettes to minors) should be understood. Interviews with a diversity of organizational and political representatives can provide most of this kind of assessment information.

ASSESSMENT TRADITIONS

Before describing the various components of analysis, we briefly review the background of various assessment traditions. The terms *community analysis* and *community diagnosis* are used interchangeably in the literature, although analysis, strictly speaking, precedes diagnosis. The term *community diagnosis* surfaced in the 1950s (Morris, 1975) and was introduced to the health planning field in the mid-1960s. The content of community diagnosis was later reformulated by Bennett (1979). Green and Kreuter's (1980) pioneering work, *Health Education Planning*, added a broader social diagnostic framework to this applied discipline. The World Health Organization (1982) has published a handbook for community health workers in the developing countries based on the community diagnosis concept. Dever's (1980) community model has also contributed to community diagnosis methodology. More recently, Haglund (1988) has written about community diagnosis within the Swedish context. Other guides include Baker's (1977) *Assessment of Health Status and Needs in Developing Countries*, Blum's (1981) *Planning for Health*, and Dignan and Carr's (1986) *Program Planning for Health Education and Health Promotion*.

Community analysis has evolved independently from three basic traditions that follow different paradigms: the medical science approach, the health planning approach, and the community development approach. Elements from all three approaches can be found in assessment practice today.

The *medical science approach* equates health with the absence of disease and health improvements with the application of medical science and technology to the community. The medical concept of community analysis in Sweden, for example, dates to the eighteenth century, when the Swedish Collegium Medicum requested that district medical officers record patterns of epidemic and endemic diseases each year and encouraged them to describe important factors that influenced these disease patterns in terms of demography, environmental health hazards, and living habits. The medical science approach to community analysis lacks direct citizen involvement and relies on diagnosis by experts.

The *health planning approach* emphasizes technical needs assessment strategies. The focus is on improvements in delivering medical and preventive services. The Canadian Lalonde report (Epp, 1986) using this approach started a worldwide chain of national reports addressed to disease prevention. Various World Health Organization (1981) goal statements for the year 2000 reflect to some degree the health planning approach. In the United States, *Objectives for the Nation* (U.S. Department of Health and Human Services, 1980) and the surgeon general's report, *Healthy People* (U.S. Department of Health and Human Services, 1979), reflect the health planning influence.

During the last decade in the United States the comprehensive Health Planning Act (1965) focused planning on service delivery through health service agencies (HSAs) at the regional and national levels. Although legislative authority for this program was terminated in 1987 (Sofaer, 1988), little planning in the domain of prevention and wellness services was attempted during its operational phases. In fact, most American communities lack systematic planning mechanisms for health promotion development and/or coordination among current providers. Priority areas for new health interventions are often determined by individual health providers in the community. Efforts to develop a planning process, however, usually follow a needs assessment model adapted from community social service planning (Dignan & Carr, 1986; McKillip, 1987). Health promotion planning, however, is usually isolated from other social service planning in U.S. communities. This fragmentation in planning between health and social service areas is common and requires new approaches and solutions by policy and legislative leaders.

The *community development approach* views health in the broader context of social and economic improvement and views citizen empowerment as vital to improvement in health status. Better health, in large part, is seen as the result of improvements in social and educational levels and involves improved quality of life as well as access to medical and preventive services. Community members are encouraged to take greater responsibility for and control of their own health care. Community development emphasizes community cooperation. Advocates of this approach include Freire (1970), Duhl (1986), and Biddle and Biddle (1985).

The community development (or community organization) approach emphasizes direct citizen participation in the community analysis process and encourages a grass-roots or "bottom-up" decision-making process rather than a "top-down" health planning approach, where "experts" determine the community's health promotion agenda and new initiatives. Other contributors to this literature and approach include Nix (1978), Schwebbel (1973), Bracht (1988), and Rifkin (1988). Currently, the Kaiser Family Foundation is using community development approaches in its several health promotion projects in western and southern states. The Model Standards Project (American Public Health Association, 1985) and the Centers for Disease Control's (1987) PATCH represent other current efforts to apply this approach.

Health promotion planners following the community development paradigm view the community as both the *context* in which an educational program operates and the *vehicle* through which institutional changes in attitudes, practices, and policies can be effected. The information gathered for community analysis facilitates a developing partnership among organizations, civic leaders, and groups who play an important intervention role as channels of program dissemination.

COMPONENTS OF COMMUNITY ANALYSIS

The purposes of community analysis for health promotion are to identify resources, problems, and opportunities and to set priorities for planning and developing an action program. The quantitative or descriptive aspect of this analysis has five components:

(1) a demographic, social, and economic profile compiled from census or local economic development data resources

(2) a health risk profile (including behavioral, social, and environmental risks)

(3) a health/wellness outcomes profile (morbidity/mortality data)

(4) a survey of current health promotion programs

(5) special studies of target groups, awareness levels, perceived needs, organizational capacity, and so on

Table 4.1 summarizes these components of community analysis, including objectives and typical data sources and methods.

Preintervention Analyses: Quantitative Data Components

General Community Profile (Socioeconomic)

First, geographic boundaries of the community must be defined in terms of political units or service areas. Data for this area of assessment include geographic, demographic, social, and economic factors. It is important to describe the community's population by age, sex, and racial or ethnic heritage. Other social variables may include family structure, marital status, housing conditions, education levels, immigration, divorce rates, voting participation, crime rates, and available quality-of-life measures. Economic indicators may include employment, labor force characteristics, poverty and related welfare and social security beneficiary rates, general business conditions, and major economic developments. Communities with high unemployment or recent economic recession may have fewer resources and be less capable of achieving commitment to a "health focus" agenda.

Health Risk Profile

The health risk profile has three main components: behavioral risk, social risk, and environmental (physical/chemical/biological) risk. Comprehensive assessment methods for each of these areas are available in the work of other authors (e.g., see Dever, 1980; Green & Kreuter, 1980); we present here a brief summary of the salient features to be assessed.

The *behavioral risk assessment* includes dietary habits and use of drugs, alcohol, and tobacco, as well as patterns of physical activity. If previous studies are not available, planners may choose to conduct their own surveys of community residents regarding health behaviors and perceptions of health problems and needs. Examples of survey

Table 4.1

Summary of Community Analysis Components

Analysis Question	Objectives	Typical Data Sources
Preintervention: Quantitative		
General community characteristics, structure, and history: What are the geographic features of this community? What are its unique concerns, health-related community agendas, and recent civic actions?	Analyze demographic, economic, and social characteristics of the community as they impinge on health and health promotion efforts.	Wide range of social-economic sources: census information, economic development, and social service data. Historical and other social indicators.
Health risk profile: What are the behavioral, social, and environmental risks to the population and/or special subgroups?	Determine actual and/or perceived health risk levels. Includes behavioral (e.g., smoking), social (e.g., high unemployment), and environmental (e.g., chemical hazards) risks.	Local health screening surveys or past risk factor studies from state or national sources and registries; behavioral risk factor telephone surveys.
Health-wellness outcomes assessment: What are the levels of ill health and disability? Indicators of wellness?	Determine local morbidity/mortality and disability levels for various conditions and diseases.	Epidemiologic measures; past health or quality-of-life studies. Selective utilization of regional and national data sources.
Community health promotion survey: What programs, resources, skills, and provider groups already exist? What is the level of participation in these programs? In what areas is there a need to develop or expand?	Assess programs in local institutions and groups. Obtain supply and demand levels of health promotion. Monitor organizational changes over time.	Current community inventories used to develop data base through contacts with local informants: health departments, local medical clinics, hospitals, wellness programs, and so on.
Specialized studies: What special target groups exist? Can they facilitate dissemination? What do these groups want to do?	Develop implementation strategies specific to program target groups. Identify some groups as targets of intervention (smokers), others as resources for intervention (physicians).	Systematic surveys or key informant interviews of special target groups.

(Continued)

Table 4.1

Summary of Community Analysis Components (Continued)

Analysis Question	Objectives	Typical Data Sources
Preintervention: Qualitative		
Community leadership study: Who are the people to help or hinder a community project? How do people want to participate?	Assess community influentials and key organizations. Develop list of names for possible membership on citizen boards or task forces. Develop past strategy for partnership approach with the communities.	Can be done separately or as part of community health promotion survey; interviews with organizational officials and reputed influentials; past studies when available.
Community readiness: What campaigns and initiatives is the community ready for?	Anticipate problems, community issues, and possible conflicts. Determine areas of greatest interest and potential energy.	Information from behavioral risk factor surveys, key informants, organizational officials, and archival materials.
Intervention Period		
Tracking/monitoring survey of changes occurring in community: What does the intervention consist of?	Track programs in major institutional sectors (health, business, etc.). Document social/health changes and unusual events that provide broader context for interpreting findings.	Weekly tracking and collection of data from local field staff with monthly feedback. Interviews and unobtrusive measures.
Monitoring from period of first contact all project-general activities that occur: Areas include community mobilization, formation of boards, media use, events scheduled, meetings/promotional activities, and legislative activity.		

instruments include the National Health Promotion and Disease Prevention Survey (Thornberry, Wilson, & Golden, 1986) and the Health Hazard Appraisal Index (Travis, 1977). Questions about medical care utilization by individuals or groups, self-care activities, and perceived needs can be included. Utilization of alternative health care programs (e.g., holistic medicine) can also be assessed.

Social indicators of risk are less commonly studied, but their utility may be of increasing importance. The stress of long-term unemployment, isolation, and/or poor education has been associated with poor health status. On the other hand, recent research suggests that positive health outcomes are related to social support mechanisms. New approaches to measuring social supports and networks are being reported in the literature. Gottlieb (1985) discusses variables that can be used to measure the source and strength of social networks. Hansson (1988) has utilized the concepts of social network, social support, and social influence in a theoretical model that has been empirically tested and found to be useful in the field of health.

Environmental factors associated with health risks include the local quality of the physical environment, including water, soil, air, climate, and housing characteristics. Representatives of local and state environmental agencies should be interviewed to identify special problems in a particular community's environment.

Health/Wellness Outcomes Profile

The community's health/wellness profile reflects the distribution of illness and well-being in the community. This profile may consist of health indicators or single factors reflecting the health status of individuals or defined groups. According to Dever (1980) and Abelin (1986), some of the most useful indicators are age-specific death rates, proportional mortality ratios, unnecessary deaths, potential years of life lost, and morbidity and mortality rates. The profile may contain composite measures summarizing data for defined target groups, such as adolescents or women.

Community Health Promotion Program Survey

Before planning or undertaking new health initiatives, it is important to have a complete description of current health promotion efforts in the community. One way to identify current programs in a community is to consult with key community informants on the status of community programming (Neuber, 1980). However, such efforts may be limited by the restricted experience and perspectives of these informants. As experts from the community, they have a better and more complete knowledge than do outsiders, but unless they have had to pull together a summary of current programs for some purpose, their knowledge is incomplete and often fragmented. A more comprehensive and objective procedure to describe health promotion programs is often needed.

An early effort to provide such a description of community health programs can be found in the Community Resource Inventory (CRI) procedure developed by the Pennsylvania Heart Health Project (Cohen, Felix, & Yopp, 1986). The Minnesota Heart Health Program developed an expanded assessment instrument (The Community Health Promotion Survey, Weisbrod, 1989) which has the advantage of providing quantitative indicators of community health promotion activities allowing evaluation over time of specific changes in the status of programming. For a discussion of its use, see Weisbrod, Pirie, Bracht and Elstun, 1990. In assessing a community's health promotion program status, we want to know where the community is concentrating its efforts—what areas of health have the most activity. An examination of program activities helps us judge the breadth of opportunities available to individuals in improving their health and highlights the areas of health where opportunity is low. Examining the variety of programs in relation to participation helps us assess the market for additional programming.

Specialized Community Studies

For planning purposes there may be a need to secure additional information on the characteristics of selected social groups of the population. In the Minnesota Heart Health Program, for example, data on membership in community groups and associations were obtained (Carlaw, Mittelmark, Bracht, & Luepker, 1984). Church membership was high in all three cities, ranging from 43% to 48%. Thus churches were considered as sites for community awareness and educational programs. Membership in sports and recreation groups ranged from 22% to 28%. About 50% of the groups that citizens belonged to provided some type of health information. Thus already-existing channels for health information dissemination were utilized.

Understanding attitudes and practices among professionals in a community can be useful in developing and complementing programs. In one Minnesota Heart Health study (unpublished), physicians were surveyed about their ideas and practices regarding cardiovascular disease risk and prevention activities. The survey determined that physicians felt most effective in hypertension control and prevention and least effective in reduction of weight, blood cholesterol level, and smoking. Based on this information, physician education programs focused initially on skills for risk reduction and health behavior change. Later, protocols and management systems were introduced into many medical clinic practices in order to improve systematic prevention practices among primary care physicians and their staffs.

A related survey of 421 other health professionals (nurses, pharmacists, dentists) found that less than one-third of respondents felt they had a substantial positive effect on individuals with health problems or heart disease risks. Improving professional effectiveness was identified as a program goal.

Preintervention Analyses: Qualitative Data

Study of Community Leadership

Involvement of community leaders is essential to program success. The identification of influential persons and organizations should begin early in the community diagnosis process. Various approaches to studying community leadership and decision-making processes are detailed by Finnegan, Bracht, and Viswanath (1989). There are essentially four approaches to an analysis of influence and leadership: positional, reputational, decision-making, and community-reconnaissance forms of analysis. These alternative methods are based on different assumptions about community power structure and function. They were developed originally in formal sociological studies of communities primarily in the United States, but they have their roots in ethnographic methods. Their current applicability to other societies has not been evaluated.

The "modified positional-reputational approach" as reported by Nix (1978) identifies different types of influentials based on leadership function (legitimizers, effectors, activators, and general public). The method also reveals community factions and key coordinating groups or centers of decision making whose involvement (or noninterference) may be critical for a health program's success.

A brief survey form is used to collect information. Basically, during personal interviews with leaders, the interviewer begins by describing the need or the proposed project and then answers any questions the interviewee might have about it. Next, the interviewer queries for information. Included are questions about other community leaders who might have interest in the subject or experience in other communitywide projects. The interviewee names other respected leaders and "doers" in the community. Examples of prior successful or unsuccessful community programs in health or other areas are also requested in these interviews. Finally, information is gathered on organizations that might be interested in or important to the success or failure of such a program.

These interviews are not only a tool for community analysis but a first step in the community organization process, because they introduce the project or purpose of the study to the community. The reputational survey may result in 50-100 interviews, depending on the size and complexity of the community. The opinion leader survey period usually takes several weeks. In one Minnesota community of about 35,000, leadership interviews were conducted with 30 informants who named the most influential leaders in each community sector. The total number of times a leader was named served as a guide in making decisions about the makeup and size of the local citizen board and its related task forces.

In larger and more complex communities, the leadership study may include 150 to 200 interviews. Leadership influence may operate differently in larger communities, where an individual's influence may extend only as far as his or her own organizational boundaries. In larger communities, personal influence is enhanced by formal organizational authority, but it is exercised largely through coalitions. A guide to contacting key members and institutional sectors of the community is provided in the Appendix to this chapter.

Assessing Readiness and Opportunity for Change

A critical area of qualitative diagnosis is the determination of readiness for and commitment to community change. If a leadership study has been completed, information about the attitudes and expected level of participation of key community actors will have been obtained. A behavioral risk factor survey will pinpoint personal perceptions of needs and priorities among the general public. Recent health demonstrations point to the importance of developing issue awareness before substantive community problems can be dealt with or changed. Developing local awareness then may be a prerequisite of goal setting and developing cooperative strategies for action. The extent to which a community shares a common vision of the future and has had a record of past successful achievements is a good measure of how likely it is to become activated toward a new goal.

Sometimes the inability to act on a problem occurs because the community lacks experience in utilizing or developing resources in a concerted way. Conflicting agendas may not allow groups to prioritize communitywide problems or opportunities readily. Past leadership conflicts may impede groups' working together. Project organizers must recognize that participating organizations (e.g., voluntary health organizations) are unlikely to substitute new collaborative goals quickly for their own long-standing goals. Redefinition and/or modification of collaborative goals may be required.

Cottrell (1977) has developed a construct for viewing community competence. A competent community is one in which the various component parts have the following abilities:

(1) They are able to collaborate effectively in identifying the problem and needs of the community.
(2) They can achieve a working consensus on goals and priorities.
(3) They are able to agree on ways and means to implement the agreed-upon goals.
(4) They can collaborate effectively in the required actions.

These abilities represent, of course, an idealized model of community readiness. They serve as a general guide rather than a predictive set of absolute requirements. Interviews with key informants and organization officials can identify past achievements or conflicts and existing organizations or networks that will be needed. Focus group interviewing methods (see Krueger, 1988) can often be useful in this type of assessment. Locating sources of energy and enthusiasm is one goal in this analysis. Identifying target markets for programs is another. Project organizers need to examine their own objectives and energies as well. Does the sponsoring group have the experience to build a perception of credibility and trust in the community? Are project objectives consistent with the values of local community participation and ownership? Does the project maximize local resources? Are the project organizers prepared to be flexible in program design and/or implementation?

SUMMARY

Successful implementation of community health promotion programs and interventions depends in large part on accurate analysis and understanding of many community and social factors. A community's history, including past collaboration among various sectors, is important, yet it is sometimes overlooked in the assessment process. Specialized studies of target groups may be required. Community analysis is a comprehensive process used to assess health needs, organizational resources, leadership patterns, and potential for change. Results of these various analyses reveal not only a great deal about a community's health needs, but also the community's agenda in working toward program implementation.

APPENDIX:
KEY COMMUNITY SECTORS, LEADERS, AND
ORGANIZATIONAL CONTACTS

This summary list of key organizations and contacts can be useful in planning overall community assessment studies, especially the leadership survey.

Media

- newspapers (publisher/editor, feature editors, and so on; nondaily papers, including shoppers' guides; circulation data and geographic area covered)
- radio stations (market area served and target audiences)
- TV stations (market area served and target audiences)
- billboard or other major advertisers (any "public service" space available?)

For each of the above, (a) note key contact persons (e.g., who has the health beat, who is the news director or public service director) for channels that have good local coverage, and (b) limit data collection to highly accessible sources (such as marketing reports).

Health Care Providers/Facilities

- Identify types and numbers of health personnel.
- List public and private health agencies, insurers (e.g., Blue Cross/Blue Shield), and HMOs. List the full range of health care programs and populations served, from acute to chronic, including any alternative health care programs (acupuncture, wellness centers, and the like).
- List associations and societies for professional providers, including physicians, dentists, chiropractors, nurses, nutritionists/dietitians, pharmacists, social workers, and other health care providers.
- Identify officers, regular meetings, newsletters.

- List hospital and clinic administrators, directors of various departments and hospital board members.
- List public health board members.

Educational Institutions

- List school districts serving the geographic area being defined as your community.
- For each district, list schools (by type: elementary, middle, junior high, high) serving students from your community. Note whether school serves only your community or estimate what proportion of its students come from your defined community. List key school board members and principals.
- For each school, list number of students per grade and number of classrooms per school, if applicable (e.g., for elementary).
- Include similar information on private and/or parochial schools serving the community.

Government Agencies

- List key agencies: county executive, mayor's office, city manager, judicial, congressional representatives, safety and planning offices.
- Describe above agencies: size, staff, key programs.
- Obtain copies of any smoking control and other related health ordinances (city and county) and review legislative history of any attempts to change ordinances in the last five years.
- Characterize city and county employment by location and size, and any health projects by government (Fire Department, police, emergency aid).
- Describe general political climate.

Economic/Commercial Organizations

- Identify worksites and businesses from Chamber of Commerce reports, public documents. List key CEOs, company presidents.
- Estimate proportion of employees at large businesses who live in target community.
- Obtain data on unemployment rates.
- Enumerate cigarette and food vendors, wholesalers, and distributors.
- Enumerate key businesses with health concerns or programs (EAPs).

Labor Organizations

- List major trade unions.
- Describe local union coverage, history of business-labor relations.
- Describe health program benefits.

Religious Groups

- Identify existence of any interfaith council or council of churches and synagogues.
- Describe general characteristics of church attendance and primary affiliation.

Voluntary and Private Organizations

- List relevant voluntary organizations (health and social services).
- Collect annual reports.
- For each organization, note numbers of committees, volunteers, and so on.
- List self-help and mutual assistance groups

Other Organizations

Other useful organizations may include social, cultural, and sports groups that serve to enhance social intervention.

- List significant coalitions, associations, groups, service clubs, and so on.
- List community meeting places (e.g., community center, recreational facilities and parks).
- List special communitywide events, sponsors, key activists in organizing.

Summary of Leadership Contacts

Summarize the community leadership of each sector/organization and key individuals according to the following areas:

- media
- health and medical
- education sector
- government, political
- economic (business/labor)
- religious
- social and human services
- voluntary association

REFERENCES

Abelin, T. (1986). Positive indicators in health promotion and protection. *WHO Statistical Quarterly, 39,* 353-364.

American Public Health Association. (1985). *Model standards: A guide for community preventive health services* (2nd ed.). Washington, DC: St. Mary's.

Baker, T. (1977). *Assessment of health status and needs in developing countries.* New York: Springer.

Bennett, F. J. (Ed.). (1979). *Community diagnosis and health action: A manual for tropical and rural areas.* London: Macmillan.

Biddle, W. W., & Biddle, L. (1985). *The community development process: The rediscovery of local initiative.* New York: Holt, Rinehart & Winston.

Blum, H. L. (1981). *Planning for health: Generics for the eighties.* New York: Human Sciences.

Bracht, N. (1988, August). Community analysis precedes community organization for cardiovascular disease prevention. *Scandinavian Journal of Primary Health Care* (Suppl. 1), 23-30.

Carlaw, R. W., Mittelmark, M. B., Bracht, N., & Luepker, R. (1984). Organization for a community cardiovascular health program: Experiences from the Minnesota Heart Health Program. *Health Education Quarterly, 11,* 243-252.

Centers for Disease Control. (1987, April). *The community, state and CDC: Partners in a planned approach to community health.* Atlanta, GA: Center for Health Promotion and Education, Division of Health Education.

Cohen, A. S., Felix, M. R. J., & Yopp, R. (1986). Measuring community change in disease prevention and health promotion. *Preventive Medicine, 15,* 411-421.

Cottrell, L. S., Jr. (1977). The competent community. In R. Warren (Ed.), *New perspectives on the American community* (pp. 535-545). Chicago: Rand McNally.

Dever, G. (1980). *Community health analysis: A wholistic approach.* Germantown: Aspen System Corporation.

Duhl, L. (1986). *Health planning and social change.* New York: Human Sciences.

Dignan, M., & Carr, P. (1986). *Program planning for health education and health promotion.* Philadelphia: Lea & Febiges.

Epp, J. (1986). Achieving health for all: A framework for health promotion. *Scandinavian Journal of Public Health, 77,* 393-407.

Finnegan, J. R., Bracht, N., & Viswanath, K. (1989). Community power and leadership analysis in lifestyle campaigns. In C. T. Salmon (Ed.), *Information campaigns: Managing the process of social change.* Newbury Park, CA: Sage.

Freire, P. (1970). *Pedagogy of the oppressed.* New York: Penguin.

Gottlieb, B. (Ed.). (1985). *Social networks and social support.* Beverly Hills, CA: Sage.

Green, L. W., & Kreuter, M. (1980). *Health education planning: A diagnostic approach.* Palo Alto, CA: Mayfield.

Haglund, B. (1988). The community diagnosis concept: A theoretical framework for prevention in the health sector. *Scandinavia Journal of Primary Health, 6*(Suppl. 1), 11-21.

Hansson, B. (1988). *Social network, social support and health in elderly men: A population study.* Unpublished thesis, Lund University, Department of Community Health Sciences.

Krueger, R. (1988). *Focus groups: A practical guide for applied research.* Newbury Park, CA: Sage.

McKillip, J. (1987). *Need analysis: Tools for the human services and education*. Newbury Park, CA: Sage.

Morris, J. N. (1975). *Uses of epidemiology* (3rd ed.). Edinburgh: Churchill Livingstone.

Neuber, K. (1980). *Needs assessment: A model for community planning*. Beverly Hills, CA: Sage.

Nix, H. L. (1978). *The community and its involvement in the study planning action process* (HEW Publication No. CDC 78-8355). Washington, DC: Government Printing Office.

Rifkin, S. B. (1988). Primary health care: On measuring participation. *Social Science in Medicine, 26*(9), 931-940.

Schwebbel, A. (1973). A community organization approach to implementation of comprehensive planning. *American Journal of Public Health, 63*.

Sofaer, S. (1988). Community health planning in the United States: A postmortem. *Family & Community Health, 10*(4), 1-12.

Thornberry, O. T., Wilson, R. W., & Golden, P. M. (1986). The 1985 Health Promotion and Disease Prevention Survey. *Public Health Reports, 101*, 566-570.

Travis, J. (1977). *Wellness workbook for health professionals*. Mill Valley, CA: Wellness Resource Center.

U.S. Department of Health and Human Services. (1979). *Healthy people: Report of the surgeon general*. Washington, DC: Government Printing Office.

U.S. Department of Health and Human Services. (1980). *Public health service—promoting health/preventing disease: Objectives for the nation*. Washington, DC: Government Printing Office.

Warren, R. (1969). A community model. In R. Kramer & H. Specht (Eds.), *Readings in community organization practice*. Englewood Cliffs, NJ: Prentice-Hall.

Weisbrod, R. R. (1989). *How to use the community health promotion survey*. Unpublished manuscript.

Weisbrod, R. R., Pirie, P. L., Bracht, N. F., & Elstun, P. (in press). Worksite health promotion in four midwest cities. *Journal of Community Health*.

World Health Organization. (1981). *Development of indicators for monitoring progress towards health to all by the year 2000*. Geneva: Author.

World Health Organization. (1982). *The place of epidemiology in local health work* (WHO Offset Publication No. 70). Geneva: Author.

Chapter 5

STRATEGIES AND STRUCTURES FOR CITIZEN PARTNERSHIPS

NEIL BRACHT
JULIE GLEASON

This chapter focuses on strategies to enhance citizen participation in health promotion and expands on principles of community involvement discussed in several preceding chapters. In Chapter 1, Green and Raeburn discussed community action as the critical enabling process for community health promotion. The social change models reviewed in Chapter 2 assume active citizen involvement. Community organization principles presented in Chapter 3 are, of course, based on a fundamental premise of citizen action and local ownership. In Chapter 4, we recommend that community analysis methods incorporate citizen and lay leader efforts in the identification of need and in the assessment of community readiness for change.

The content of this chapter provides a more focused look at what is known about the citizen involvement process and strategies to enhance community action. The role of nongovernment organizations in health promotion is highlighted. We begin with a definition and review of the literature on citizen participation, including a discussion of the motivations of those who become involved. Various ongoing structures for building effective partnerships between professionals and communities are described. The formation of citizen boards and their roles, functions, and vulnerabilities are also described.

Experience from the 10-year, three-community Minnesota Heart Health Program (MHHP) provides a backdrop for some illustrations used in this chapter. The Minnesota model utilized *community boards* to initiate partnerships for communitywide health promotion programs to prevent heart disease. The 11-community COMMIT project (National Cancer Institute Heavy Smoker Trial) also has used the citizen board model. In the Minnesota project these boards represented numerous sectors of community. They began initially as advisory groups to the university-based project, but evolved into independent nonprofit corporations exercising final control over the maintenance and long-term implementation of heart health and related activities in their communities. At the conclusion of the MHHP, 73% of programs were being continued by local community sponsors. Other results documenting local involvement and ownership of programs and activities of this partnership arrangement are presented later in this chapter.

As mentioned in Chapter 3, there are several alternative approaches to organizing local groups for active participation and involvement. While influenced by the successes of the Minnesota partnership model, we have studied many intervention programs both nationally and internationally, and we discuss other approaches below, in the section on selecting organizational structures.

The term *citizen participation* is used in this chapter to embrace many forms of citizen action for community problem solving, including self-help groups. We define the term as follows:

Citizen participation is the social process of taking part (voluntarily) in formal or informal activities, programs, and/or discussions to bring about a planned change or improvement in community life, services, and/or resources.

From a theoretical perspective, citizen participation can be seen either as a dependent variable, where causes of participation are identified, or as an independent variable, where consequences of participation are analyzed (Voth & Jackson, 1981). L. Green (1986) notes, however, that "the principle of participation has not been systematically codified in health education with a cohesive set of constructs, definitions and propositions, but even in its crude form it serves to explain a wide range of behavioral phenomena in health" (p. 212).

Indicators or measures of citizen involvement include opportunity for and level of decision making or advising, amount and duration of time devoted to goal activities, representativeness of citizen and leader groups formed, degree of local ownership perceived and/or achieved, satisfaction with the processes of participation, and, finally, achievement and long-term maintenance of goals. Additional participation indicators have been developed by Rifkin, Mueller, and Bichmann (1988).

The content and perspective of this chapter are drawn principally from North American and Western European experiences and research findings. Applications to citizen participation beyond that context should be approached cautiously. The community development and anthropological literature suggest various cross-cultural styles (some passive, others more active) in coping with and responding to perceived community problems or opportunities. The third annual Healthy Cities Conference on community action and citizen participation (held in Pecs, Hungary, in 1989) provided ample evidence of the diversity to be found in this field.

Is citizen involvement a necessary requirement for achieving health promotion goals? Can citizen input be bypassed or ignored without untoward consequences? The research base for these questions is not readily available. Local and national values or legislative considerations frequently determine the degree to which citizens are engaged in social change goals. Limited evaluative studies plus anecdotal evidence suggest that when organizers seek out and utilize citizens, community health outcomes are better realized and long-term maintenance of program effects is enhanced.

CITIZEN PARTICIPATION: A REVIEW

Many community improvements, including public health enhancement, result from direct citizen concern and action. Historical studies of organized social life reveal distinct urban and rural forms of civic change (see, e.g., Eisenstadt & Schachar, 1987). Complex urban environments often develop more formal avenues and infrastructures through which citizen involvement is mediated and realized. Informal, ad hoc citizen approaches are more frequently seen in rural areas or small towns and villages. Regardless of geographic and community structural determinants, citizen involvement or participation (these terms are used interchangeably) is widely observed and reinforced as a social norm of community life.

Perceptions of the social benefits of citizen participation are generally positive. Official government bulletins (e.g., Council of Europe, 1980) often espouse active citizen participation. Surveys in North America document high rates of volunteer involvement and successful civic action projects (American Can Corporation, 1986). U.N.

documents recommend wider use of citizen participation strategies (see, e.g., Leparski & Nussel, 1987; World Health Organization Office of Health Promotion, 1986). Chavis, Stucky, and Wandersman (1983) suggest that "creating partnership and linkages between social scientists and citizens can improve the quality of research, enhance the potential for its utilization and help people help themselves" (p. 430). Ashton, Grey, and Barnard (1986) discuss community action strategies within the new World Health Organization Healthy City initiatives. Many health, social service, and sports associations depend entirely on volunteer support and effort. In the workplace, greater employee participation in decision making has been a general trend.

A recent review of social and community intervention programs in the field of mental health and community psychology shows promising short-term results but points up the need for more citizen and consumer involvement:

> Needed for the next generation of social and community interventions are fewer individual and more collective efforts designed in concert with the groups and communities we seek to assist. Designing and conducting such programs with greater ecological sensitivity to issues of process and context will help insure that effective interventions endure after initial results have been published. (Gesten & Jason, 1987, p. 456)

While citizen involvement may be desired and frequently called for, studies of citizen participation in community development programs show a mixed record of success (Gittel, 1980; Kweit & Kweit, 1981). Voth and Jackson (1981) cite anecdotal evidence of citizens spontaneously mobilizing and achieving important objectives, but conclude that "the citizen participation process is not easily stimulated or managed for policy purposes. Furthermore, the proportion of citizens involved may be limited and these may be primarily community elites" (p. 11). In the United Kingdom there are a number of groups who argue for a role in planning and setting objectives for health services. However, "two groups with the least involvement are the work force and the community" (A. Green, 1987, p. 132). Even when consumers are given a voice, experiences reported by Pecarchik, Ricci, and Bardin (1976, p. 73) from the Mon Valley Health and Welfare Project in the United States have shown that the presence of consumer representatives on the management board does not in itself guarantee meaningful consumer participation in decision making and planning. This was also true of Office of Economic Opportunity programs during the 1960s and 1970s.

Representatives from 26 European countries, Canada, and Australia have concluded that "attention be given to educating, or allowing lay people to participate in the creation, implementation and evaluation of health promotion, disease prevention, treatment and support programs" (Euro Reports and Studies 95, 1983, p. 12).

On the more positive side, the Vannas Project in Sweden sought to include community and consumer expectations in changes at a local primary care center (Westman, Andersson, & Eriksson, 1987). In the United States, citizen involvement in local health centers and programs generally has been successful. Simmons (1975), Cleary, Kichen, and Ensor (1985), and Kizer (1987) document several successful health education projects involving citizen action. Citizen health commissions in Cuba (Minkler, 1980-81) and consumer cooperatives in Japan (Sonada, 1988) offer additional examples of successful citizen involvement.

Motivation of Active Participants

Several researchers have studied the characteristics and motivations of those who actively participate in formal or voluntary associations. Wandersman and Giamartino (1980) found that participation was more likely among those who were concerned about their neighborhood, had more experience in community leadership, and felt that competent colleagues could be enlisted to support the project. Smith (1975) noted distinct social class differences among participants he studied (generally they came from higher socioeconomic levels). More recent studies show a wider spread of participation by age, sex, and race. Young adults (14 to 17 years) contribute more volunteer effort than any other age group, but one of four persons over 75 years is still active in volunteer programs. Some 38% of minority groups volunteer and participate in community activities, as do 40% of those characterized as poor. There has been an increase of men reporting participation in volunteer activity (45% male versus 51% female).

In summarizing factors that contribute to successful citizen participation, Voth and Jackson (1981) list the following as important:

- good faith on the part of the sponsoring group or agency
- clearly defined authority of citizen groups
- availability of resources
- ability of citizen groups to create and sustain an effective organization that they control

Our eight years of intensive experience with three distinct communities and their citizen boards in the Minnesota Heart Health Program suggest six additional factors for successful citizen activation:

- early and extensive knowledge of community history, organizational resources, influence structures, and interorganizational networks, including past successful or unsuccessful efforts at change
- early identification and open discussion of resistance forces or barriers to change that exist in the community (could include lack of government funding and/or commitment)
- clearly stated roles and time commitments for community participants/volunteers
- commitment of project sponsors to partnership and/or local ownership from the beginning of a project (may require active consultation and involvement following the project demonstration period; includes training time to develop skills for long-term maintenance)
- planned reinforcement (recognition and/or tangible benefits) of citizen participants built into program development and design stages
- timely use of conflict-resolution strategies when issues or disagreements cannot readily be resolved

From a review of what is known about citizen participation, we can summarize the social and programmatic benefits most frequently mentioned in various studies. Citizen involvement in planning for community change is a way of doing all of the following:

- pretesting the feasibility and acceptability of new programs or ideas
- gaining wide citizen support and the efforts of volunteers
- incorporating local values, attitudes, and symbols into implementation plans
- gaining access to local leaders, resources, and technical skills not otherwise available
- building the lay person's point of view into program delivery
- developing local skills and competencies for future community development/opportunities
- forcing coordination among loosely structured agencies and organizations, both public and private
- negotiating conflicts among political factions and special interest groups
- ensuring local ownership and long-term maintenance

CITIZEN INVOLVEMENT IN
HEALTH PROMOTION: RECENT EXPERIENCES

Citizen involvement in health promotion can run the gamut from manipulation and tokenism to actual control. Various levels of citizen participation are possible. In most social action projects or health promotion programs a *partnership* arrangement of community citizens (usually initiated by a core group of community leaders) is combined with the knowledge and talents of vested change agents and government specialists. This has been particularly true of demonstration projects in chronic disease prevention during the last 10 to 15 years, beginning largely with the North Karelia Project in Finland (Puska, Nissinen, & Tuomilehto, 1985; Puska, Salonen, Tuomilehto, Nissinen, & Kottke, 1983). The U.S.-based Minnesota (Carlaw, Mittelmark, Bracht, & Luepker, 1984; Mittelmark, 1986), Pawtucket (Lefebvre, 1986), and Stanford (Farquhar, Flora, & Good, 1985) Heart Health projects and Pennsylvania County Health Improvement Project (Stunkard, Felix, Yopp, & Cohen, 1985) have used citizen involvement in conjunction with local professional and voluntary services to achieve desired risk-reduction goals for heart disease at the community level. Citizen action is basic to the PATCH (Planned Approach to Community Health) programs of the Centers for Disease Control. This is true also for the several community health demonstration projects sponsored by the Kaiser Family Foundation now operating in the western and southern United States. In short, citizen action is a key component of many current prevention-oriented projects.

While much of community organization theory (Cox, Erlich, Rothman, & Tropman, 1979) suggests that the impetus for community change comes from grass-roots groups, with change efforts primarily directed by citizens themselves, social improvements also are governed by many external factors, organizations, and policies. Grass-roots influence is but one, albeit important, factor in change. Few communities are independent of larger regional, federal, and international social and economic influences. Bureaucratic social planning models can be combined with advocacy models and grass-roots approaches. Peterson (1988) has analyzed the relationship between "top-down" and "bottom-up" strategies in Sweden. Balance and integration between the two are recommended. Wakefield and Wilson (1986) review evidence of the importance of leadership opinions in health campaigns.

In Minnesota, citizen leadership boards were developed in the three demonstration communities to build a partnership strategy between university and community. These boards developed into "independent" nonprofit organizations overseeing and maintaining health promotion activities. Local activation of citizen health boards in both Australia and New Zealand is also under way (Wakefield & Wilson, 1986). Some Scandinavian countries are reassessing the complementary use of nongovernment organizations in health programs and policies (Stonmarck, 1988). MacNair (1980) has written extensively on community partnership organizations.

Such semiautonomous boards pose certain problems. First, long-term maintenance and fiscal support for these ad hoc groups is clouded. Will they ever have sufficient funds and influence to maintain program effort? Second, use of citizen groups may seem out of place in highly structured public systems of health care in some countries. Third, in the United States, citizen community health councils or coalitions add yet another layer to an already fragmented and complex health services system. Notwithstanding these serious organizational and funding issues, one major advantage of citizen boards is that such groups represent a relatively *neutral* arena for the broad-based requirements of community health promotion. In a partnership model, health professionals (the experts) "stretch" to join with citizens (often the doers). The control and direction of programs can be a mutual undertaking. If citizen-based organizations are shown to be effective initiators of programs, policymakers should consider legislative and fiscal support for their continuation. Of course, publicly financed services must also play a vital role in program maintenance.

In the North Karelia project, the official public health service provides many of the professional and technical services required for heart disease risk intervention, but a citizen advisory group and voluntary heart association organization have played a major implementation role in program dissemination, education, and support. In Minnesota the citizen boards have played a similar role, but, with their more autonomous structure, resemble the "linking pin" concept discussed and promoted by Aldrich (1979). According to Aldrich, community organizations and their leaders can be seen as forming interorganizational networks or loosely coupled systems. Aldrich believes that community "organizations that produce goods, deliver services, maintain order or challenge the established order are fundamental building blocks of modern societies and must stand at the center of the analysis of social change" (p. 149). Aldrich identifies the linking pin organization as a type of organization geared to citizen involvement.

Such an organization has extensive and overlapping ties to different parts of other organizational networks and can play a central role in community integration and coordination. Since health promotion and wellness systems are not solidly established in all societies, linking pin organizations have a good chance of survival because they are moving into an unoccupied niche. Of course, as previously mentioned, the survival of such organizations is at risk because of their lack of structural traditions, support, and long-standing visibility.

To summarize, cooperation among private, public, and voluntary sectors in communitywide intervention programs is not only desired but required if new broad-based community goals are to be realized. Few citizens have the skill to design the sophisticated social marketing and media campaigns often necessary to create program awareness. Technical and professional experts are usually needed. The consumer perspective can be beneficial to professionals and government experts who design intervention strategies. In short, cooperative partnership among experts, consumers, and community leaders is desired. This cooperation extends to research efforts as well, including effective feedback and dissemination between scientists and citizens (Chavis et al., 1983).

SELECTING ORGANIZATIONAL STRUCTURES TO FACILITATE CITIZEN INVOLVEMENT

Mobilizing citizen action usually begins with the establishment of a structure to accommodate the formation and coordination of citizen effort. The type of structure decided upon varies by community type, size, program goals, past organizing experiences, and preferences for decision-making styles of the core organizing or motivating group. Minority populations may have developed distinctive organizing structures as well (for example, the role of the Black church).

A core group of concerned citizens and professionals usually initiates the action process. The group may select or identify a key person or organization to coordinate initial activities. This coordinator may be either a professional or a lay community leader. The group serves as a catalyst for assessing local needs and developing preliminary notions about what type of structure best accommodates citizen involvement and participation. Although the various structures or models have some classification purity, successful programs are likely to use aspects from several models.

Types of Citizen Partnership Structures

Leadership board or council. This model brings together existing leaders and/or community activists to work together toward a common goal, such as smoke-free environments or accident prevention. Generally, the board includes leaders from diverse community sectors or groups who are identified as necessary for achieving project goals. Boards recruit additional volunteers, who serve on action-oriented task forces. This model has been used successfully in the three-community Minnesota Heart Health Program.

Coalition. This model uses linked organizations and groups to address community issues. Existing organizations combine talents and resources to collaborate on problem solution. The formation of a new communitywide or regional coalition of groups and organizations is customary to tackle new community problems, although it is possible to enlist an existing coalition. Coalitions tend to be fluid, with organizations free to enter or leave. Coalitions for smoke-free societies have been quite active in recent years. Committed leadership is important to coalition success. Considerable effort must be directed toward interorganizational communication.

"Lead" or official agency. In this model, a single existing community agency or organization is identified as the primary liaison for health promotion activities in the community. This model is useful when the agency is an "obvious choice" or a community's political context, past history, and/or available resources dictate the selection of a credible and well-established agency, either public or private. In Pawtucket, the local hospital was the principal community sponsor of heart health activities in collaboration with other groups and organizations. For a discussion of this approach, see the Mexican-American community case study presented in Chapter 13 of this volume.

Grass-roots. This model reflects the use of informal structures in a community. Change efforts are less planned and more spontaneous. This model is often used by people who are not represented by formal structures (e.g., public housing residents). Mobilization often occurs through direct involvement with neighborhood residents (Burghardt, 1982, pp. 19-20). Self-help and mutual support groups often emerge from citizen advocacy efforts (Hatch & Kickbusch, 1983). Freire (1973) enforces this approach in building critical consciousness among citizens. Some grass-roots efforts have evolved into consumer cooperatives, through which local control is better achieved. Other grass-roots movements have had major impacts on policy decisions (e.g., improved care of the mentally ill and developmentally disabled). Brownlea (1983) discusses rural and urban grass-roots models that have worked.

Citizen panels. New forms of citizen monitoring and advocacy are emerging in partnership with bureaucratic organizations. Citizen panels can be either appointed or elected, and their task is circumscribed. Usually a five- to 10-member panel works cooperatively with government bodies to shape program policy and monitor program performance (e.g., a panel set up to monitor a waste disposal project). The panel structure could operate in highly bureaucratized systems with no tradition of direct citizen effort.

Networks and consortia. Network structures are less formal and hierarchical than coalitions. Networks develop more spontaneously and bring together persons who have a common commitment and who can act as catalysts for community action. Networks seem best suited to short-term goals for which collaborative action can be assured and long-term organizational resources and support are not of fundamental concern (an example is rapid support for proposed legislation). Parent and school groups organizing against drunk drivers or neighborhood groups fighting crime are examples of network action. A consortium is somewhere in the middle between a coalition and a network. Work-site consortia to promote health have been described by Basch, Zelasko, and Burkholder (1985) and Pelletier, Klehr, and McPhee (1988). Consortia tend to be relatively professional in nature and to link organizations in a formal way. The resources of several organizations can often be more effective in a coalition effort.

The organizational structures described above are not static. They can evolve into new or modified forms. Government and research groups generally benefit when citizen organizations exercise leadership control. Local ownership includes the prerogative to make changes and even "mistakes" in organizing and planning. Issues related to the adherence to research protocols (if present) must be discussed openly with citizen boards. Mittelmark discusses this in more detail in Chapter 6.

ROLE OF CITIZEN BOARDS

If local citizen involvement is a desired element of broad-based community health enhancement projects, how is it best realized? What process is involved? Using community boards as one model or structure of organizing, we discuss, based on experiences of the Minnesota project, two of the most important components of facilitating effective participation: formation and evolution of a citizen board and the roles and functions of task forces.

Board Development and Evolution

As discussed in Chapter 3, community groups play an important role in all five stages of organizing for health promotion. For example, in Stage 1, a detailed community analysis is done in cooperation with community leaders and potential participating organizations. After analysis and discussion, a citizen group is formed to begin planning. Initially, several leading citizens with stated interests in or known commitments to the project are solicited for membership. They are asked to suggest names of others they think might be helpful to the program. These names usually are similar to those found in a leadership survey analysis (Bracht, 1988). Invitations are issued both to heads of organizations and to individuals previously identified as community leaders. This group represents the major sectors of the community, including commercial, volunteer, political, educational, religious, recreational, medical, public health, and media (see Chapter 3, Table 3.3). The board may or may not be staffed by paid employees. It elects its own officers and sets its own bylaws. Special effort to interest and recruit minority group representatives is imperative. This is discussed further in the case studies presented in Part V.

An evaluation of local community boards in the MHHP showed that retention of founding members (after a seven-year period) was over 50%, indicating strong long-term community involvement and interest. Additionally, 73% of all programs initiated in the communities are now operated by local private and public organizations.

A critical step in board development is improved information and knowledge about the target issue. In one city, board members and their spouses were invited to a retreat, where workshops were held to give them more information on MHHP goals and board members had the opportunity for informal interaction with professional staff. Because board members need sufficient time to "digest" a complex health program, a six- to 10-month period is usually required in order to assist lay boards in developing more local control and directions.

A board's first anniversary can be a time to recognize accomplishment and to acknowledge the beginning of a new phase of board ownership and independence. In each of the three MHHP communities, a significant programmatic issue or decision-making conflict between the university and the community occurred about one year after project initiation. Local staffing problems brought board and university representatives to the negotiation table. Community board members were clearly moving away from a strictly advisory role. These events suggest that in developing community boards, one should look for community organizers who are skilled at conflict resolution and should also anticipate the need for increased independence and project restructuring.

In summary, the major functions of an initial citizen planning group and its successor organization include (a) participation in decisions about the overall intervention plan, (b) review of the accuracy of the community analysis profile, and (c) commentary on budgets, personnel, facilities, and subcontracting activities. As the more permanent community board emerges, the initial planning group members may need to continue to assist new board members in clarifying their mission, identifying tasks, enlarging community representation, and increasing community acceptance of the project.

Roles and Functions of Task Forces

Although the community advisory board represents the major sectors of the community and provides initial project legitimation, a broad public health program needs additional volunteer help and wider representation. A series of task forces made up of many additional volunteers, some professional and some lay, reporting to the larger community advisory board can be established. A task force, as indicated by the name, is a group focused on a particular assignment. This means that task forces help in narrowing the scope of a large community project to manageable component parts. The focus on improved health curricula in schools or standardization of communitywide blood pressure measurements are examples of such focused activities. Task forces provide opportunities to bring additional professionals into a contributing voluntary role. A school curriculum for health promotion might, for example, bring together a curriculum director, a principal, a teacher, a school nurse, and a community parent representative. As volunteers leave task forces, some may be considered for more permanent assignments on the community board, such as the executive or budget standing committees. This placement and/or reassignment of volunteers is of critical importance to the success of any program. To be successful, a volunteer program must use sound management techniques, including systematic documentation of effort and performance. Liability protection for volunteers is one issue that needs attention, and local or state statutes must be reviewed.

SUMMARY

Numerous communitywide demonstrations have documented the important contributions made by local citizen groups and leaders. We have reviewed the literature on citizen participation and summarized its general conclusions. Various structures for organizing and facilitating citizen involvement have been presented. The community board model of the MHHP has been used for illustrative purposes in this chapter. Regardless of which structure is chosen, several conditions stand out as important in assuring successful collaboration among the interested parties in any community health project. Early and continuing clarification of project activities and goals is critical. Mutual trust needs to develop, and real community decision making must take place. The field director's role is a most important one, and he or she must be able to initiate and maintain a process for continued participation and successful retention of community volunteers. Finally, and most important, successful collaborations reflect a commitment to mutual consultation and the maximization of local ownership opportunities.

REFERENCES

Aldrich, H. (1979). *Organizations and environments.* Englewood Cliffs, NJ: Prentice-Hall.

American Can Corporation. (1986). *Report on model community programs.* Greenwich, CT: Author.

Ashton, J., Grey, P., & Barnard, K. (1986). Healthy Cities: WHO's new public health initiative. *Health Promotion, 1*(3).

Basch, C. E., Zelasko, S., & Burkholder, B. (1988). An alternative approach for worksite health promotion: The consortium model. *Health Education Quarterly, 15*, 22-24.

Bracht, N. (1988). Community analysis precedes community organization for cardiovascular disease prevention. *Scandinavian Journal of Primary Health Care* (Suppl. 1), 23-30.

Brownlea, A. (1983). *Grassroots initiative in health care: Urban and rural models that work.* Brisbane, Australia: Griffith University.

Burghardt, S. (1982). *Organizing for community action.* Beverly Hills, CA: Sage.

Carlaw, R. W., Mittelmark, M. B., Bracht, N., & Luepker, R. (1984). Organization for a community cardiovascular health program: Experiences from the Minnesota Heart Health Program. *Health Education Quarterly, 11*, 243-252.

Chavis, D., Stucky, P., & Wandersman, A. (1983, April). Returning basic research to the community: A relationship between scientist and citizen. *American Psychologist*, 424-434.

Cleary, H., Kichen, J., & Ensor, P. (1985). *Advancing health through education: A case study approach.* Palo Alto, CA: Mayfield.

Council of Europe, European Public Health Committee. (1980). *What can be expected from health education programmes?* Strasbourg: Author.

Cox, F., Erlich, J., Rothman, J., & Tropman, J. (Eds.). (1979). *Strategies of community organization: A book of readings* (3rd ed.). Itasca, IL: Peacock.

Eisenstadt, S., & Schachar, A. (1987). *Society, culture, and urbanization.* Newbury Park, CA: Sage.

Euro Reports and Studies 95. (1983). *Primary health care in industrialized countries: Report on a WHO meeting.* Bordeau: World Health Organization.

Farquhar, J., Flora, J., & Good, L. (1985). *Integrated comprehensive health promotion programs.* Palo Alto, CA: Kaiser Family Foundation.

Freire, P. (1973). *Education for critical consciousness.* New York: Seabury.

Gesten, E., & Jason, L. (1987). Social and community interventions. *Annual Review of Psychology, 38,* 427-460.

Gittel, M. (1980). *Limits to citizen participation.* Beverly Hills, CA: Sage.

Green, A. (1987). Is there primary health care in the UK? *Health Policy and Planning,* 2(2), 129-137.

Green, L. (1986). The theory of participation: A qualitative analysis of its expression in national and international health policies. *Advances in Health Education and Promotion, 1,* 211-236.

Hatch, S., & Kickbusch, I. (1983). *Self-help and health in Europe: New approaches in health care.* Copenhagen: World Health Organization.

Kizer, W. M. (1987). *The healthy workplace: A blueprint for corporate action.* New York: John Wiley.

Kweit, R., & Kweit, M. (1981). *Implementing citizen participation in a bureaucratic society.* New York: Praeger.

Lefebvre, C. (1986). *Pawtucket Heart Health Program: Methods used for cultural change.* Paper presented at the Hasselby Conference on the Role of Community Analysis and Focus Groups in Community Intervention Studies, Stockholm.

Leparski, C., & Nussel, E. (Eds.). (1987). *Country-wide integrated non-communicable diseases intervention programme, protocol and guidelines for monitoring and evaluation procedures.* Berlin: Springer-Verlag.

MacNair, R. (1980). *Community partnership organizations: A better way to gain participation in health programs.* Atlanta, GA: U.S. Department of Health and Human Services, Centers for Disease Control.

Minkler, M. (1980-81). Citizen participation in health in the Republic of Cuba. *Quarterly of Community Health Education, 1*(1), 73.

Mittelmark, M. (1986). Community-wide prevention of cardiovascular disease: Education strategies of the Minnesota Heart Health Program. *Preventive Medicine, 15,* 1-17.

Pecarchik, R., Ricci, E., & Bardin, N. (1976). Potential contribution of consumers to an integrated health care system, *Public Health Reports, 91*(1), 72-76.

Pelletier, K. R., Klehr, N., & McPhee, S. (1988). Developing workplace health promotion programs through university and corporate collaboration. *American Journal of Health Promotion, 2*(4), 75-81.

Peterson, B. (1988). *Health policy development and local implementation: How to keep head and tail together.* Paper presented at the National Conference on Healthy States, Brisbane, Australia.

Puska, P., Nissinen, L. A., & Tuomilehto, J. (1985). The community-based strategy to prevent coronary heart disease: Conclusions from the ten years of the North Karelia Project. *Annual American Review of Public Health, 6,* 147-193.

Puska, P., Salonen, J. T., Tuomilehto, J., Nissinen, A., & Kottke, T. E. (1983). Evaluating community-based preventive cardiovascular programs: Problems and experiences from the North Karelia Project. *Journal of Community Health, 9*(1), 49-63.

Rifkin, S., Mueller, F., & Bichmann, R. (1988). Primary health care: On measuring participation. *Social Science Medicine, 26*(9), 931-940.

Simmons, J. (1975, October). Making health education work. *American Journal of Public Health, 65,* 1-49.

Smith, D. H. (1975). Voluntary action and voluntary groups. In A. Inkeles, J. Coleman, & N. Smelser (Eds.), *Annual review of sociology* (Vol. 1, pp. 247-270). Palo Alto, CA: Annual Reviews.

Sonada, K. (1988). *Health promotion and consumers' cooperative movements in Japan.* Paper presented at the Second International Conference on Health Promotion, Adelaide, Australia.

Stonmarck, S. (1988). *The role of non-governmental organizations in mobilization for healthy public policy.* Paper presented at Second International Conference on Health Promotion, Adelaide, Australia.

Stunkard, A. J., Felix, M. R. J., Yopp, P., & Cohen, R. Y. (1985). Mobilizing a community to promote health: The Pennsylvania County Health Improvement Program (CHIP). In J. C. Rosen & L. J. Solomon (Eds.), *Prevention in health psychology* (pp. 143-190). Hanover, NH: University Press of New England.

Voth, D., & Jackson, V. (1981). *Evaluating citizen participation: Rural and urban community development* (Working Paper). Washington, DC: Center for Responsive Governance.

Wakefield, M., & Wilson, D. (1986). Community organization for health promotion. *Community Health Studies, 10,* 444-451.

Wandersman, A., & Giamartino, G. (1980). Community and individual difference characteristics as influences on initial participation. *American Journal of Community Psychology, 2,* 217-229.

Westman, G., Andersson, S., & Eriksson, C. (1987). Initiating change in primary care: The Vannas Project—its realization and evaluation. *Scandinavian Journal of Primary Health Care, 5,* 27-34.

World Health Organization Office of Health Promotion. (1986). *Health promotion: Concept and principles in action.* Copenhagen: Author.

Chapter 6

BALANCING THE REQUIREMENTS OF RESEARCH AND THE NEEDS OF COMMUNITIES

MAURICE B. MITTELMARK

Professional groups and community groups interact at many levels. Citizen involvement (as discussed in Chapter 5) often occurs in collaboration with government, industry, voluntary organizations, and universities. In academic medicine and public health, this can take the form of extending preventive services to the community, volunteer activity by community residents on behalf of the academic institution, and joint projects such as health awareness campaigns or fund drives to benefit new programs or facilities. A special instance of town-gown relations occurs when formal community health projects are undertaken that include a significant evaluation and research component. Such projects can range from community-initiated and -managed projects in which an external group is used as consultants to scientific programs of community health research primarily conceived and funded by, for example, a university faculty group and carried out in the neighborhood "laboratories" of the community.

In this chapter the focus is on academic-community relationships, and I draw on experience from several U.S. and international projects in order to review the opportunities and pitfalls of such collaborative ventures. Whatever the origin and purpose of such community health research projects, they share with all social experimentation the challenge of maintaining scientific rigor in method and measurement while simultaneously allowing the flexibility to accommodate the diverse needs and expectations of the community at large.

SOCIAL EXPERIMENTATION

General guidelines for the management of social experiments have been developed. The Social Science Research Council, for example, has offered recommendations in five areas: the need to negotiate about the study design, the need to tailor methods and procedures to the particular climate of a community, the need to maximize application of the study to real-life problems, the need for constant quality assurance and control, and the need to study not only outcome, but also the process of change, asking both what effects occurred and *how* they occurred (Riecken & Boruch, 1974).

The first two of the council's recommendations are particularly relevant to the issue of balancing practical and scientific needs in community health research. These points are briefly paraphrased (and somewhat embellished) as follows. Negotiation, implying ready willingness to compromise on ideal approaches to the problem at hand, is necessary if the study design is to be realistic. Part of the process is clarifying objectives and developing a practical plan for the work, but the key activity is *negotiation*. This may have greatest significance in the design of the study. Flexibility in determining the design of field studies has been aided by the development in recent years of practical texts on the subject (Judd & Kenny, 1981; Rutman, 1977).

Although rare as yet, formal agreements have been used for some joint research and demonstration projects involving academic and community groups. One recent example of this occurred in a collaboration between the East Harlem Council for Human Services, Inc. (EHCHS) and the Department of Community Medicine at Mount Sinai School of Medicine in New York City (Merino, Rose, & Boch, 1982). The EHCHS was the product of a grass-roots movement by young Puerto Rican activists, who sought help from Mount Sinai in establishing a neighborhood health center. The EHCHS obtained funding for the center from the U.S. Public Health Service and engaged the Mount Sinai investigators as collaborators to provide technical assistance and consultation help with project management, and provide services.

The unique aspect of the collaboration was the adoption early in the program of a formalized planning model to define clearly the roles and responsibilities of the community agency and the academic center. A

Phase	Role of Community Agency	Role of Department of Community Medicine
(I) Planning the planning	(1) Recognize a community health problem.	← Respond to community request for assistance.
	(2) Decide to address the problem.	← Agree to work with community, study problem.
	(3) Select program goals.	← Assist with articulation of goals.
(II) Preparation of the plan	(1) Select the approach, design a preliminary model.	← Study resources, propose solutions, design preliminary model, organize planning team.
	(2) Refine model, specify tasks required to actualize model.	← Refine model, specify tasks required to actualize model.
	(3) Write and submit proposal.	← Organize proposal, assist with funding sources, participate in site visits.
(III) Program implementation	(1) Design a timetable.	← Assist with timetable.
	(2) Implement the program.	← Assist with selection of key staff.
	(3) Evaluate the program.	← Design evaluation process.
	(4) Modify according to the evaluation results.	← Propose solutions.

SOURCE: Merino et al. (1982, Figure 1). Reprinted by permission.

Figure 6.1. The Planning Model

schematic representation of the model is shown in Figure 6.1. On its face, this planning model seems comprehensive enough to accommodate a wide range of community health projects, including both research and service programs. By adjusting the elements of the planning model, virtually any collaborative agreement could be formalized, helping significantly to clarify roles and expectations. Of course, agreements must be fluid enough to accommodate the changing circumstances of a collaboration as the project develops and matures.

There is a clear need to tailor interventions and other study procedures to fit the social and political climate of the community. It is a truism that there is no such thing as a packaged social intervention that can be used "right out of the box." This is true even for communities that appear to the casual observer to be quite homogeneous. In one major multicommunity study of cardiovascular disease prevention in the Midwest, the Minnesota Heart Health Program (MHHP), it was discovered early that the same *process* of planning and community organization could be used in the different communities involved in the program, but that specific educational approaches had to be adapted to meet the unique needs of each community (Mittelmark et al., 1986).

ACTION RESEARCH

This collegial perspective on the involvement of community groups in decision making about health research and service in community settings has roots in several behavioral science disciplines, notably social work and psychology (Cox, Erlich, Rothman, & Tropman, 1979; Bracht, 1978, pp. 243-260; Jones, 1985). Key developments in this perspective can be traced readily to Kurt Lewin, perhaps the most prolific and influential figure in the field of applied social psychology. Lewin's work and writings have had direct significance for contemporary community health research, since a good many of the behavioral scientists in the field are trained in the Lewinian tradition. This tradition goes back to the years of World War II and immediately after, when Lewin launched many innovative field studies of behavior change in diverse and often difficult settings (Lewin, 1948). Characteristically, Lewin sought involvement of research participants, factory workers, and housewives, for example, as active collaborators in all aspects of his work.

In recent times, Lewin's approach, termed *action research*, is evident as a principal element in virtually all the major community-based cardiovascular disease research and demonstration projects being conducted in the United States. For instance, its central role in the theoretical framework of the MHHP has been described by Mittelmark et al. (1986), and numerous specific examples of its application have been published. As a concrete example, the Pawtucket Heart Health Program fully involved workers and management in decision making about how health promotion programs at the work site would be carried out and assisted volunteer task forces of employees in using needs assessment data to establish their own health improvement priorities, to implement and revise programs, and to reset goals as necessary (Lasater et al., 1984).

PATTERNS OF RELATIONSHIPS BETWEEN ACADEMIC AND COMMUNITY GROUPS

Collaborative relationships between academic and community groups can take several forms. In some cases, the academic group develops the plan, obtains the funding, and leads the project, and the community collaborator is, in a sense, the junior partner in the effort. In other cases, their roles are reversed; in yet others, roles change as the project moves through its different phases.

Wandersman (1981) has provided a useful framework to describe relationships between organizational partners. A key aspect of his analysis relates to *decision-making power*. The power of a group can range from strictly advisory to a position of full authority. It is not simply vagueness in terminology that results in certain community groups being called "community advisory boards" while others are called "boards of directors." The central difference is that a board of directors can hire and fire staff, while an advisory board cannot. On the other hand, advisory boards are not powerless. Their principal instrument of power is the potential to withdraw from association with a project whose leadership or direction they disapprove. Disillusionment and withdrawal may occur also when advice given is not often enough taken.

Wandersman categorizes program participants into three major groups: *residents*, who are the individuals the program targets; *helpers*, including professional and nonprofessionals, who perform a range of tasks to form or maintain an organization; and government *officials*, who fund, oversee, or monitor projects. These concepts of role, status, and power can be adapted to classify typical relationships between academic and community groups involved in community health research.

Partnership Status

All parties to a community health program are in a partnership of sorts. These partnerships may exhibit all of the variations characteristic of a professional partnership (silent compared with managing, junior, and senior partners) and changes in the partnership (new partners joining, junior partners becoming senior partners, and partners leaving). Whatever their status, power, and level of responsibility, partners share one characteristic, and that is that all partners in an enterprise have some degree of ownership of it. In this sense, contributing groups in community health research and demonstration programs can be thought of as being either junior or senior partners, though over time the partnership status of a group may very well change. Examples of each of these partnership models, and suggestions for maintaining satisfactory collaboration in each of them, are given in later sections of the chapter.

Vested Interests of Contributing Partners

In a community research project, the usual partners are one or more academic groups and one or more community groups. The term *academic group* is meant to include individuals and collections of individuals in specialized academic centers, traditional scholastic departments, medical schools, schools of public health, or the "scientific" branches of local, state, or federal agencies. The common characteristic of these academic groups is that their principal interest in the project rests with the evaluation of the intervention and dissemination of results to professional peer groups.

Community groups include both formally and informally constituted groups, either permanent or temporary. Included are government units, private for-profit businesses and health organizations, and not-for-profit organizations. The common characteristic of community groups is that their vested interest rests primarily with the need to provide the community with health services.

Though they are not central to the present analysis, two other groups that are critical to the conduct of community health programs should at least be mentioned: (a) the population of residents the project is intended to serve, and (b) the program's line staff—health educators, for example (who, as an aside, must be artful at negotiating the boundaries separating the service population, the academic group, and the community group; see Minkler, 1978, for a discussion of this issue).

Program Stage

As a community health research and demonstration program progresses from the planning stage through the early implementation phases and on to maturity, the vested interests of the various partners hold relatively constant. Academic groups continue to be most interested in the scientific project, and community groups continue to be motivated mostly by the service needs of the community. However, as the program moves through its natural stages, the partnership arrangement of the contributing groups may change, with junior partners taking on seniority and vice versa.

Various patterns of partnership are illustrated in the following sections, drawing from current community health research and demonstration programs around the world. Emphasis is placed on management strategies that help protect the vested interests of all parties to the partnership.

THE COMMUNITY GROUP AS SENIOR PARTNER

The national experience with community research and demonstration programs dates mostly from the 1960s, when many social action programs were launched to deal with poverty and its consequences. Characteristically, these programs were designed and implemented by community social service agencies, and academic groups were involved as consultants to study the effectiveness of the programs (Brophy, Maisto, Burstein, & Chan, 1977).

The North Karelia Project

A contemporary example of this partnership model is the Finnish North Karelia Project (National Public Health Laboratory of Finland, 1981). Epidemiological observations of regional differences in cardiovascular morbidity and mortality within Finland stimulated the governor of the county (state) of North Karelia and other community leaders to seek national aid to reduce the cardiovascular disease problem in North Karelia. Parliament passed legislation to provide needed resources, and the National Finnish Heart Association took responsibility for organizing the community-based program. The project was conceived as a national pilot program wherein the community-based approach would be carefully tested. Within just two years, the project evolved into an official activity of the regional health administration. By the fourth year, activities had been integrated into the basic health services at village-level health centers. Thus community leaders were the key in stimulating government actions to deal with the public health problem, and the Finnish system very quickly institutionalized the program as an official part of the health service.

The scientific study of the program was undertaken by investigators at the University of Kuopio and other academic institutions. This included the design of the evaluation, surveys of risk factors, and surveillance of morbidity and mortality. There was, of course, collegial exchange about all aspects of the program, and university investigators certainly contributed to the education program, just as government and community leaders contributed to the evaluation. However, because the locus of control of the project was in the community, certain features of the study design were dictated by political considerations more than by scientific ones. Perhaps the prime example of this was the decision to locate the intervention program in North Karelia and assign the neighboring county of Kuopio as the study reference area. The investigators would surely have preferred to assign counties to experimental conditions randomly, but this could not be accommodated under the circumstances.

Community Dog Litter Cleanup Campaign

Another example of the community in the role of senior partner is the collaboration that evolved during the 1970s between a group of researchers at De Paul University and Chicago neighborhoods that sought to control dog litter (Jason, McCoy, Blanco, & Zolik, 1980). Initially, concerned community leaders brought the problem to the attention of the university group, which followed up by conducting modest surveillance and intervention programs. The publicity from this effort stimulated other groups to consult the De Paul group, and additional community studies were undertaken. The role of the university group evolved to include significant contributions both to evaluation and to intervention, but community leaders and groups maintained "ownership" of the litter control effort. Nevertheless, the investigators were concerned about the possibility that community residents would feel dominated by the scientists and undertook to avoid this first by becoming familiar with the community and its culture and then by involving community members as partners in the design of evaluation and intervention initiatives.

Community Groups as Evaluators

The notion that community groups might be partners in evaluation activities, as occurred in the dog litter cleanup campaign, is not commonly held. Nevertheless, as implausible an idea as this may seem, it is one with which the American social action movement has substantial experience, mainly through the community mental health movement that was stimulated by the federal Community Mental Health Centers Act of 1963. The provisions of the act encouraged evaluation by citizens and, in practice, this has included diverse activities, ranging from short site visits to the establishment of evaluation committees for whom the professional evaluator is a resource (Weiss, Monroe, Bray, Davis, & Hunt, 1977).

Researchers as Diagnosticians

In some community health research partnerships, the researcher's role is that of diagnostician, with responsibility to collect data to aid in health *planning* rather than in health program *implementation* (Morris, 1975). Reports on the Vermont Health Risk Survey (Novick, Jillson, Coffin, & Freedman, 1985) and Swedish Skarborg County Study (Haglund, Isaacsson, Ryden, & Råstam, 1983) show the academic group in the role of community diagnostician.

THE ACADEMIC GROUP AS SENIOR PARTNER

Several community health research programs in the cardiovascular disease prevention area illustrate the situation in which the academic group is the senior partner and the community group is the junior partner. However, all these have been planned so that authority and responsibility will gradually shift to the community group, to help ensure that the programs become incorporated in the fabric of the community.

For example, Farquhar and his colleagues (1984) at Stanford University have introduced terminology to help differentiate educational contributions made to a community project by outside experts (exogenous activities) and by community groups (endogenous activities). An important feature of the Stanford model of disease prevention in communities is the goal of using exogenous resources early in the life of a project to stimulate endogenous support as the program unfolds. The example is given of how smoking classes initiated by the Stanford group were eventually incorporated as a standing service of a county health department.

As a second example, the MHHP intended from the outset that its communities would gradually assume control over the programs (Carlaw, Mittelmark, Bracht, & Luepker, 1984). From the time of the initial meeting with community leaders in each of the three intervention towns of the MHHP, university researchers stated the hope and expectation that the partnership between university and community would evolve, with the community emerging as senior partner in the latter stages of the project. They saw this as vital to the long-term viability of the heart health program. This plan is depicted in Table 6.1, which illustrates expected changes in the collaborative arrangement at different stages.

This plan was at once a benefit and a liability to the program. The program gained additional importance in the eyes of community leaders when they realized that evolving community control was a prime objective of the MHHP. Conversely, there was some tension between the academic group and the community groups as discussions proceeded about the exact timing of the changes in the community's role from junior to senior partner. It was difficult, for example, for the project staff who organized citizen task forces to learn to serve those task forces rather than lead them. This problem was exacerbated because, early on, some leadership by staff was indeed needed.

Also from the MHHP come quite concrete examples of ways in which ascendancy of the community group has been signaled. In the twin towns of Fargo, North Dakota, and Moorhead, Minnesota, a significant event in the evolution of the community group was its decision to seek incorporation as a not-for-profit organization charged to maintain the heart health program as a permanent activity in the community (Murray, 1986). With this significant step, the community group moved from having the limited responsibility of an advisory body to being an independent group with fund-raising authority and management responsibility. A similar process of formal incorporation has occurred in the other two MHHP communities, Mankato and Bloomington, both in Minnesota.

As a final example of the shift in partnership roles, early in the program in Mankato, the MHHP established an interagency council for blood pressure control that within one year became totally independent and successfully competed for state block grant funding to carry out its work (Blackburn, Grimm, Luepker, & Mittelmark, 1985). Representatives of the MHHP continue to serve on the council, but only as

Table 6.1

Steps in Education and Community Involvement for the
Minnesota Heart Health Project

Phase I Step I	Step II	Phase II Step III	Step IV
community analysis	development of task forces	development of social system support	organizational commitment to an improved social environment
identification of geographical and interest sector representatives to serve on heart health board	extension of community participation through committees, thus diffusing awareness and involvement	organization of skill-building sessions and workshops in churches, school districts, trade unions, service, and health clubs, etc.	employers encourage and reinforce consistent heart healthy behavior through financial and other incentive systems
education of board members in essential components and proposed scope of education program	development by T.F. and committees of alternatives and choices to act positively for heart health (enabling factors)	social system support of behaviors conducive to heart health	insurance companies, banks, and related organizations provide favorable rates for heart healthy families and individuals
members identify interest as task force chairpersons and in executive committee	gradual modification of community values and norms to support heart healthy behaviors	strengthening of community norms and values	

researchers as initiating partners————————— community as initiating partners

SOURCE: Carlaw et al. (1984, Table 1). Reprinted by permision.

members in good standing, with no greater or lesser status than any other council member.

Training of Community Leaders

A key strategy in helping community leaders to understand the scientific and public health issues of a community project (and in preparing them to join in and eventually control decision making) is formal training. This is needed to overcome a communications (and knowledge) gap between community groups and academic groups; scientists often may not be sufficiently concerned with the perceived needs of the community and tend to focus on study endpoints that are of little consequence to the community. Lay groups, on the other hand, may be resistant to proposals that are indicated by research findings, due to financial or other considerations.

Hayman, Hochbaum, and Hoffman (1979) have experimented with a variety of training conference formats to provide a venue for interchange to reduce this communication gap. An evaluation of the approach shows that attenders perceive formal conferences to be effective in providing a meeting ground for the exchange of ideas between researchers and community health practitioners.

Apparently, specialized training retreats serve several needs. An extended meeting gives members of academic and community groups time to get to know one another. Frequently, even in a relatively small community, such a retreat gives community leaders the chance to become better acquainted, contributing ultimately to a more effective community group.

Some of these programs have been quite elaborate. The North Karelia Project (McAlister, Puska, Salonen, Tuomilehto, & Koskela, 1982), the Montevideo (Minnesota) Heart Health Project (Luepker et al., 1981), and the MHHP (Carlaw et al., 1984) all used weekend retreats with overnight accommodations; the Minnesota retreats included spouses of the invited community leaders, following the rationale that involvement of community leaders' families would help personalize the health issues and potential for improvement. A major difference in strategy was that North Karelia timed its retreats to start five years after the education program was launched. The Minnesota retreats were the initial project activities, occurring before any public education was undertaken (no data are available on the comparative effectiveness of these strategies).

BALANCED PARTNERSHIPS

In some projects, it can be quite difficult to determine who is the senior partner and who is the junior partner. When resources are contributed in almost equal amounts by the academic and the community groups, partnership status may shift back and forth, depending on which group is best equipped to tackle the problem of the moment. Such a program is the Pennsylvania County Health Improvement Program (CHIP), located in Lycoming County. Because external funding for the program was minimal, the state health department program organizers depended totally on the community to provide facilities for the project. When the initial choice of space in a local hospital did not work out, the community steering committee arranged an alternative location (Stunkard, Felix, Yopp, & Cohen, 1985).

SUMMARY

Collaborations between academic and community groups for the purpose of mounting and maintaining community health research projects are substantially strengthened when both parties approach the relationship as a true partnership. Partnerships are dynamic relationships, with power often shifting as the project progresses from planning to implementation and on to completion. There is a tradition in behavioral science in which certain individuals involved in a study are called "experimenters" while others are called "subjects." This is a fading tradition, with subjects today more and more often referred to as "participants." In community-based research, an even newer concept is emerging, one that suggests "collaborators" as the label most appropriate for the community groups and leaders whose support is critical to the establishment and maintenance of the project.

Using this approach requires flexibility on the part of academic groups, both in the process of designing studies and in analyzing the community health research studies being conducted by others. Strong study designs and methods can be employed nevertheless, if investigators are willing to devote time and energy to building the community partner's understanding of the research issues that confront the project. More often than not, an informed community group will be as demanding of quality in research design as are its academic colleagues.

REFERENCES

Blackburn, H., Grimm, R., Luepker, R. V., & Mittelmark, M. (1985). The primary prevention of high blood pressure: A population approach. *Preventive Medicine, 14,* 466-481.

Bracht, N. (1978). *Social work and health care: A guide to professional practice.* New York: Haworth.

Brophy, M., Maisto, S., Burstein, L., & Chan, A. (1977). Evaluation of community action programs: Issues and alternative. In R. D. Coursey, G. A. Specter, S. A. Murrell, & B. H. Hunt (Eds.), *Program evaluation for the health professions: Methods, strategies, participants* (pp. 205-224). New York: Grune & Stratton.

Carlaw, R. W., Mittelmark, M. B., Bracht, N., & Luepker, R. (1984). Organization for a community cardiovascular health program: Experiences from the Minnesota Heart Health Program. *Health Education Quarterly, 11*, 243-252.

Cox, F., Erlich, J., Rothman, J., & Tropman, J. (Eds.). (1979). *Strategies of community organization: A book of readings* (3rd ed.). Itasca, IL: Peacock.

Farquhar, J. W., Fortmann, S. P., Maccoby, N., Wood, P. D., Haskell, W. L., Taylor, C. B., Flora, J. A., Solomon, D. S., Rogers, T., Adler, E., Breithouse, P., & Weiner, L. (1984). The Stanford Five City Project: An overview. In J. D. Matarazzo, S. H. Weiss, J. A. Herd, N. E. Miller, & S. W. Weiss (Eds.), *Behavioral health: A handbook of health enhancement and disease prevention* (pp. 1154-1165). New York: John Wiley.

Haglund, B. J. A., Isaacsson, S. O., Ryden, L., & Råstam, L. (1983). Health profile of Skarborg County 1977: A Swedish rural cross-sectional study. *Scandinavian Journal of Community Health, 10*(2), 67-80.

Hayman, C. R., Hochbaum, G., & Hoffman, H. I. (1979). Communications between community health researchers and practitioners: Evaluation of an attempt at improvement. In H. C. Schulberg & F. Baker (Eds.), *Program evaluation in health fields* (Vol. 2, pp. 435-442). New York: Human Sciences.

Jason, L. E., McCoy, K., Blanco, D., & Zolik, E. S. (1980). Decreasing dog litter: Behavioral consultation to help a community group. *Evaluation Review, 4*(3), 355-369.

Jones, E. F. (1985). Major developments in social psychology during the past five decades. In G. Lindsey & E. Aronson (Eds.), *Handbook of social psychology: Vol. 1. Theory and method* (3rd ed., pp. 64-96). New York: Random House.

Judd, C. M., & Kenny, D. A. (1981). *Estimating the effects of social interventions.* Cambridge: Cambridge University Press.

Lasater, T., Abrams, D., Artz, L., Beaudin, P., Cabrera, L., Elder, J., Ferreira, A., Knisley, P., Peterson, G., Rodrigues, A., Rosenberg, P., Snow, R., & Carleton, R. (1984). Lay volunteer delivery of a community-based cardiovascular risk factor change program: The Pawtucket experiment. In J. D. Matarazzo, S. H. Weiss, J. A. Herd, N. E. Miller, & S. W. Weiss (Eds.), *Behavioral health: A handbook of health enhancement and disease prevention* (pp. 1166-1170). New York: John Wiley.

Lewis, K. (1948). Action research and minority problems. In G. W. Lewin (Ed.), *Resolving social conflicts.* New York: Harper.

Luepker, R. V., Brown, J. W., Sobel, J. L., Jeffery, R. W., Pechacek, T. F., Hall, N., & Jacobs, D. R. (1981, November). *Mass media campaign for cardiovascular disease prevention.* Paper presented at the 109th Annual Meeting of the American Public Health Association, Los Angeles.

McAlister, A., Puska, P., Salonen, J. T., Tuomilehto, J., & Koskela, K. (1982). Theory and action for health promotion: Illustrations from the North Karelia Project. *American Journal of Public Health, 72*, 43-50.

Merino, R., Rose, D. N., & Boch, S. J. (1982). A medical school's involvement in the development of a community-based health center. *Journal of Community Medicine, 8*(2), 130-140.

Minkler, M. (1978). Ethical issues in community organizations. *Health Education Monographs, 6*(2), 199-210.

Mittelmark, M. B., Luepker, R. V., Jacobs, D. R., Bracht, N. F., Carlaw, R. W., Crow, R. S., Finnegan, J., Grimm, R. H., Jeffery, R. W., Kline, F. G., Mullis, R. M., Pechacek,

T. F., Perry, C. L., Pirie, P. L., & Blackburn, H. (1986). Community-wide prevention of cardiovascular disease: Education strategies of the Minnesota Heart Health Program. *Preventive Medicine, 15*, 1-17.

Morris, J. N. (1975). *Uses of epidemiology.* Edinburgh: Churchill Livingstone.

Murray, D. M. (1986). Dissemination of community health promotion programs: The Fargo-Moorhead Heart Health Program. *Journal of School Health, 56*(9), 375-381.

National Public Health Laboratory of Finland. (1981). *Community control of cardiovascular disease: Evaluation of a comprehensive community program for control of cardiovascular diseases in North Karelia, Finland, 1972-1977.* Copenhagen: World Health Organization, Regional Office for Europe.

Novick, L. F., Jillson, D., Coffin, R., & Freedman, M. (1985). The Vermont Health Risk Survey and the design of community wide prevention health programs. *Journal of Community Health, 10*(2), 67-80.

Riecken, H. W., & Boruch, R. F., (Eds.). (1974). *Social experimentation: A method for planning and evaluating social intervention.* New York: Academic Press.

Rutman, L. (Ed.). (1977). *Evaluation research methods: A basic guide.* Beverly Hills, CA: Sage.

Stunkard, A. J., Felix, M. R. J., Yopp, P., & Cohen, R. Y. (1985). Mobilizing a community to promote health: The Pennsylvania County Health Improvement Program (CHIP). In J. C. Rosen & L. J. Solomon (Eds.), *Prevention in health psychology* (pp. 143-190). Hanover, NH: University Press of New England.

Wandersman, A. (1981). A framework of participation in community organizations. *Journal of Applied Behavioral Sciences, 17*(1), 27-58.

Weiss, C. I., Monroe, J., Bray, C., Davis, H., & Hunt, B. (1977). Evaluation by citizens. In R. D. Coursey, G. A. Specter, S. A. Murrell, & B. H. Hunt (Eds.), *Program evaluation for the health professions: Methods, strategies, participants* (pp. 325-338). New York: Grune & Stratton.

Part III

COMMUNITYWIDE
INTERVENTION STRATEGIES

Chapter 7

ROLES OF MEDIA IN COMMUNITY-BASED HEALTH PROMOTION

JUNE A. FLORA
DIANA CASSADY

Communities across the United States are organizing themselves to improve the health of their citizens. In this movement toward self-improvement, community health agencies are making use of local resources. These local resources include media. These community-based efforts along with the use of media are inspired by positive models such as the nationally funded community-based research and demonstration projects to prevent cardiovascular disease (CVD) (Blackburn, Luepker, Kline, Bracht, & Carlaw, 1984; Farquhar, Fortmann, et al., 1985; Farquhar, Maccoby, & Wood, 1985; Farquhar et al., 1977; Lasater et al., 1984). Other model projects aim to prevent alcohol-related problems and teenage pregnancy (National Institute of Alcohol and Alcohol Abuse, 1983; Vincent, Clearie, & Schlucheter, 1987).

However, while research projects demonstrate the effectiveness of media in health promotion programs, several obstacles prevent local agencies from replicating these successes. One obstacle is the transfer of knowledge from research reports to local health professionals. Journal articles emphasize results, rarely including details about the

AUTHORS' NOTE: The work represented in this chapter was supported in part by U.S. Public Health Service Grant HL21906 from the National Heart, Lung and Blood Institute to John W. Farquhar, M.D., principal investigator. We extend our appreciation to two people who reviewed early versions of the chapter, Carol Baume and Louise Miller. Their comments and insights added considerably to the final product.

design of media components, especially when these components are related to program promotion (Flora & Wallack, 1990). Second, research projects often have substantial funding that is not readily available to local health agencies. These two factors make it difficult for local health agencies to translate research into practice.

In this chapter, we attempt to make existing research applicable to community settings by discussing the potential of media in the context of limited resources and experience. We begin by delineating roles that the mass media can play in health promotion programs. We then outline some of the possibilities of cooperation with local media organizations and gatekeepers, as a means for overcoming budgetary constraints. The roles of media organizations in community-based interventions and a description of how these roles can be used in planning are discussed. We conclude by identifying guidelines for the integration of media and media gatekeepers in community health program planning and implementation.

DEFINITIONS OF MEDIA

We use the term *media* to refer to media channels, the paths by which the message reaches the receiver—whether it arrives visually, in auditory form, or as written text. The term as used here includes the mass "broadcast" media, such as network television and national newspapers, as well as the smaller "narrowcast" media, such as specialized cable television, magazines, and local newsletters.

Individual media channels can be distinguished by (a) the extent to which they target specific audience subgroups, (b) the senses affected, (c) the size and characteristics of the audience reached, (d) the possibility of message repetition, (e) message duration, (f) the opportunity for feedback, (g) the amount of receiver control, (h) the type of message coding, and (i) the power of message preservation (McGuire, 1981; Schramm, 1982). Network television, for example, exemplifies a mass medium that has limited ability to target specific well-defined audiences. Targeting audiences through nationwide television is a much more expensive endeavor (involving message design, production, and placement) than is, for example, distributing booklets to individuals at specific workplaces or direct mail to an existing list of individuals whose behavior is known. If, however, the target audience is blue-collar workers in the United States, television may be less costly than reaching workers through thousands of individual workplaces across the nation.

The mass media are often designed to reach everyone, as in a presidential address or news about the recent earthquake in California. But just as frequently, the mass media are used to address particular audiences. Consider, for example, the success of soap operas that reach only a certain segment of the total population, or the Super Bowl, which is not watched by everyone, but by a large, well-defined segment. Television programs can be directed toward audience segments—youth, women, or the marginally literate.

In the mass media, such as network television and nationally distributed newspapers, audience targeting is done through message placement and message design. Smaller or more narrowcast media (e.g., booklets, magazines, cable TV, local radio, local computer networks) can reach particular audience subgroups more efficiently (Flora, Maibach, & Maccoby, 1989). For example, the Stanford Three Community Study (TCS) used a single Spanish-language radio station and newspaper to reach Spanish speakers (Maccoby & Alexander, 1979). In larger urban areas, however, the Spanish-language media may be more diversified, with different stations reaching different segments of the Spanish-speaking audience.

MEDIA MESSAGES IN HEALTH INTERVENTIONS

Media messages vary in comprehensibility, the number of arguments presented, one-sided or two-sided arguments, and style of presentation (e.g., humorous or dramatic), to mention a few (Petty & Cacioppo, 1981). Media messages can be the primary agent for change in a community health promotion program or solely a means to promote existing services. We distinguish four roles of media messages in public health interventions: (a) primary change agent, (b) complement to other interventions, (c) means of recruitment and promotion of services and programs, and (d) provider of support for life-style (health) changes. Flora, Maibach, and Maccoby (1989) have reviewed these four roles elsewhere, but because of their importance to understanding media in community based health promotion, we cover each role again, in detail.

In the first role, *media as primary change agent,* media are the primary or sole means of influencing the targeted endpoint, whether knowledge gain, shifts in social norms, or behavior change. Health professionals commonly use media alone to achieve health promotion goals (Flora, Maccoby, & Farquhar, 1989; Flora & Wallack, 1990). The Stanford TCS, for example, compared two different types of interventions, mass media alone and mass media supplemented with intensive face-to-face counseling (Farquhar et al., 1977; Maccoby, Farquhar, Wood, & Alexander, 1977). The results illustrated that media alone can achieve change in some behaviors, such as diet, but that other more addictive habits (e.g., smoking) require additional face-to-face interaction. (Farquhar et al., 1977; Maccoby et al., 1977). At the end of the first year of intervention, the supplemented intervention was more effective at reducing cardiovascular disease risk. By the end of the second year of intervention, risk reduction was equal in both intervention communities, while the control community had increased its rate of risk. However, at the end of the third year, the community educated by the mass media alone showed a loss in the maintenance of effects, while the community having supplemental counseling sustained effects (Maccoby & Solomon, 1981). It should be noted that although there were differences in the sizes of the effects, all changes were significantly different from controls.

A more recent example of media as primary change agent is the collaboration of the National Cancer Institute (NCI) and the Kellogg Company. This collaborative effort produced dramatic effects on health behavior (e.g., cereal purchases) through the use of media (Freimuth, Hammond, & Stein, 1988). The Kellogg Company developed a national media campaign to promote bran cereal consumption and NCI's Cancer Information Service (CIS) toll-free number. It consisted of seven 30-second television commercials, public relations materials, and special cereal packaging. The NCI's recommendation to consume a high-fiber/low-fat diet was a prominent message in the campaign. During the two years of the campaign, the number of people reporting eating high-fiber diets to reduce cancer risks more than doubled (from 2% to 5%), while the awareness of fiber as a preventive for cancer more than tripled (from 9% to 32%). Bran cereal sales also increased, and over 50,000 people either called or wrote the NCI with further questions (Freimuth et al., 1988; Levy & Stokes, 1987).

Media can also be used as a *complement or supplement* to other interventions. That is, media can be integrated into a program that combines multiple channels of communication (e.g., television, print, and face-to-face). In Flay's (1987) review of 40 smoking cessation programs, he reports that mass media campaigns utilizing multiple channels were reasonably successful in changing knowledge and attitudes about smoking and, in some instances, smoking behavior. Furthermore, mass-mediated smoking cessation clinics that provided printed materials were more effective than those that did not, and mass-mediated clinics with social support groups were most effective.

In an innovative example of media supplementation, Flay and colleagues (1986) mounted an ambitious smoking prevention and cessation program combining television news, school-based prevention training, family viewing, and parental quitting with self-help materials. Both television and classroom delivery separately influenced overall program acceptance as measured by participation, satisfaction, and perceived program efficacy. Television and classroom delivery interacted to influence perceived program efficacy positively (Brannon et al., 1989).

Another good example of media as complement comes from Finland. In the North Karelia Project, Puska and colleagues (1987) worked with a national television station to carry out a 15-part multi-risk factor television series over six months. The show featured health experts and a group of eight participants who attempted to change their health behaviors. The show and an accompanying workbook were promoted heavily nationwide on TV and through newspapers, and even more intensively in schools, markets, and work sites and through trained opinion leaders. Results were positive, showing a graded effect: Those who participated in the TV show reported more changes than those who watched less; and those who lived within the boundaries of North Karelia, the project's home, reported more changes than those in any other part of the country. These results support the hypotheses that mass media yield a more powerful effect when used in conjunction with supplementary health education efforts (Flay, 1987; Puska et al., 1987).

In the third role, as a *promoter* of programs, media are used to familiarize audience members with health behaviors, products, and services, and to encourage them to participate in programs. This is perhaps the most commonly ascribed role for media in health promotion, and probably the best known by the public (Flora & Wallack, 1990). King, Flora, Fortmann, and Taylor (1987), in a study of the quitting rates of a smoking contest, examined the ways that participants found out about the event. Promotion efforts included television public service announcements (PSAs) produced by the station, newspaper ads, and distribution of fliers through schools, libraries, workplaces, and physicians' offices. Participants most often mentioned TV as the way they learned about the contest.

Another interesting example is a multimedia tap-water scald burn prevention program, in which both television and utility bill inserts were used to raise awareness about the dangers of tap-water scald burns. The program also offered free thermometers for testing the water temperature of residential water heaters (Klatcher, 1987). Approximately 19% of subscribers requested thermometers. Over 60% of those who also had access to their water heaters tested the water temperature, and 50% of those whose water temperature exceeded the recommended level lowered their thermostats. An interesting observation about the relative effectiveness of different media is that many more respondents remembered seeing television ads than remembered inserts in their utility bills (30% versus 5%), yet the utility company's records show that over 67% of the thermometer requests were actually received through the bill insert process.

In the fourth role, media as *supporter of life-style change*, media reinforce messages, support health changes, encourage maintenance of change, and keep health issues on the public agenda. While media as a reinforcer of change has not been well investigated in health, it has been documented in other areas of media use (e.g., political communication). Lazarsfeld, Berelson, and Gaudet (1948) have shown that one of the most powerful effects of political campaigns is to support the audience's existing beliefs about candidates.

In the Stanford studies (the TCS and the Stanford Five City Project [FCP]), televised public service announcements were regularly used to serve a dual change and support function (Flora, Maccoby, & Farquhar, 1989). In the FCP, formative research from smokers revealed that many smokers who had relapsed were so concerned about coping with urges that they were hesitant to reinitiate quitting, and that many recent quitters were afraid their urges would never go away. In response to these data, the staff developed a series of PSAs composed of testimonials by local citizens who had quit smoking. Successful quitters discussed their urges, the diminishing strength of these urges, and their method for coping with the urges to smoke.

The role selected for media depends on program outcome objectives, staff expertise, organizational resources, and the level of participation of media organizations in the community health promotion effort. For example, health organizations experienced in using media and creating behavior change programs may work in collaboration with local media organizations to use media as a complement. On the other hand, health agencies with existing behavior change programs and/or limited resources for media production and organizational collaboration may decide to use media only as a means for promoting existing efforts (Flora & Wallack, 1990).

MEDIA GATEKEEPERS
AND HEALTH PROMOTION

In order to create an effective media component in a health promotion program, it is essential to win the support of local media organizations and their leaders. Because media organizations often serve a gatekeeping function with respect to health information, we will use the terms *media organizations* and *gatekeepers* interchangeably. Practitioners should keep in mind that there are multiple gatekeeping positions within media organizations. For example, in television, PSA directors, programming directors, news directors, public relations representatives, and even sales managers are all important gatekeepers of media airtime. Some health projects have budgets set aside for media production and are able to hire staff with media expertise. Others must rely on media gatekeepers to donate all that is required to produce and air (or print) health messages.

Because local health agencies rarely have the luxury of extra monies for new staff of special programs, an alternative is to enlist media organizations in health education programs. Media organizations, including television and radio stations, newspapers, and magazines, can be innovative and resourceful collaborators in local health promotion efforts. Media gatekeepers and their organizations have played a variety of roles in community health promotion efforts, from a minimum of health news coverage to initiating health promotion programs. In a survey of Black media and health professionals on efforts to prevent AIDS in the Black community, both health agency and media staff agreed that media can play several roles in disseminating health information. Roles include "objective news transmitter" and "cooperative participant" (Ehigator, 1988). However, there was no agreement as to the frequency with which media organizations played these roles: Many more health professionals considered the media to be "cooperative participants" than did media professionals. In addition, media professionals identified two additional but less frequently occurring roles: equal partner in the health promotion process and community leader in the prevention of AIDS.

The roles that local media gatekeepers/organizations play in health promotion have considerable impact on program design. This section reviews the advantages and disadvantages of working with media organizations, identifies roles of media organizations in health promotion, and reviews some ways in which health agencies have successfully incorporated these roles into the design of health promotion programs.

Like other organizations in the community, such as social service groups, law enforcement organizations, and health care agencies, media organizations have an interest in the welfare of the community and actively participate in community decision making. At times, the most serious community problems require the collaborative efforts of all community organizations. One successful example of this is a communitywide effort to reduce teenage pregnancy (Vincent et al., 1987).

There are both advantages and pitfalls when health promotion agencies begin to collaborate with other organizations. By sharing the responsibility for a complex and expensive program, several organizations can together achieve goals for the community that would not be possible through the efforts of only one organization. This is particularly true when underfunded community-based health agencies and relatively resource-rich local media combine forces. The success of this approach is related to the extent to which organizations can maintain their individual identity in the decision-making process or agree to have a common identity as, for example, an advisory board or consortium. It also depends on whether organizational representatives can meet their institutional needs (such as number of participants, fund-raising, or program development) through participation in a cooperative effort.

Health agencies regularly enlist the aid of media organizations in health promotion efforts (Flora & Wallack, 1990). At the very least, this can mean contacting a television station about airing broadcasting public service announcements (PSAs). It can also involve much more, such as proposing extended news coverage of a health program, collaborating with the media organization in program planning, or requesting financial support. But before the media organization is contacted, the health agency staff must determine what role the media organization should play to meet the goals of the program and the role they would like to play relative to the media agency. Mutual decision making about roles is best, with each agency clarifying its available resources, program goals, and expectations regarding organizational benefits.

To facilitate this process, we have defined three roles that media organizations can play and have played in community-based health promotion: (a) media organization as news producer, (b) media organization as equal partner, and (c) media organization as health promotion leader.

Media organization as news producer. News producers fulfill a traditional news coverage function for the community. At times, health issues enter the news arena. For example, most media covered the release of a new cholesterol-lowering drug when it was approved by the Federal Drug Administration in 1987. However, far fewer cover ongoing cardiovascular disease prevention efforts at the local level.

This emphasis on newsworthiness directs media organization attention to how a health promotion program fits into the larger context of local or national health issues. This focus tends to limit participation in health promotion to news coverage, and may exclude the possibility of other types of contributions, such as program production, financial support, or publicity for community events.

If some local media organizations limit their role to covering news, health promotion agencies can couch their program goals in these terms. The San Francisco AIDS Foundation's campaign targeting intravenous drug users is one example of this. In planning their campaign to encourage drug users to clean their needles with bleach, the staff determined that extensive news coverage would supplement paid media messages (newspaper ads and billboards) and would be free of charge. To get media attention, campaign planners emphasized national findings that IV drug users are one of the fastest-growing groups affected by AIDS. By associating a local program with national news, the organization effectively caught the attention of media organizations that play the role of objective news producer. Seizing news opportunities by writing press releases, engaging in creative epidemiology (presentation of epidemiological data in new and interesting forms), creating news with created events, and reacting in a timely manner to the general news environment are other ways to enhance local news coverage (National Cancer Institute, 1988).

Media organization as partner. Media organizations can also play the role of equal partner in community health promotion. This can involve several levels of participation, from planning the media component of a program to participating in overall program planning.

In planning a health promotion program, the first step is to review the program goals in light of the type of resources and technical assistance required to meet these goals. Local media organizations may be able to supply many of these resources. For example, a television station interested in equal partnership in a health promotion program could mean financial backing for some or all of the program, integrated television coverage on that station's news and other locally produced shows, production of public service announcements, and production and distribution of print materials.

Media organization as leader. Media organizations have also initiated programs without the assistance or request of a health promotion agency. In these cases, media organizations are leaders in community health promotion. Many media organizations initiate public service projects, contact local health gatekeepers, and organize events.

Media organizations have taken a leadership role in promotion in several different ways. A Northern California television station became one of the first to advertise condoms. This provoked extensive news coverage of the ads and the health issues of AIDS and sexually transmitted disease. In taking this leadership role, the television station paved the way for other stations to advertise condoms and to promote similar health-related discussions in other parts of the country. In another example, a local television station sponsored a communitywide race for CVD prevention. It was inspired, in part, by many other CVD prevention activities in the community, but the race itself was initiated by the station, and after the larger CVD prevention program was completed. The race continues to be sponsored jointly by the station and a local hospital.

INTEGRATING MEDIA INTO
COMMUNITY-BASED HEALTH PROMOTION

The process of establishing a community-based health promotion effort involves many steps, from setting up an advisory board or other organizational body to analyzing problems and planning interventions. Mass media and media organizations may be involved in several of these steps; in this section we will outline a process for integrating media organizations and media-based interventions into the health promotion process. These steps are based on the health communication research literature, the conditions for successful media use in behavior change discussed earlier in this chapter, and more than a decade of experience using the media in CVD prevention trials (the TCS and FCP). Note that the sequence of the steps may vary somewhat depending on the source of the program, be it a single agency or a consortium of agencies. The steps are discussed in turn below.

(1) Conduct a media resource assessment. This is a first step toward defining media and media organization roles in health promotion. There are three parts to completing an assessment of media resources in the community: identify existing communication opportunities, learn about individual media gatekeepers, and create your own opportunities (Durazzo, Flora, & Foote, 1988).

Even small communities can have many existing media to use in health promotion efforts. Media channels include television, radio, newspapers, and magazines, and each of these may have many outlets. Within the media channels, there are many possible media outlets to identify and record. For example, television stations include UHF and VHF stations, college stations, and cable access. Radio stations, often numerous, include all AM and FM stations, college stations, and public radio. And beyond the major daily newspapers distributed in the community, there may be small-circulation newspapers that serve special populations, such as businesses, shoppers, residents of certain geographic locations, or speakers of foreign languages. Other, more narrowcast media include newsletters, cable TV, and home and office computer networks. An inventory of each of these channels will provide an overview of communication opportunities. Such an inventory includes the name and phone number of the gatekeepers, the audience of the media outlet, the formats of the outlet, and ratings or market share information.

Next, within each communication channel, specific opportunities should be identified. Each channel of communication harbors many different health message outlets. In television, for example, news broadcasts, public affairs shows, special programs, commentary and talk shows, magazine programs, community service programs, PSAs, and community calendars are potential channels for disseminating health information.

Learn gatekeepers' interests and conflicts. Is the media organization restricted in what issues it will promote because of its advertisers? How is news handled by different organizations? Do news directors always feel compelled to present an opposing point of view (Flay & Burton, 1988)? This type of information will help the health professional have a deeper understanding of media organizations and will reduce nonproductive effort as well as enhance informed negotiation.

Health agencies can also create their own communication opportunities outside the existing ones. This requires taking a proactive rather than reactive stance. It also involves substantial lead time and expertise in planning and dealing with the media. The only limit to these opportunities is imagination. For example, in the Spanish-language campaign of the FCP, the manager of the largest Spanish-language radio station and the FCP production consultant devised a special series of radio novellas that were presented in 5-minute segments and that continued over 50 or more segments. The unique elements of this effort were the length of the individual segments and their continuation over time. The radio station aired segments of the series at 8:30 in the morning and 1:30 in the afternoon. This series was a cooperative effort in which the station provided time, promotion, call-in lines, and consultation, and the FCP provided scripts, direction, production, and coordination.

When completed, the media resource assessment will be a comprehensive inventory of "media outlets" and the potential of those outlets as resources in community-based health promotion. With an inventory of media resources close at hand, it is also much easier to make use of all possible media channels in the community and plan a truly integrated, comprehensive media campaign.

(2) Analyze the role of media organizations. An assessment of local media organizations through interviews with gatekeepers can shed tremendous light on their role in the community. This requires collecting information about each organization, either through interviews with managers of media organizations and community leaders or by an informal content analysis of the media. A detailed history of each organization's participation in community service projects, public statements about community issues, policies about community involvement, and contributions to other organizations or projects will help health agencies determine the level of resources already committed to community projects, prior commitments to certain agencies or causes, and level of interest in working with community agencies.

A health agency may develop a very clearly stated role for a local media organization. However, the organization's definition of its own role in the health promotion program will be influenced by factors such as its past relations with the health agency, interaction with other health promotion organizations, history of activity in health promotion, and its public service agenda. In working with media organizations, health agencies need to understand the demands already placed on media organizations. This understanding comes from learning about the media and media organizations. Part of the success of the Stanford TCS and the FCP was the close working relationship staff developed with local media organizations.

(3) Determine the role of mass media in health promotion programs. As intervention planning takes place, so should a systematic process of defining the role of mass media in relation to health promotion. Should it be primary education, complement, promotion, or support? A primary role for media would be more appropriate in a program that seeks to create awareness of an issue or to change knowledge. In a program that seeks to change health behavior, media might be more effective in a complementary or promotional role.

Logistical considerations also affect the role of mass media in a health promotion program. Time constraints may prohibit using media in a promotional role because it takes a relatively long time to make contacts and organize press conferences and other media events. On the other hand, staff expertise in media production would facilitate using media in a primary role. Finally, although mass media and media organizations can play very important roles in a health promotion program, their roles do not have to be equal. For example, if a media organization is a partner in the program, this does not mean that mass media will play a primary role in the intervention. Mass media will probably play a large role, as it is in the interest of the media organization to promote the program it is sponsoring, but media use does not rule out a strong face-to-face component of the program.

(4) Implement media-based programs. Once the roles of the media and media organizations are determined, then the program planner can implement the program in the community. Outcome objectives, the extent and nature of formative research, and outcome evaluation plans can also be defined at this time. The process of implementation is complicated by the need to coordinate the schedules and resources of multiple organizations. Feedback and communication among the collaborating agencies are essential to achieving successful outcomes.

(5) Evaluate media efforts. Evaluation of media-based efforts should include both the quantitative outcomes of the program and the qualitative outcomes of satisfaction of working with media organizations and carrying out media-based programs. This evaluation process allows health agencies and media organizations to exchange feedback that will strengthen relations and ultimately improve programs.

CONCLUSION

The media are a community health promotion resource that is sometimes left untapped or not used to its full potential. As a means to make the best use of media at the local level, this chapter has offered a rationale for distinguishing between the roles of media and media organizations. There is a potentially large yet distinct role that each can play in health promotion. One is a tool used by a health promotion agency; the other is an active participant. Because of this difference, different criteria and methods are used to determine program roles for mass media messages and media organizations. Understanding the potential roles of mass media in supporting health promotion, incorporating lessons from successful media-based programs, and working cooperatively with media organizations can increase the impact of community-based health promotion programs.

REFERENCES

Blackburn, H., Luepker, R. V., Kline, F. G., Bracht, N., & Carlaw, R. (1984). The Minnesota Heart Health Program: A research and demonstration project in cardiovascular disease prevention. In J. D. Matarazzo, S. H. Weiss, J. A. Herd, N. E. Miller, & S. W. Weiss (Eds.), *Behavioral health: A handbook of health enhancement and disease prevention* (pp. 1171-1178). New York: John Wiley.

Brannon, B. R., Dent, C. W., Flay, B. R., Smith, G., Sussman, S., Pentz, M. A., Johnson, C. A., & Hansen, W. B. (1989). The television, school, and family project: The impact of curriculum delivery format on program acceptance. *Preventive Medicine, 18,* 492-502.

Durazzo, R., Flora, J. A., & Foote, D. (1988). *Working with the media: Getting your issue on your community's agenda.* Menlo Park, CA: Applied Communication Technology.

Ehigator, A. A. (1988). *The role of media in disseminating AIDS prevention information to the Black community of the San Francisco Bay Area.* Unpublished master's thesis, Stanford University, Department of Communication.

Farquhar, J. W., Maccoby, N., & Wood, P. D. (1985). Education and community studies. In W. Holland, R. Detels, & G. Knox (Eds.), *Oxford textbook of public health* (pp. 207-221). Oxford: Oxford University Press.

Farquhar, J. W., Maccoby, N., Wood, P. D., Alexander, J. K., Breitrose, H., Brown, B. W., Jr., Haskell, W. L., McAlister, A. L., Meyer, A. J., Nash, J. D., & Stern, M. P. (1977). Community education for cardiovascular health. *Lancet, 1,* 1192-1195.

Farquhar, J. W., Fortmann, S. P., Maccoby, N., Haskell, W. L., Williams, P. T., Flora, J. A., Taylor, C. B., Brown, B. W., Jr., Solomon, D. S., & Hulley, S. B. (1985). The Stanford Five City Project: Design and methods. *American Journal of Epidemiology, 122,* 323-334.

Flay, B. R. (1987). Mass media and smoking cessation: A critical review. *American Journal of Public Health, 77,* 153-160.

Flay, B. R., & Burton, D. (1988). *Design and characteristics of health campaigns.* Paper presented at the conference, Mass Communications and Health: Complexities and Conflicts, Palm Springs, CA.

Flay, B. R., Pentz, A. A., Johnson, C. A., Sussman, S., Mesell, J., Scheier, L., Collins, L. M., & Hansen, W. B. (1986). Reaching children with mass media health promotion programs: The relative effectiveness of an advertising campaign, a community-based program, and a school-based program. In G. B. Leather (Ed.), *Health education and the media* (Vol. 2, pp. 149-154). Oxford: Pergamon.

Flora, J. A., Maccoby, N., & Farquhar, J. W. (1989). Communication campaigns to prevent cardiovascular disease: The Stanford community studies. In R. E. Rice & C. K. Atkin (Eds.), *Public communication campaigns* (2nd ed.). Newbury Park, CA: Sage.

Flora, J. A., Maibach, E., & Maccoby, N. (1989). Role of mass media in health promotion. In L. Breslow (Ed.), *Annual review of public health.* Palo Alto, CA: Annual Reviews.

Flora, J. A., & Wallack, L. (1990). Health promotion and mass media use: Translating research into practice. *Health Education Research, 5,* (1), 73-80.

Freimuth, V. S., Hammond, S. L., & Stein, J. A. (1988). Health advertising: Prevention for profit. *American Journal of Public Health, 78,* 557-561.

King, A. C., Flora, J. A., Fortmann, S. P., & Taylor, C. B. (1987). Smokers' challenge: Immediate and long-term findings of a community smoking cessation contest. *American Journal of Public Health, 77,* 1340-1341.

Klatcher, M. L. (1987). Prevention of tap water scald burns: Evaluation of a multi-media injury control program. *American Journal of Public Health, 3,* 337-354.

Lasater, T., Abrams, D., Artz, L., Beaudin, P., Cabrera, L., Elder, J., Ferreira, A., Knisley, P., Peterson, G., Rodrigues, A., Rosenberg, P., Snow, R., & Carleton, R. (1984). Lay volunteer delivery of a community-based cardiovascular risk factor change program: The Pawtucket experiment. In J. D. Matarazzo, S. H. Weiss, J. A. Herd, N. E. Miller, & S. W. Weiss (Eds.), *Behavioral health: A handbook of health enhancement and disease prevention* (pp. 1166-1170). New York: John Wiley.

Lazarsfeld, P., Berelson, B., & Gaudet, H. (1948). *The people's choice.* New York: Columbia University Press.

Levy, A., & Stokes, R. (1987). Effects of a health promotion advertising campaign on sales of ready-to-eat cereals. *Public Health Reports, 102,* 398-403.

Maccoby, N., & Alexander, J. (1979). Use of media in lifestyle programs. In P. Davidson (Ed.), *Behavioral medicine: Changing health lifestyles* (pp. 351-367). Alberta, Canada: Banff International Conferences on Behavior Modification.

Maccoby, N., Farquhar, J. W., Wood, P., & Alexander, J. (1977). Reducing the risk of cardiovascular disease: Effects of a community-based campaign on knowledge and behavior. *Journal of Community Health, 24,* 100-114.

Maccoby, N., & Solomon, D. (1981). Heart disease prevention: Community studies. In R. E. Rice & W. J. Paisley (Eds.), *Public communication campaigns* (pp. 105-126). Beverly Hills, CA: Sage.

McGuire, W. J. (1981). Theoretical foundation of campaigns. In R. E. Rice & W. J. Paisley (Eds.), *Public communication campaigns* (pp. 41-70). Beverly Hills, CA: Sage.

National Cancer Institute. (1988). *Media strategies for smoking control* (National Institutes of Health Publication No. 89-3013). Rockville, MD: National Institutes of Health.

National Institute of Alcohol and Alcohol Abuse. (1983). *Prevention plus: Involving schools, parents, and the community in alcohol and drug education* (DHHS Publication No. 84-1256). Rockville, MD: National Institutes of Health.

Petty, R. E., & Cacioppo, J. T. (1981). *Attitudes and persuasion: Classic and contemporary approaches.* Dubuque, IA: Wm. C. Brown.

Puska, P., McAlister, A., Niemensivu, H., Piha, T., Wijo, J., & Koskela, K. (1987). A television format for national health promotion: Finland's "Keys to Health." *Public Health Reports, 102,* 263-269.

Schramm, W. (1982). Channels and audiences. In G. Gumpert & R. Cathcart (Eds.), *Inter/media: Interpersonal communication in a media world* (pp. 78-92). New York: Oxford University Press.

Vincent, M. L., Clearie, A. F., & Schlucheter, M. D. (1987). Reducing adolescent pregnancy through school and community-based education. *Journal of the American Medical Association, 57*(24), 320-321.

Chapter 8

INVOLVING WORK SITES
AND OTHER ORGANIZATIONS

GLORIAN SORENSEN
RUSSELL E. GLASGOW
KITTY CORBETT

An integral component of community health promotion efforts is the involvement of diverse organizations central to the community. Work sites, places of worship, fraternal and civic organizations, recreation clubs, and other community organizations provide ideal sites for promotion and support of health behavior or policy changes. Work sites and other organizations may also promote communitywide events or activities sponsored by other agencies. Such organizations are often eager to promote health and wellness programs as part of their mission. Through these sites, health promotion organizers may be able to target groups who are often underserved by traditional health promotion programs, such as low-income or minority groups. Programs conducted in organizations and work sites also have access to "captive audiences" for whom participation is made easier by the convenience of the setting (Nathan, 1984).

Participating organizations may also offer opportunities to establish intervention strategies that foster structural and cultural changes supportive of long-term maintenance of health behavior changes. Environmental changes such as nonsmoking policies, fitness facilities, or cafeteria modifications reinforce the messages being communicated through direct education programs while also building peer support for health behavior change. Changes in the social norms of the organization are likely to support long-term maintenance of individual changes.

This chapter describes a process for working with work sites and other organizations that encourages long-term incorporation of health promotion goals into their organizational structure. Such "ownership" and incorporation is increased through early participation in planning and program promotion. Not all organizations have the commitment or the resources to be involved. Targeting highly motivated groups is usually the best way to begin attracting wider organizational participation in the community. Considerable research has been devoted to work-site health promotion, and methods for designing, promoting, implementing, and evaluating such programs have been developed (Fielding, 1984; O'Donnell & Ainsworth, 1984; Sloan, Gruman, & Allegrante, 1987). Although similar approaches apply to other organizations, work sites have received more attention. Our discussion in this chapter focuses primarily, but not exclusively, on work sites, although methods for involving other organizations in the community are discussed. Intervention strategies appropriate for work-site settings are generally applicable to religious, ethnic, recreational, service, and fraternal organizations. Work sites and other organizations may also be excellent channels for targeting minority and low-income groups, also addressed later in this chapter.

BUILDING COMMUNITY SUPPORT
FOR WORK-SITE INTERVENTIONS

Each work site may be viewed both as an independent social structure with its own "corporate culture" and as an integrated member of the broader community. This broader community role links it to such groups as the chamber of commerce, professional organizations, and unions, as well as to providers of work-site intervention programs, such as health voluntary agencies, hospitals, and private consultants. Success in work-site health promotion efforts depends upon a sound understanding of the culture and norms of the work site and its linkages to the broader community. Involving members of community organizations in planning and implementing programs is also critical to success and can be pursued at two levels. First, work-site or organizational representatives can participate in the general community needs analysis (see Chapter 4). Second, a similar analysis process is applied within the individual work site: Internal needs assessment or marketing research provides information on employee concerns and interests and guidance in tailoring the intervention to the work site. Steps in establishing

Table 8.1

Steps to Establishing Successful Work-Site Health Promotion Programs

---

(1) Build community support.
    (a) Assess community norms, culture, and activities.
    (b) Establish community advisory board.

(2) Assess work-site culture and social norms.
    (a) Capitalize on opportunities to facilitate the program.
    (b) Identify and modify existing barriers.

(3) Solicit top management and union support.

(4) Use employee input in planning.
    (a) Conduct employee surveys.
    (b) Appoint employee steering committee.
    (c) Appoint work-site liaison.

(5) Provide ongoing programming with environmental and social supports.

(6) Conduct periodic program evaluation.

---

work-site programs are shown in Table 8.1. The first step is to build support for programs by soliciting work sites' participation in community analysis and planning.

Work-Site Participation in Community Analysis and Planning

Community analysis is a systematic process for gaining information about the community that will guide planning and intervention. This process identifies key community players, including work-site leaders and providers of health promotion programs, gaps in existing services and community resources, and factors influencing program adoption. The community needs assessment may also be one of the first contacts with community and work-site leaders, who play a critical role in raising community awareness of health promotion efforts.

One aspect of the community analysis is a general assessment of the business and labor community's "culture" and history. Do work sites have a history of activities or environmental changes promoting healthy behaviors? How extensively have the mass media covered work-site health concerns? What other community issues may divert employers' and employees' attention and energy away from concern about health? Which health issues are of greatest priority to the business and labor community? Have they been able to work together successfully or are there adversarial relationships or turf issues of which one must be aware?

Several sources exist for addressing these questions. First, printed materials may provide important background information. Listings of work sites and their characteristics (e.g., size, types of industry) generally are available from the local chamber of commerce, a state business census, or the Yellow Pages. Newspapers and public documents provide a sense of community concerns and information on other service providers. More in-depth information can be obtained from individual or group interviews with community leaders or health promotion providers.

Successful communitywide health promotion programs depend on active citizen involvement and the tailoring of programs to the community's needs and interests. These requirements can be addressed by the early formation of a community board or "wellness council." Such boards include business and labor leaders and providers of health promotion programs (Kizer, 1987). The board may decide to establish a special task force on work-site and organizational programs. Such a task force functions as

(1) a *catalyst* for the support and involvement of local business and labor leaders;

(2) a *source of information* on ways to tailor programs to community needs;

(3) a *liaison* between employers and community service providers (e.g., health voluntary organizations such as the American Lung Association, American Heart Association, and the American Cancer Society; the YMCA and other nonprofit organizations) and service vendors (e.g., hospitals, employee assistance programs, health clubs);

(4) a *clearinghouse of information* for employers on health information, community resources, and effective implementation models of health promotion;

(5) a *coordinator* in sponsoring communitywide health promotion activities; and

(6) a *support* for ongoing program implementation.

Members of both the community advisory board and the task force are likely to be representatives of work sites that are already providing health promotion programs for employees or that are at least interested in such services.

In some communities, structures like work-sites consortia may already exist that will meet the goals of work-site health promotion efforts. Current providers may be willing to expand health promotion services if community analysis provides convincing information on the market for them. In most cases it will be necessary to respect existing relationships among health providers and avoid overlap and duplication of existing services. A community board can play a central role in handling issues of competition and resource allocation for both communitywide programs and individual work sites and organizations.

Another important advantage of an integrated communitywide program is the impact that leadership can have on the social norms of the business community. Employers may adopt health promotion programs on recommendations from their peers. Contacts with work sites not yet involved may be most effectively initiated by other business leaders who can vouch for the benefits of participation. Work sites first to adopt new ideas and programs are pacesetters and models for others (Rogers & Shoemaker, 1971). Such work sites are likely to be most willing to commit sufficient resources to attain and sustain program success. Initiating programs in companies most ready for change and most likely to succeed with health promotion efforts is likely to enhance the attractiveness of participation for other companies. Working first with high-profile companies such as media producers or large work sites will further build community awareness of and confidence in program efforts. Building relationships with work sites less ready for change is likely to take more time, but requests for program publicity may lay the groundwork for later on-site activities. Once a track record of community success is established, providers should target work sites with significant numbers of employees from underserved or high-risk groups, such as minorities and low-income groups. Following the development of the broader community support network, attention can turn to analysis and planning activities for individual organizations. These are discussed in the next section.

Marketing Health Promotion in the Work Site: Work-Site Analysis and Planning

Just as community analysis forms the basis for designing effective communitywide strategies, analysis of the concerns and culture of target work sites and organizations is used to identify factors that affect program and policy adoption within the work site. Successful interventions result from a twofold effort: (a) capitalizing on opportunities and resources that can assist program and policy adoption, and (b) identifying existing and potential barriers and eliminating or diminishing them where possible (see Table 8.2).

Although many employers and employees may be receptive to health promotion programs, it is unrealistic to expect a universal welcome. By anticipating work-site concerns, community boards may find ways to address potential barriers effectively. The differing perspectives of management and employees are described below and can be assessed through the work-site analysis (O'Donnell & Ainsworth, 1984; Sloan et al., 1987).

From the management perspective, barriers to adoption of health promotion programs and policies include the following:

- *Management attitudes:* Some managers may feel that health promotion is outside the mandate of their organizations, may prefer to maintain the status quo, or may believe that health behavior changes are unrelated to health outcomes.
- *Concern with potential consequences:* Management may believe that health programs or policies would not provide enough benefit to employees, would increase conflict between management and employees, or would provide only negligible economic benefits.
- *Participation costs:* Some managers may think that spending work time on health issues will interfere with productivity or that programs cost too much.
- *Competing priorities:* Competing concerns may include other health-related programs offered, including employee assistance, drug abuse prevention, and injury prevention programs, or other company concerns such as collective bargaining and economic growth or decline.

From the perspective of employees, barriers may include these:

- *The perception of inappropriate interference in personal lives:* Some employees may view health behaviors as "life-style" issues outside management's concern.
- *Confidentiality:* This issue may be a concern, especially where biochemical assessment (i.e., "drug testing") or the collection of personal data is involved.
- *Diversion of attention from competing issues:* Some union members have leveled this charge in response to health promotion efforts. For instance, nonsmoking policies and smoking cessation programs have been criticized

Table 8.2

Advantages of and Barriers to Work-Site Health Promotion

Advantages	*Barriers*
For the employer	
possible improved employee morale and productivity	resistance to change and other management attitudes
possible reduction in health care costs	concern about potential consequences
enhanced recruitment and retention of employees	participation costs
corporate image	competing priorities
For the employee	
access and convenience	perceived inappropriate interference in personal life
reduced cost	confidentiality
participation with co-workers	diversion of attention from competing issues
social and environmental support for behavior change	release time and other logistics of program delivery
For the provider	
access to large numbers of people	logistics of program delivery
ability to target underserved groups	
opportunity for long-term, repeated interventions	
social support for the intervention message	
possibility of changes in the environment and social norms	

as a "smoke screen" camouflaging other hazards perceived as more serious to worker safety.

- *The logistics of program delivery:* Inconvenient timing and location of program offering can often reduce participation rates. Even when the company top management allows release time, an employee's direct supervisor may not support it.

The work-site analysis will provide information on management's and employees' attitudes toward health promotion, both essential elements to program success. Managerial enthusiasm will quickly filter down through the organizational hierarchy; employees will also sense any ambivalence or disinterest on the part of their supervisors. Having top executives actively and visibly involved is critical to program success. At the same time, promoters must generate support and enthusiasm among workers, particularly in companies having organized unions. Low participation may result if a health promotion program is seen as a management attempt to divert attention from employee concerns about working conditions rather than as a fringe benefit. Since employers generally are the sponsors of work-site health promotion programs, program promotion often focuses on their concerns. Nonetheless, unions may also choose to sponsor health promotion programs, and should be included in marketing efforts.

Community boards and program providers can address these barriers to participation by contrasting them with potential benefits. In general, participation in health promotion efforts is consistent with work sites' long-term goals of survival, profitability, and productivity (O'Donnell & Ainsworth, 1984). Information on health promotion presented to employers must emphasize the benefits of involvement. Although there is little systematic evidence that health promotion is a cost-effective means of decreasing health care costs (Warner, Wickizer, Wolfe, Schildroth, & Samuelson, 1988), the potential for tangible benefits is real.

Understanding how these potential benefits fit with what employers hope to obtain from a program is a key step in marketing health promotion programs to employers. This information may be collected during the work-site analysis. Some work sites may provide programs in response to employee requests. These employers may be primarily interested in programs from an employee morale or public relations perspective (Brownell, 1986). At other work sites, the primary motivation may be the potential savings resulting from healthier employee life-styles; in such cases, reputable estimates of dollar savings can greatly bolster the program's chances of adoption. Yet such benefits must not be oversold. With the possible exception of smoking cessation and hypertension detection and follow-up treatment programs, the potential cost benefits of occupational health programs—especially relatively short-term payoffs—are not clearly established (Glasgow & Terborg, 1988; Warner, in press).

A company's image and visibility in the community are likely to be enhanced by its demonstration of concern and responsibility for employee well-being. These programs may have favorable effects on turnover, morale, and satisfaction among present employees, and may also increase the attractiveness of the work site to prospective employees. Improved morale may contribute to increased performance and productivity. In the long run, preventive measures may reduce the cost of benefits, including health and life insurance and worker's compensation.

In addition to assessing perceived barriers to and benefits of participation, the work-site analysis includes learning about employee characteristics and the work site's history, if any, of health promotion efforts. The potential market or audience may be examined according to groups that may have differing interests in and/or needs for health promotion (Kotler, 1984). Examples of different target markets include those working on the night shift or employees' family members. Such an assessment is particularly important in work sites having a high proportion of groups often hard to reach with health promotion programs, such as low-income or minority groups. Decisions must be made about which groups to target and how best to reach and intervene with each of them. An approach that explicitly sets priorities and directs promotional activities toward these various market segments should increase program success.

Further information about the work site can be gleaned from employee surveys and interviews with management and labor representatives. Interviews may elucidate challenges to be met and alert providers to potential "land mines" such as the existence of segments of a company that feel disenfranchised, poor employee-management relations, and negative experiences with employee assistance programs, safety and accident prevention, or past health promotion efforts. An employee survey can be useful for assessing the work-site climate, designing the program to fit employee needs, and establishing a baseline for evaluating program effectiveness. A survey's usefulness can be enhanced in two ways: (a) It should be completed by a large proportion of employees to provide a representative, unbiased view of employee attitudes; to achieve this, strong endorsement from top labor and management officials and assurances of confidentiality are vital. (b) The survey should include questions on issues of particular interest to the work site to personalize the survey and further involve work-site representatives in its results.

In summary, the work-site analysis lays the groundwork for integrating health promotion into the culture and norms of the work site. With a perspective on the priorities of management and employees, the health promotion provider can anticipate potential problems in program implementation and capitalize on existing supports within the work site.

The Process of Health Promotion in Work Sites

As noted above, the process of working with a single work site mirrors that of establishing excellent health promotion activities communitywide. First, community and work-site analyses provide the background for tailoring the program to the specific site. Second, involvement of community or work-site members in a work-site steering committee better assures a sense of commitment and ownership.

The initial meeting with work-site representatives often sets the tone for what is to follow. This first meeting should give the employer an accurate but positive impression of the potential program and a realistic understanding of the potential benefits of participation. The health promotion provider should begin to understand the organization and contextual factors (e.g., upcoming reorganization, seasonal layoffs, rotating shifts, collective bargaining agreements) that are particularly likely to affect program participation and success.

Work-site analysis, as discussed previously, involves assessing the "corporate culture" and evaluating work-site receptivity and barriers to health promotion efforts. The work-site analysis will also guide the level of participation solicited, which may vary from posting program announcements to writing letters of endorsement to printing newsletter tips to providing volunteers. Existing resources and committees should be used whenever possible, including existing health or safety committees that may assist in planning and implementation.

The work-site steering committee can provide direction for health promotion efforts, help to channel employee involvement and ownership, provide feedback on program options, and greatly assist in promotion and recruitment. A productive steering committee is likely to include the following: (a) a member of management who has decision-making authority and is respected by employees; (b) one or more representatives of labor/union interests, preferably elected by workers; and (c) "peer opinion leaders" from each of the primary market groups one hopes to have an impact on, also chosen by employees. We recommend involving at least two employee or labor representatives, including a union steward if applicable, from the outset of negotiations and planning. While members who support health promotion objectives can contribute substantially to program direction, involving subgroups who disagree with program objectives may help to defuse opposition. For example, committees addressing nonsmoking policies should include smokers to assure that their concerns are considered.

To clarify what is expected of the work site and what the work site can expect from the provider, a written statement may be presented during early discussions with the company. For example, responsibility for scheduling rooms for classes or posting notices of program activities may be assigned to an employee liaison designated by the company. Additionally, any program costs to be incurred by the company members of the steering committee may be documented to assure clarity and to prevent later misunderstandings. Such a statement should also describe services provided to the work site.

An integrated plan for informing employees about the program can be developed in cooperation with the work-site steering committee, based on results from the work-site analysis. Committee members and other knowledgeable insiders can help in tailoring publicity and using internal lines of communication, such as word-of-mouth promotion, as much as possible. Multiple, repeated announcements of program activities using different promotional channels (e.g., employee newsletters, posters, flyers, point-of-contact displays) keep the program in the public eye. Where feasible, another strategy is to conduct a series of no-obligation informational meetings for all employees during work hours (Klesges & Glasgow, 1986). Publicity should also address anticipated barriers to participation (Orlandi, 1986). In summary, it is critical to devote sufficient time and planning to program promotion. Even the most efficacious program will not prove cost-effective if employees are not aware of it and do not participate.

INTERVENTION STRATEGIES

The primary goal of organizational health promotion is to produce the greatest possible impact on specified health-related behaviors among employees or members of an organization given limited money and resources. In oversimplified terms, sitewide impact is a combined function of rates of participation and behavior change among participants and nonparticipants. The reach of a program is generally inversely related to its effectiveness. Thus programs reaching large numbers generally produce lower rates of behavior change than do direct education programs, which generally attract fewer participants. Even if a program is successful for 90% of participants, if only 2% of all employees participate its impact is negligible. Combining various strategies is likely to ensure the broadest reach and greatest impact (Nathan, 1984; Stachnik & Stoffelmayr, 1983).

Experience with a range of behavioral problems suggests that there is usually no one treatment strategy that guarantees success. The most successful programs employing multifaceted, multicomponent interventions rely on two principles: flexibility and reaching employees at various "stages of change" (Prochaska & DiClemente, 1983). This approach identifies four major stages (precontemplation, contemplation, action, maintenance/relapse) describing receptiveness to behavior change. The goals of health promotion include progression from one stage to another to produce lasting behavior change. Effective intervention strategies need to aim at persons in every stage of change. For example, those who are "contemplating" change will probably not commit themselves to participating in a series of lengthy meetings, but might be willing to watch a videotape or pick up a self-help pamphlet.

Work sites and other organizations, as well as individuals, can be reached at different stages of change or receptivity to health promotion (Bulow-Hube & Morisky, 1987). Some organizations may be willing to construct state-of-the-art on-site fitness facilities, allow employees time off work to attend classes, or cover the costs of participation in structured intervention activities; others will not. Offering an array of intervention options increases the likelihood of attracting a broad range of employers. Providing feedback on initial surveys and anticipating likely barriers to program participation based on company characteristics and health promotion history are important steps in creating high initial interest in a program.

As shown in Table 8.3, health promotion programs can be classified according to three intervention strategies: motivational/incentive approaches, educational/skills training, and environmental/social support activities. In general, to meet the needs of persons in varying stages of change, intervention programs should provide options within at least two, if not all three, of these categories. Within each of these types of programs, formats can vary from low-contact (and usually low-cost) activities to very intensive, time-consuming, and expensive delivery systems.

Motivational/Incentive Strategies

These activities involve procedures to encourage employees either to initiate behavior change attempts (e.g., sign up for a stress management class, try to diet for a week) or to maintain relatively new behavior

Table 8.3

Types of Work-Site and Organization Health Promotion Programs

---

(1) motivation and incentive strategies

  • screening
  • health risk appraisals
  • incentives for behavior change or participation
  •, contests or lotteries

(2) educational/skills training activities

  • self-help materials
  • computer-assisted instruction
  • classroom instruction
  • individual counseling

(3) environmental and social support activities

  • restructuring the physical environment: cafeteria changes, point-of-choice food
    labeling, nonsmoking policies
  • building social support: buddy systems (e.g., Adopt-a-Smoker), involving family
    members (e.g., developing take-home materials)

---

changes (e.g., continue exercising three times per week, stay off ciga-rettes). The two most common motivational approaches are (a) screen-ing and health risk appraisals (Blair, Piserchia, Wilbur, & Crowder, 1986; Weiss, 1984) and (b) incentive programs or contests.

Health risk appraisal (HRA) involves the systematic collection of information on individual and family health history, risk factors (e.g., blood pressure, serum cholesterol levels), and health-related behaviors. There are a wide variety of specific health hazard appraisal systems of varying cost, complexity, and validity; most involve constructing an estimated life expectancy or risk score by comparing a person's health profile to morbidity and mortality statistics associated with known risk indicators. Most systems also estimate the risk reduction likely to result from changing one or more health-related behaviors. HRAs are often used as kickoff events for behavior change programs, and when offered at the work site (without charge during work hours) they can attract as many as 75% of employees (Blair et al., 1986). HRAs can provide valuable needs assessment and baseline information, and appear to have important motivation effects.

However, the value of health risk appraisals has often been uncriti-cally accepted. Different HRAs produce different risk estimates, and the validity of the risk and life expectancy calculations used for most

HRA assessments is unknown (Wagner, Beery, Schoenbeack, & Graham, 1982). Users of HRAs should assess the match between their target population and the population used in developing the HRA; for example, many data bases do not include women and minorities, whose risk profiles may differ substantially from those of a White male sample. Many HRAs also base their recommendations on 10-year mortality estimates, which may be an inappropriate outcome measure for employees under 40 years of age. As a result, recommended changes may focus on alcohol consumption and exercise and overlook smoking and dietary habits important to long-term mortality. HRAs may also not be usable in all populations based on the reading level of their results, which is generally at college level or above (Bibeau & Mullen, 1987).

The other main type of motivational activity involves arranging incentives or contests for health behavior change goals. The three most commonly used approaches are guaranteed incentives or awards, contests within an organization, and challenges or competitions between organizations. Guaranteed incentives have been used by employers to reinforce a variety of behavior changes, such as losing a certain number of pounds (Brownell, 1986) or stopping smoking for a specified period of time (Shepard & Pearlman, 1985). Two important advantages of incentive programs are that they can be constructed so they (a) require little professional time to administer and (b) address issues of long-term behavior change and maintenance—an area in which many motivational approaches are lacking. Contests within organizations often take the form of lottery drawings among participants who achieve specified goals for a given month, and can also serve as promotional events. A key to the success of such contests seems to be the extent to which top management actively supports and participates in these efforts. Another important component is adequate promotion and feedback on progress. Publicly posting goals and performance (e.g., number of miles run/walked per week) can bring attention to and reinforce healthy behaviors. Competition between organizations, the final incentive strategy, has been used effectively by several community heart disease prevention programs (Elder et al., 1987; King, Flora, Fortmann, & Taylor, 1987; Pechacek, Freutel, Arkin, & Mittelmark, 1983). Such competitions can be especially effective at encouraging high levels of participation in work sites where employees identify with their companies (e.g., Brownell & Felix, 1987; Klesges, Vasey, & Glasgow, 1986).

Incentive programs of all three types can increase credibility and participant satisfaction by providing feedback on biological measures related to health risk. In programs involving biomedical screening or

HRAs, feedback in the form of change from baseline on indices such as blood pressure, carbon monoxide levels, or fitness level (VO_2 max) can be an important reinforcer of behavior change. Finally, incentive/motivational programs should be designed to encourage referral to educational or skills training activities for participants requiring assistance in achieving or maintaining their behavior change goals.

Educational/Skills Training Activities

These activities teach participants the "how-tos" of changing health-related behaviors. Options range from simply providing information on, for example, the caloric and nutritional content of various foods to developing and monitoring individualized exercise programs. If at all possible, a range of options should be offered, ranging from basic self-help approaches (e.g., manuals, audiotapes, computer-assisted programs) to more intensive group or individual counseling. The Staywell Program developed by the Control Data Corporation is an excellent example of a program providing multiple options for employees—in their case ranging from health risk appraisals only to computer-assisted instruction to life-style courses taught by health professionals (Naditch, 1986). When more time-consuming alternatives are offered, participation is greatly enhanced if employees can be given time off from work to participate and if training activities can be conducted on-site. Some employees may be self-conscious about seeking certain types of services such as employee assistance programs or stress management training, and program planners may want to consider confidential referral and individual treatment options if these are financially feasible. Within any format, participants can be usefully taught general behavioral principles such as gradual behavior change based upon goals derived from baseline data, performance feedback, and coping skills training (e.g., stimulus control techniques, assertiveness training, behavioral rehearsal of problematic situations).

Health education activities need to do more than just provide information (Meichenbaum & Turk, 1979). The better programs generally identify potential stumbling blocks (e.g., Brownell, 1988) and focus on relapse prevention strategies (e.g., Marlatt & Gordon, 1985) that teach participants to anticipate and to cope with "high-risk" situations. Framing health promotion activities as general problem-solving (e.g., D'Zurilla & Goldfried, 1971) or self-management skills (e.g., Watson & Tharp, 1981) that can also be applied to other areas of life can prepare participants for dealing with new challenges to maintaining behavior change. Often, voluntary health agencies (e.g., American Heart Association, American Cancer Society) or university-based programs (e.g., psychology or community health departments) in the local community may be able to deliver high-quality educational/skills training programs at little or no direct cost. Whatever format is adopted, involving employees who may eventually be able to assume leadership of educational programs will increase the likelihood of long-term program maintenance within the company.

Environmental/Social Support Activities

These activities fall into two primary categories: those that restructure the physical environment (e.g., changing foods available in the cafeteria, removing or restocking vending machines, introducing smoking bans) and those that attempt to maximize social support for health promotion. Environmental interventions have not received a great deal of research attention, but to the extent that they reduce opportunities to engage in harmful behaviors and enhance opportunities to pursue healthful behaviors, they should produce long-term and short-term benefits (Sorensen, Pechacek, & Pallonen, 1986). Involving the worksite steering committee or labor representatives in planning environmental interventions is necessary to ensure that employees perceive such changes not as limitations on their privileges but as benefits that promote their health.

Most research on environmental change has focused on cafeteria or point-of-purchase food selection programs (e.g., Wilbur, Zifferblatt, Pinsky, & Zifferblatt, 1981; Zifferblatt, Wilbur, & Pinsky, 1980) and smoking bans (Eriksen, 1986; Rosenstock, Stergachis, & Heaney, 1986; U.S. Department of Health and Human Services, 1989; Walsh & McDougall, 1988). The Wilbur et al. (1981) vending machine study found that making lower-calorie foods available did more to affect food choices than did providing nutrition education materials. Initial studies of smoking bans (Biener, Abrams, Follick, & Dean, 1989; Biener, Abrams, Follick, McAnulty, & Dean, 1986; Rigotti, HillPikl, Cleary, Singer, & Mulley, 1986; Rosenstock et al., 1986) have not identified significant short-term reduction in smoking rates, although recent reports suggest that smoking policies contribute to cessation as well as increased participation in cessation programs (Millar, 1988; Sorensen, Rigotti, Rosen, & Pinney, in press). Such environmental interventions convey an important message about an organization's position on employee health issues and may alter work-site social norms related to health behaviors.

The second major group of environmental support activities consists of attempts to enlist naturally existing or newly created social support systems to reinforce efforts to change behavior. For many persons the amount of social support perceived is one of the primary determinants of successful long-term behavior change (Coppotelli & Orleans, 1985; Sarason & Sarason, 1985). Strategies to involve both employees and family members have been developed, such as "Good Buddy" contests, "Adopt-a-Smoker" programs, and various buddy systems.

One important factor in producing lasting behavior changes is the development of local experts capable of maintaining health promotion efforts. Far too often, interventions consist of one-shot efforts that produce relatively dramatic initial behavior changes, but fail to sustain them; within a couple of months after the program, most employees return to their original behavior. Environmental changes are particularly important to changing social norms for long-term support of behavior change. Two additional strategies for achieving long-term behavior change are (a) to conduct repeated or ongoing classes and incentive programs (e.g., monthly contests) that encourage renewed efforts from employees who have slipped back into old behaviors, and (b) to construct networks or coalitions of employees from one or more work sites to provide a forum for ongoing discussion and support of common health promotion goals. Other strategies may be particularly useful when working in small businesses, work sites with visible unions, or work sites employing large numbers of low-income or minority group members, as described below.

ENHANCING UNION PARTICIPATION IN HEALTH PROMOTION EFFORTS

Unions historically have been ardent supporters of some kinds of health promotion programs and policies and quite ambivalent about or resistant to others. Unions' priority is to support policies that reduce workplace hazards, increase employer responsibility and liability for worker health, and improve protection of the labor force. They are generally less likely to support policies and programs that address worker behaviors believed to be life-style and personal choice issues (Brown, McCarthy, Marcus, et al., in press; Green, 1988).

An important barrier to union support of specific health promotion programs is the process by which many of these programs are introduced and implemented. They are rarely the product of mutual agreement and joint planning by management and labor. Unilateral decisions by management about any programs affecting workers may be regarded as violations of collective bargaining agreements. Collaboration between the two groups, or at least inclusion of labor leaders in discussions, is a fundamental step toward making health promotion programs acceptable to the broader work force (Marcus, Baker, Froines, et al., 1986).

Exploration of specific workplace situations may uncover significant worker dissatisfaction with the company's handling of hazards. In such cases, health promotion providers would be wise to target those issues directly in health promotion interventions either before or along with the introduction of other plans and ideas. A cancer education program, for instance, might try to counter fatalistic attitudes by providing information and screening for high-risk conditions and behaviors. Such a program is more likely to be well received if it builds from or supplements a strong and visible health and safety program in the work site.

In the context of a large work site or company served by one or more unions, the principle of management-labor consultation should be paramount. A program introduced by the union is likely to be better received than one from management. Nevertheless, the key to program and policy success here, as elsewhere, lies in the individual stakeholders and "spark plugs" who are willing and able to spend personal time and energy on the effort. These individuals may be anywhere in the organization, but, obviously, the higher their position in the management or labor hierarchy, the more clout they will have in pushing a program or policy through and making it widely acceptable.

THE SPECIAL CASE OF SMALL BUSINESSES

Since 45% of all workers are employed by companies of fewer than 100 people (U.S. Small Business Administration, 1984), small businesses are an important intervention channel. Yet it is inefficient to work individually with the large numbers of small business. Outreach efforts to small businesses and organizations ideally should involve more than just mailings, as personal contact has a greater chance of success. Since identifying and contacting the dozens, hundreds, or even thousands of such places in a community is an unwieldy task, a first step is to find umbrella associations that serve or represent large numbers of them. The local chamber of commerce is a typical candidate, as are merchants' associations, downtown coalitions, community coalitions, ministerial associations or the local council of churches, and some fraternal and service organizations, such as Lions and Rotary. Smaller companies rely heavily on outside sources of information, because they often have limited internal resources. Networking with other companies or coalitions is an important method of introducing new programs and solving implementation problems (Bulow-Hube & Morisky, 1987).

Smaller companies often use more informal and less structured decision-making and communication processes than do larger companies. Small size may be associated with a "family" rather than a "corporate" atmosphere. One employee's voice may carry considerable weight, and representatives of management are usually highly visible. Thus employee input about and top management support of health promotion take on particular significance. Also, the person responsible for health promotion in the small work site is likely to "wear many hats" and to have less formal training in health promotion issues than his or her counterpart in a large organization (Bulow-Hube & Morisky, 1987). Health promotion providers may need to identify ways of responding to programming needs despite the numerous competing responsibilities of the company's liaison.

INVOLVING ORGANIZATIONS
IN HEALTH PROMOTION

The process and methods for promoting health in work sites described in this chapter can also be applied to other community groups, such as religious and civic organizations. Community organizations serve multiple religious, social, cultural, economic, political, and helping functions. They also lend themselves well to serving health promotion, as a growing number of programs have demonstrated (Lasater, Wells, Carleton, & Elder, 1986; Roberts & Thorsheim, 1987; U.S. Department of Health and Human Services, 1987), and may be an especially effective channel for targeting underserved populations. The process is usually integrated with an assessment of the overall community's culture and norms. Interviews with community leaders are helpful in identifying organizations crucial to efforts targeted at specific groups. Broad communitywide support enhances the program's ability to gain access to community organizations. Community organizations should be represented on the community advisory board or task force that is established for program planning, promotion, and implementation.

Using Community Organizations to Target Minorities, the Poor, and Other Underserved Groups

There is a pressing public health need for outreach to minority, poor, and other underserved populations, and for creative, culturally appropriate health promotion approaches with these groups. Disparities in health status have been amply documented between persons of low and high socioeconomic status and between ethnic minorities and White Americans (U.S. Department of Health and Human Services, 1984, 1984-1986). The strongest predictor of health status differences is socioeconomic status, yet few health promotion efforts target income, education, or employment conditions in statements of purpose or in their approaches (Kaplan, Haan, Syme, Minkler, & Winkleby, 1987; Slater & Carlton, 1985). Most programs appear to assume that their standard approaches will reach minorities and the poor, although their outreach abilities and effectiveness are often inadequate (Abraham & Krowchuk, 1986; Harwood, 1981; Pasick, 1987; Ramirez, Herrick, & Weaver, 1981; Riessman, 1981; Saunders, Alcalay, & Pasick, 1987). There are very few programs that are culturally appropriate and structurally accessible.

Organizations can provide excellent opportunities to reach underserved populations. Historically, minority, low-income, and minimally educated groups have not been reached adequately through more standard health education channels. Some projects operating through community organizations have had encouraging results. Churches, for example, have been effective and willing channels for cardiovascular and cancer risk-reduction programs for Black, inner-city, and rural populations (Dressler, 1987; Hatch & Lovelace, 1980; Levin, 1984).

Other important outreach organizations in minority, poor, rural, or underserved communities may include labor unions, service groups, sports groups, social and youth clubs, grass-roots community action groups, Women, Infant, and Children (WIC) programs and food stamp outlets, the unemployment office, the Salvation Army and other charity and service organizations, and ethnic origin associations. Some of these groups may provide sites for locating hard-to-reach target populations; others may have a demonstrated ability to provide health messages and services to underserved groups (e.g., United Farm Workers, the Salvation Army, fire departments).

In using work sites and organizations to identify and work with hard-to-reach groups, special consideration should be given to several barriers beyond those already mentioned (Monrroy & Orgue, 1983; Ramirez et al., 1981; Riessman, 1981; White, Levine, & Levine, 1979):

- *Concern about differential treatment and discrimination:* Workers, unions, and management in many organizations have been sensitized to class- and race-related issues of discrimination and preferential treatment, as have the unemployed, retired, and disabled. Singling out any group for a special program or approach may draw criticism from some sectors as well as positive publicity from others.

- *Concern about control and ownership of projects:* Development of working relations between more affluent, professional, or culturally mainstream Americans and minority or poor Americans may be marked by conflict over who ultimately has control over a project. Community boards—as essential to good relations with hard-to-reach target groups as with any other community—may find themselves juggling demands from funding sources and professional providers against those of community members and grass-roots organizations.

- *Lack of trust:* Persons of minority or poor backgrounds may not welcome a health promotion program with open arms. Many factors feed this lack of trust, including communication problems between providers and persons of different class, ethnic, and language backgrounds; a history of negative experiences with organizations; perceptions of institutional racism in health facilities, including previous exclusion from programs; an association of research and health promotion with sales and marketing ploys; and concerns about the imposition or intrusion of alien ideas and practices upon them.

- *Apathy or lack of interest:* Some of the persons in our society who are most in need of health promotion efforts may be among the least interested in them. The jobless, the destitute, the deinstitutionalized mentally ill, and drug addicts may be preoccupied with less future-oriented concerns. It is a real challenge not only to locate and identify these people, but to engage them actively in programs.

- *The economic costs of participation:* An ostensibly free program may not attract the most needy because of associated expenditures that make participation prohibitive. Transportation, for instance, may involve not only paying bus fares but also buying snacks for children along the way. Program advice to consume more high-quality, low-fat protein may appear completely infeasible to poor persons. Attending a free screening may mean loss of pay for some employees, time away from a job search, or the cost of child care. Alternatively, some people may assume that *free* implies low quality; some kind of reciprocal exchange agreement may be appropriate.

- *Cultural insensitivity and ignorance:* Providers are all too often unaware of important differences in beliefs and habits of the people they serve. It is erroneous to assume homogeneity among members of an ethnic or cultural group and to apply blanket generalizations to members of a community. Many providers are ignorant about biological variation among ethnic groups, and as a result they may counsel counterproductive behaviors. The lactose intolerance of a majority of the world's adult population is a prime example of such a biological factor.

Communication difficulties due to differences in cultural values and assumptions, knowledge, language, and nonverbal communication styles can lead to misunderstandings and communication breakdowns. Language is the most basic difference, but expressive styles (e.g., ways of expressing agreement and disagreement or anger and power conflicts) may also vary significantly. Underlying some communication problems may be differences in background knowledge about social institutions. Differences in beliefs often mean differences in priorities in identifying health problems and solutions to them. For example, teen pregnancy may be defined very differently by providers and by Black teenage mothers.

With underserved and high-risk groups, providers should be fully committed to working with, or if necessary even turning a project over to, local insiders. Community ownership of a project may be critical to its success or failure, so working closely with persons of the group targeted is essential. This process may entail not only identifying local "movers and shakers," but training community members, thereby empowering them to work toward their own as well as project goals. In working with local organizations and in creating a community board, it is also important to recognize and take into account possible cultural differences in leadership selection and styles. Imposing predetermined organizational forms or structures in a community may be counterproductive to attaining goals.

Health promotion programs that cut across class and cultural lines must conform to the target group's priorities, beliefs, values, perceptions, and practices if they are to be accepted. If they are to endure, they must allow the pursuit of culturally meaningful ends through culturally acceptable means. The content of messages, their formats, and modes of delivery should be culturally relevant. Discovering existing community organizations, leaders, and alliances and building knowledge of the target group's expectations, attitudes, and usual ways of getting things done are essential steps in this process. A review of methods and strategies as discussed in other chapters, especially the case studies in Section V, in this volume may be helpful with these issues.

SUMMARY

Organizations and work sites can participate in health promotion efforts in two basic ways: (a) as program recipients who provide sites and targeted populations and (b) as partners who provide resources and ideas for carrying out program activities in a larger community. Partnership builds a higher level of interest and commitment to community-wide projects. Organizations are recruited with the objective of obtaining as much cooperation and participation as possible. Health promotion interventions in work sites and community organizations may include motivational/incentive activities, education/skills training, and environmental/social support activities. Integrating a variety of strategies in a single site is an effective means of presenting the health promotion message to persons at various stages of readiness for change. Building social and environmental supports for behavior change and repeating program offerings will promote long-term maintenance of health behavior change. Organizations can also be effective sites for reaching underserved and minority populations.

The long-term maintenance of health promotion efforts in work sites and community organizations hinges, in part, on the integration of these endeavors into broad-based strategies for community change. As described throughout this book, community change is most effectively achieved and sustained when intervention efforts are implemented in coordinated, multifaceted ways across diverse community channels.

REFERENCES

Abraham, I. L., & Krowchuk, H. V. (1986). Unemployment and health: Health promotion for the jobless male. *Nursing Clinics of North America, 21*(1), 37-47.

Bibeau, D., & Mullen, K. (1987). *Evaluating health promotion technology: Health risk appraisals.* Paper presented at the annual meeting of the American Public Health Association, New Orleans.

Biener, L., Abrams, D. B., Follick, M. J., & Dean, L. (1989). A comparative evaluation of a restrictive smoking policy in a general hospital. *American Journal of Public Health, 79*, 192-195.

Biener, L., Abrams, D. B., Follick, M. J., McAnulty, D., & Dean, L. (1986). *Effects of a restrictive smoking policy on hospital employees.* Paper presented at the meeting of the Society of Behavioral Medicine, San Francisco.

Blair, S. N., Piserchia, P. V., Wilbur, C. S., & Crowder, J. H. (1986). A public health intervention model for work-site health promotion. *Journal of the American Medical Society, 225*, 921-926.

Brown, E. R., McCarthy, W., Marcus, A., et al. (1988). Workplace smoking policies: Attitudes of union members in a high-risk industry. *Journal of Occupational Medicine, 30*(4) 312-320.

Brownell, K. D. (1986). Weight control at the workplace: The power of social and behavioral factors. In M. F. Cataldo & T. J. Coates (Eds.), *Health promotion in industry: A behavioral medicine perspective* (pp. 143-161). New York: John Wiley.

Brownell, K. D. (1988). *The LEARN program for weight control.* Philadelphia: University of Pennsylvania.

Brownell, K. D., & Felix, M. R. J. (1987). Competitions to facilitate health promotion: Review and conceptual analysis. *American Journal of Health Promotion, 77*, 28-36.

Bulow-Hube, S., & Morisky, D. E. (1987). The innovation-decision model and workplace health promotion programs. *Health Education Research, 2*(1), 15-25.

Coppotelli, H., & Orleans, C. S. (1985). *Quasi-experimentation, design and analysis issues for field settings.* Chicago: Rand McNally.

Dressler, W. W. (1987). The stress process in a southern black community: Implications for prevention research. *Human Organization, 46*(3), 211-220.

D'Zurilla, T. J., & Goldfried, M. F. (1971). Problem-solving and behavior modification. *Journal of Abnormal Psychology, 78*, 107-126.

Elder, J., McGraw, S., Rodrigues, A., Lasater, T., Ferreira, A., Kendal, L., Peterson, G., & Carleton, R. (1987). Evaluation of two community-wide smoking contests. *Preventive Medicine, 16*, 221-234.

Eriksen, M. P. (1986). Workplace smoking control: Rationale and approaches. *Advances in Health Education and Promotion, 1*(A), 65-103.

Fielding, J. E. (1984). Health promotion and disease prevention at the workplace. *Annual Review of Public Health, 5*, 237-265.

Glasgow, R. E., & Terborg, J. R. (1988). Occupational health promotion programs to reduce cardiovascular risk. *Journal of Consulting and Clinical Psychology, 56*, 365-373.

Green, K. L. (1988). Issues of control and responsibility in workers' health. *Health Education Quarterly, 15*(4), 473-486.

Harwood, A. (1981). Guidelines for culturally appropriate health care. In A. Harwood (Ed.), *Ethnicity and medical care.* Cambridge, MA: Harvard University Press.

Hatch, H. W., & Lovelace, K. (1980). Involving the southern rural church and students of the health professions in health education. *Public Health Reports 95*(1), 23-25.

Kaplan, G. A., Haan, M., Syme, S. L., Minkler, M., & Winkleby, M. (1987). Socioeconomic status and health. In R. Ambler & H. Dull (Eds.), *Closing the gap: The burden of unnecessary illness* (pp. 125-129). New York: Oxford University Press.

King, A. C., Flora, J. A., Fortmann, S. P., & Taylor, C. B. (1987). Smokers' challenge: Immediate and long-term findings of a community smoking cessation context. *American Journal of Public Health, 77*, 1340-1341.

Kizer, W. M. (1987). *The healthy workplace: A blueprint for corporate action.* New York: John Wiley.

Klesges, R. C., & Glasgow, R. E. (1986). Work-site smoking control programs. In M. Cataldo & T. J. Coates (Eds.), *Health promotion in industry: A behavioral medicine perspective* (pp. 231-254). New York: John Wiley.

Klesges, R. C., Vasey, M. W., & Glasgow, R. E. (1986). A work-site smoking modification competition: Potential for public health impact. *American Journal of Public Health, 76*, 198-200.

Kotler, P. (1984). Social marketing of health behavior. In L. W. Frederiksen, L. J. Solomon, & K. A. Brehony (Eds.), *Marketing health behavior: Principles, techniques, and applications* (pp. 23-40). New York: Plenum.

Lasater, T., Wells, B. L., Carleton, R. A., & Elder, J. P. (1986). The role of churches in disease prevention research studies. *Public Health Reports, 101*(2), 125-131.

Levin, J. S. (1984). The role of the black church in community medicine. *Journal of the National Medical Association, 76*(5), 477-483.

Marcus, A. C., Baker, D. B., Froines, J., et al. (1986). The ICWU cancer control and evaluation program: Research design and needs assessment. *Journal of Occupational Medicine, 28*(3), 226-236.

Marlatt, G. A., & Gordon, J. R. (1985). *Relapse prevention: Maintenance strategies in the treatment of addictive behaviors.* New York: Guilford.

Meichenbaum, D., & Turk, D. C. (1987). *Facilitating treatment adherence.* New York: Plenum.

Millar, W. J. (1988). *Smoke in the workplace: An evaluation of smoking restrictions.* Ottawa: Minister of Supply and Services.

Monrroy, L. S. A., & Orgue, M. S. (1983). Ethnic minority communities' health care involvement and consumer education. In M. S. Orgue, B. Bloch, & L. S. A. Monrroy (Eds.), *Ethnic nursing care: A multicultural approach* (pp. 329-345). St. Louis: C. V. Mosby.

Naditch, M. P. (1986). STAYWELL: Evolution of a behavioral medicine program in industry. In M. F. Cataldo & T. J. Coats (Eds.), *Health and industry: A behavioral medicine perspective* (pp. 323-337). New York: John Wiley.

Nathan, P. E. (1984). Johnson & Johnson's Live for Life: A comprehensive positive lifestyle change. In J. D. Matarazzo, S. H. Weiss, J. A. Herd, N. E. Miller, & S. W. Weiss (Eds.), *Behavioral health: A handbook of health enhancement and disease prevention* (pp. 1064-1070). New York: John Wiley.

O'Donnell, M. P., & Ainsworth, T. (1984). *Health promotion in the workplace.* New York: John Wiley.

Orlandi, M. A. (1986). The diffusion and adoption of work-site health promotion innovations: An analysis of barriers. *Preventive Medicine, 15*, 522-536.

Pasick, R. J. (1987). *Health promotion of minorities in California: A report to the East Bay Area Health Education Center.* San Francisco.

Pechacek, T., Freutel, J., Arkin, R., & Mittelmark, M. (1983). *The Quit and Win Contest: A community-wide incentive program for smoking cessation.* Paper presented at the World Congress on Behavior Therapy, Washington, DC.

Prochaska, J. O., & DiClemente, C. C. (1983). Stages and processes of self-change of smoking: Toward an integrative model of change. *Journal of Consulting and Clinical Psychology, 51*, 390-395.

Ramirez, A., Herrick, K. L., & Weaver, F. J. (1981). Elderly Asesino Silencioso: A methodology for alerting the Spanish speaking community. *Urban Health, 10*(5), 44-48.

Riessman, C. K. (1981). Improving the use of health services by the poor. In P. Conrad & R. Kern (Eds.), *The sociology of health and illness: Critical perspectives* (pp. 541-557). New York: St. Martin's.

Rigotti, N. A., HillPikl, B., Cleary, P., Singer, D. E., & Mulley, A. G. (1986). The impact of banning smoking on a hospital ward: Acceptance, compliance, air quality, and smoking behavior [Abstract]. *Clinical Research, 34*, 833A.

Roberts, B. B., & Thorsheim, H. I. (1987). A partnership approach to consultation: The process and results of a major primary prevention field experiment. In The Ecology of Prevention [Special issue]. *Prevention in Human Services, 4*(3/4), 151-186.

Rogers, E. M., & Shoemaker, F. F. (1971). *Communication of innovations: A cross-cultural approach.* New York: Free Press.

Rosenstock, I. M., Stergachis, A., & Heaney, C. (1986). Evaluation of smoking prohibition policy in a health maintenance organization. *American Journal of Public Health, 76*, 1014-1015.

Sarason, I. G., & Sarason, B. R. (Eds.). (1985). *Social support: Theory, research and applications.* Seattle: Martinus Nijhoff.

Saunders, F., Alcalay, R., & Pasick, R. (1987, May 6-7). *Health promotion for ethnic, minority communities.* Paper presented at the California Consensus Conference on Health Promotion.

Shepard, D. S., & Pearlman, L. A. (1985). Health habits that pay off. *Business Health, 2*(4), 37-41.

Slater, C., & Carlton, W. (1985). Behavior, lifestyle, and socioeconomic variables as determinants of health status: Implications for health policy development. *American Journal of Preventive Medicine, 1*(5), 25-33.

Sloan, R. P., Gruman, J. C., & Allegrante, J. P. (1987). *Investigating employee health: A guide to effective health promotion in the workplace.* San Francisco: Jossey-Bass.

Sorensen, G., Pechacek, T. F., & Pallonen. U. (1986). Occupational and work-site norms and attitudes about smoking cessation. *American Journal of Public Health, 76*(5), 544-549.

Sorensen, G., Rigotti, N., Rosen, A., & Pinney, J. (in press). The effects of a work-site nonsmoking policy: Evidence for increased cessation. *American Journal of Public Health.*

Stachnik, T. J., & Stoffelmayr, B. E. (1983). Work-site smoking cessation program: A potential for national impact. *American Journal of Public Health, 73*(12), 1395-1396.

U.S. Department of Health and Human Services. (1984-1986). *Report of the Secretary's Task Force on Black and Minority Health* (8 vols.). Washington, DC: Government Printing Office.

U.S. Department of Health and Human Services. (1984). *Health indicators for Hispanic, Black, and White Americans* (Series 10, No. 148). Washington, DC: Government Printing Office.

U.S. Department of Health and Human Services. (1987). *Churches as an avenue to high blood pressure control* (NIH Publication No. 87-2725). Washington, DC: Government Printing Office.

U.S. Department of Health and Human Services. (1989). *Reducing the health consequences of smoking: 25 years of progress: A report of the surgeon general* (DHHS Publication No. CDC 89-84111). Washington, DC: Government Printing Office.

U.S. Small Business Administration. (1984). *The state of small business: A report to the president.* Washington, DC: Government Printing Office.

Wagner, E. H., Beery, W. L., Schoenbeack, V. J., & Graham, R. M. (1982). An assessment of health hazard/health risk appraisal. *American Journal of Public Health, 72*, 347-352.

Walsh, D. C., & McDougall, V. (1988). Current policies regarding smoking in the workplace. *American Journal of Industrial Medicine 13*, 181-190.

Warner, K. E. (1987). Selling health promotion to corporate America: Uses and abuses of the economic argument. *Health Education Quarterly, 14*(1), 39-56.

Warner, K. E., Wickizer, T. M., Wolfe, R. A., Schildroth, J. E., & Samuelson, M. H. (1988). Economic implications of workplace health promotion programs: Review of the literature. *Journal of Occupational Medicine, 30*(2), 106-112.

Watson, P. L., & Tharp, R. G. (1981). *Self-directed behavior: Self-modification for personal adjustment.* Monterey, CA: Brooks/Cole.

Weiss, S. H. (1984). Health hazard/health risk appraisals. In J. D. Matarazzo, S. H. Weiss, J. A. Herd, N. E. Miller, & S. W. Weiss (Eds.), *Behavioral health: A handbook of health enhancement and disease prevention* (pp. 275-276). New York: John Wiley.

White, P. E., Levine, L., & Levine, S. (1979). Community health organizations and resources. In H. E. Freeman, S. Levine, & L. G. Reeder (Eds.), *Handbook of medical sociology* (pp. 347-368). Englewood Cliffs, NJ: Prentice-Hall.

Wilbur, C. S., Zifferblatt, S. M., Pinsky, J. L., & Zifferblatt, J. (1981). Healthy vending: A cooperative pilot research program to stimulate good health in the marketplace. *Preventive Medicine, 10*, 85-93.

Zifferblatt, S. M., Wilbur, C. S., & Pinsky, J. L. (1980). Changing cafeteria eating habits. *Journal of the American Dietetic Association, 76*, 15-20.

Chapter 9

INVOLVING COMMUNITY HEALTH PROFESSIONALS AND SYSTEMS

RUSSELL V. LUEPKER
LENNART RÅSTAM

Health professionals and medical institutions play a pivotal role in a community-based program. Physicians, nurses, dentists, nutritionists, dietitians, and others, their professional societies, and hospitals, clinics, and health agencies can contribute in several key areas:

- providing legitimation and communitywide acceptance of the planned health programs
- providing technical input
- providing guidance about local health care practices
- participating in program leadership and planning
- making structural alterations in the health care delivery systems to incorporate the program into the community

In each of these areas, all professional disciplines and organizations play a role. In general, however, the involvement of physicians is particularly important because of their leadership in the health care sector and their contacts with most citizens through direct medical services. This leadership pertains regardless of the structure of the system for provision of medical care (e.g., socialized or nonsocialized). However, physicians' relative impact on the five items above may differ between systems under market and government control.

There are some well-known barriers to professional involvement in health promotion programs. These are independent of the system of medical care, but may vary in their relative impact:

- The system of graduate training and professionalization generally emphasizes acute rather than preventive activities.
- Preventive services are uncommonly rewarded and poorly delivered relative to disease-oriented care. As a consequence, they rarely have the same institutional support as acute care services.

These conditions are changing as health care providers increasingly recognize the importance of preventive services and incorporate those services in their practices. In the United States, this is promoted by multiple federal programs that emphasize the necessity of increased effectiveness in the area of cholesterol reduction and blood pressure. These programs are supported by physician education programs as well as public awareness initiatives.

In Sweden, this change is enhanced by the Health Care Act of 1983, which guides activities of the socialized health care system. It explicitly declares that the health care sector includes preventive programs and that, consequently, public resources must be allocated accordingly. As budget is limited, this means a relative change in support from acute care to preventive strategies. Whether change will follow remains to be evaluated. However, this change can be accelerated by an effective community program. Examples of this will be given below, both from the market-oriented U.S. health care sector and from the socialized Swedish system.

BACKGROUND

There is general agreement today about the importance of both mass strategies and high-risk-oriented preventive programs. Hospitals and clinics need to give sound prevention advice to patients at risk for disease. At the same time, mass strategies have to be implemented. Health professionals have unique potential to participate in and to support community programs in several ways. The first is at the *clinic* level, where practitioners are uniquely positioned to provide information to patients about preventive behaviors and maintenance of health (Relman, 1982; Wechsler, Levine, Idelson, Rohman, & Taylor, 1982). Second, health professionals can participate at the *community* level, where their involvement on boards and committees and in other voluntary activities helps to provide leadership and to integrate the program fully into the community to ensure that it complements rather than competes with existing activities. It is clear that professional attitudes and behaviors toward disease prevention and health promotion can have great impact on societal norms and trends (Schucker, Wittes, Cutler, et al., 1987). Third, at the *personal* level, health professionals' commitment to a healthy life-style increases their effectiveness, credibility, and enthusiasm as role models for patients and community leaders (Maheux, Pineault, & Beland, 1987). It is clear that professional attitudes and behaviors toward disease prevention and health promotion programs are improving and consequently that efforts to involve this group at all three levels are supported by the current trends (Angard et al., 1986; Taylor, 1981).

There are many barriers to preventive practice. These have recently been reviewed by Kottke, Blackburn, Brekke, et al. (1987) and range from lack of knowledge to lack of perceived patient demand and commitment to the health professional. The basic education of health professionals rarely emphasizes health promotion and disease prevention-oriented practice. The foundation of basic science, often coupled with conservative norms, creates negative attitudes toward change in clinical practice that involves using more social science-based skills and knowledge. Thus it is seen that physicians are less prone than the general public to advocate life-style-based strategies for health promotion (Schucker, Bailey, Heimbach, et al., 1987; Schucker, Wittes, et al., 1987). It is likely that this reluctance also reflects professional feelings of losing control over health-related matters in the society, previously entirely possessed by the medical community. However, effective educational approaches to preventive practice are available. Most programs undertaken today are in postgraduate education, commonly workshops aimed at teaching preventive practice. While attendance generally represents the fraction of the practicing health professionals that are already active and "converted," Swedish experience suggests that professional education emphasizing prevention programs can be readily implemented (Råstam, 1988).

Recent experience in Pawtucket, Rhode Island, indicates that a targeted educational campaign can involve substantial proportions of practicing community physicians in prevention-oriented continuing medical education (Carleton, Banspach, Block, et al., 1987). This approach requires a focused effort and active recruiting of practitioners to the program. Thus experience suggests that continuing professional education may be an important vehicle for enhancing a community program.

While participation of health professionals is critical in the volunteer structure of a community health promotion program, relatively little has been written about initiating and maintaining that involvement. Nonetheless, voluntary health organizations such as the American Heart Association, the American Cancer Society, and others have traditionally emphasized the involvement of health professionals in their voluntary boards. This approach has been particularly successful with the Heart Association, where it is required that 50% of all board members be health professionals. The inclusion of these individuals not only aids in legitimating the program but provides a source of advice and consultation on technical health issues.

In addition to formal service on advisory boards, health professionals play critical roles in the institutions they represent. Health promotion programs, with few exceptions, must involve hospitals, clinics, and similar providers of health services. The involvement and commitment of health professionals appears to be an essential ingredient in obtaining the commitment of the institution. Recent efforts with hospital antismoking policies recognize the critical role of health professionals in their acceptance and implementation (Kottke et al., 1985).

Although there are, to our knowledge, no health professional education programs that formally require that students make a commitment to personal healthy life-styles, the types of individuals who enter the health professions, highly educated and affluent, tend to demonstrate more positive life-style attitudes and behaviors. For example, physicians are less likely to be smokers and more likely to be interested in physical fitness than their age contemporaries (Sobal, Valente, Muncie, et al., 1985; Wyshak, Lamb, Lawrence, et al., 1980). Similar experience is suggested for dentists and pharmacists (Garfinkel et al., 1986).

ORGANIZATIONAL APPROACHES TO INVOLVEMENT

Assessment of Community Resources

The involvement of health professionals in a community program requires a planned approach. Starting with community diagnosis (described in Chapter 4), the key health staff are identified. Generally, the program then proceeds to the formation of advisory committees of activated and representative physicians, nurses, and so on. In highly organized systems like the Swedish, however, it is often necessary to start in the formal health organizations, which will themselves nominate candidates, to legitimate the program among political and professional decision makers.

The professional community and its institutions are further involved through continuing education and support for preventive clinical practice. For example, medical institutions can be offered aid in reorganizing their delivery systems to facilitate screening and patient education programs.

Early identification of incentives for this change is essential. These frequently depend on the reimbursement system. With a fee-for-service health care sector, as in parts of the United States, preventive care can be promoted as a method for expanding practice by the identification of new groups of patients in need of care. With a socialized system, these factors will act as constraints and referral plans that control work load; for example, for dietitians this may be a legitimate way to support involvement in the program. It is obvious that careful analysis of such barriers for participation must be individually mapped before implementation.

Staffing/Coordination

The selection of a key professional person to coordinate efforts in the health professional community is a particularly important decision. Diversity of professional groups and multiple organizations make this selection difficult. The individual chosen needs to have the respect of health professionals and must feel comfortable organizing and providing initiative. The ability to work with physicians is critical. While a physician as a staff person would be ideal from a disciplinary standpoint, in a fee-for-service system this is not realistic due to salary expectations. However, in some fixed-salary systems, including the Swedish, this is possible and even promoted by legislation. In our experience, a physician who takes on such a position must retain a certain level of clinical activity to be able to keep the professional respect of colleagues and the health care community. If the physician is not identified with the professional role, his or her involvement may even be detrimental to the program.

A practical choice for such a staff position is often found in other health disciplines. Good choices are nurses, health educators, nutritionists, and pharmacists. The individual must be comfortable with a proactive role with all professional groups and institutions. For example, a nurse who can relate only to nurses' groups would not be acceptable. He or she must be able to work with hospital administrators, physicians, and others. The individual placed in this position should have multiple contacts within the health care community and be able to organize the health professional and physician advisory boards described below.

If the organization sponsoring the health promotion effort is unable to have paid staff to work with the health professional community, a volunteer organization may be necessary. In this circumstance, it is also necessary to identify a leader to assume major responsibility for the activities in this area. Again, a health professional should be sought, and an interested physician can be of considerable assistance. The volunteer, however, must be willing to devote substantial time and will need considerable clerical and administrative staff support to carry out the program. It is likely that a program run by volunteers will be of smaller scope, and hence fewer effects may result.

The size of the staff, whether paid or volunteer, depends on the size of the organizing effort. With larger populations and more complex tasks, more staff and resources are obviously necessary. The impact of the program on the health care community and professionals is closely related to the amount of effort expended.

Committees

Health professionals' committee. A volunteer health professionals' committee can provide significant assistance to a community program. It can be a resource for ideas, volunteer effort, and input into the health institutions in the community. As with any effective committee, it should be broadly representative. It is critical that no single group from a profession or an institution dominate the committee. This is particularly crucial in an era of increasing competition among health professions and health care institutions. It must be assured that local project ownership is not violated, so the group identifies it as their committee. The committee can provide technical advice and access to professional organizations. The selection of such a committee should include input from community leaders, major health care organizations, and institutions in the community. Included should be suggestions from professional societies, trade unions, and government organizations. The committee's work should be focused on specific tasks with finite goals. For example, it may provide a focus for continuing education or a method of ensuring environmental change for eliminating smoking in hospitals.

Physicians' advisory committee. In addition to their membership on a broadly representative health care committee, physicians should also be specifically organized into a separate committee. This committee should represent all elements of the physician community, including hospital staff, primary care facilities (large group practices, HMOs, and primary care centers), public health agencies, medical schools, and other organizations.

Early contacts with physicians and recruitment of physicians to advisory committees and other groups need to be in the hands of colleagues. Contacts through individuals perceived to be experts in the same field may be the only reasonable way to approach and involve this usually hard-to-engage group. An active physician volunteer who has the respect of colleagues is a good choice.

The physicians' advisory committee performs several functions. First, it is a source of legitimation for the community program. When questions are asked and issues raised, they are frequently of a medical nature. The appropriate group to respond to these inquiries should be community physicians. Such response should as far as possible reflect consensus among community physicians, and the physicians' advisory committee is a perfect vehicle for developing consensus on such matters. In addition, a physicians' advisory committee serves as a source of technical expertise for the program. It is important to have this group review community health education plans for medical accuracy and credibility. This role is a particularly important one.

Finally, this group serves as an important conduit to the major medical institutions in the community. Activated physicians who are involved in decision making and advice giving usually carry the credibility of the institution they represent. They also provide a resource by which the program can approach medical institutions to initiate new programs and institutionalize practices that are supportive of the program.

EDUCATION APPROACHES
FOR HEALTH PROFESSIONALS

Continuing education remains a primary method of delivering information to and enhancing prevention skills in the health professional community. It is a common practice, and systems exist for support and implementation. The approach to physicians differs to some extent from that of other professionals, and so it is treated separately.

Physicians

In the United States, licensing regulations require annual credit hours for physicians, supporting a system of continuing medical education (CME). Traditionally, workshops on prevention gather small audiences. However, a changing environment, with the recognition by many health care providers of a lack of education in prevention services, may change this. In addition, patient demand for preventive services and better educational programs will make them more attractive.

To develop a CME program, it is important to have the support and legitimation of local and/or national professional organizations. Those might include medical schools, medical societies, hospitals, or other organizations that traditionally provide postgraduate training. Common sponsorships bring mailing lists, facilities, and the legitimation of the cosponsoring organizations.

To make a CME program for community disease prevention most effective, it is axiomatic that high participation rates among physicians in the community are necessary, and this requires close liaison with the local medical society, hospital medical staff groups, and other organizations of physicians. Invitations to outside expert speakers, convenience of meeting sites and times, and multiple mailings or other solicitation to participate all encourage a larger audience.

The current thinking in CME suggests that physicians are well aware of the scientific arguments for prevention. Although it is important to mention these arguments, particularly when there is controversy, these should form only a minor portion of a prevention and health promotion workshop. Instead, the workshop should focus on delivering practical skills for prevention in the outpatient setting. Physicians are generally interested in knowing how to deliver services efficiently and how to be effective counselors. They need information on how to use other health professionals and colleagues for referral. Although the specific approach will depend on the topic and disease focus as well as the state of readiness in the physician community, a concentration on practical skills for preventive practice is usually needed and well received.

Recent experience suggests that when the education goal is to develop specific clinic programs, using problem-oriented education may be specially helpful. In such cases, it is helpful to include all clinic staff, who work together to develop strategies for implementation. This will facilitate further work (Råstam, 1988).

Other Health Professionals

Like physicians, other health professionals have established systems for continuing education, frequently supported by state law and the requirements of professional organizations. Here also, close cooperation with professional organizations and institutions is critical to legitimating and encouraging participation in continuing education and the uniqueness of prevention-oriented workshops. In these groups, recruitment may be of less an issue than for physicians.

As for physicians, scientific justification for disease prevention/ health promotion efforts should not be the sole basis of workshops for other health professionals. Practical skills such as those used in measurement and counseling should provide a central focus of the program. These workshops can be taught by a wide variety of health professionals from both inside and outside the discipline of the audience. Practical training sessions including hands-on experience can add to the effectiveness of these workshops.

Professional Meetings

In addition to sponsoring continuing education efforts, a community program needs to reach the broader constituency of health professionals through their professional organizations. Thus the program must be prepared to have expert speakers willing to present the program to medical societies, nurses' associations, hospital staff meetings, and other similar groups. This has the advantage of reaching many health professionals who may not attend CME workshops in the specific topical area. It allows them to gather information about the program, ask questions, and potentially be supporters of the effort. These presentations need to begin early in the community program, and they must be informative. Later presentations should update the groups on program progress and issues.

Because most program chairpersons for traditional health professional organizations are volunteers, frequently with limited budgets, they are usually pleased to have speakers made available to them. It is important that the program speaker be perceived as an expert in the health professionals' group and be able to answer scientific and technical questions about the program. An effective community program should have new presentations ready at least annually for various relevant professional groups. If issues arise or controversy exists, it may be necessary to have more frequent presentations as well as smaller discussions with professional groups.

In choosing groups to approach, it is important that professional groups representing physicians be included. Physicians are less likely to come to meetings than are other health professionals, so presentations to groups such as county medical societies or hospital staff meetings may reach only a small fraction of practitioners. Several different approaches should be considered. For other health professional groups, these presentations may be more easily performed, as their organizations may be more broadly representative and better attended. Local circumstances should dictate approaches.

INVOLVING PROFESSIONALS
IN INTERVENTIONS

Institutions

The attitude of medical institutions on health promotion and disease prevention issues is an important one. For example, medical institutions make an important statement when they have a cigarette smoking ban on their premises. Such a policy is a clear message to employees, patients, and the general community as to the attitude of the institution regarding the importance of not smoking. It can be viewed as a caring, concerned approach to the problem, particularly when linked to active smoking cessation programs for employees and patients. The encouragement of such environmental programs in health care institutions is an important support to a community program.

To implement such programs, sensitivity to the workings of an individual health care institution is important. Involving hospital or clinic administrators or, if health care is socialized, even local politicians can be particularly helpful. Working from within the system, they have the opportunity to be advocates for new policies and approaches to health promotion/disease prevention. Supporting these individuals with factual material and information that will help convince their colleagues is an important element in the program.

Such environmental programs offer wider opportunities than just restrictive policies. For example, the routine measurement of blood pressure, laboratory standards, and appropriate flagging of abnormal values may be addressed. Specific work-site programs for hospital staff, such as time for exercise, healthy cafeteria selections, routine screening, and other health promotion approaches are also valuable. Finally, medical institutions can take a leadership role through collaborative arrangements to support other community organizations, such as schools, parks, and industry, in their own health promotion and environmental programs.

Screening Programs

The involvement in screening for related risk factors for disease is probably the least controversial way that health professionals can support a community health promotion program. In its traditional form, screening aims at identifying subjects at risk for disease who need follow-up care. This is an important component of the program, and, where valid methods exist, it should be included. Inherent in the screening program must also be agreed-upon principles for referral. A sudden flood of referred patients to an already overloaded clinic may well become the start of a controversy that has the potential of hurting the program. Physicians not involved may also feel that patients are "stolen" from their clinics. Close cooperation with as many community physicians as possible is therefore necessary before the screening program is set up.

With the present emphasis on patient education for life-style change, the screening program can form an important vehicle for population-oriented health promotion. The concept of screening education means that in the screening situation every individual is seen as an opportunity for individualized health education, related to the patient's own risk factor pattern and life-style (Murray et al., 1986). The opportunity for risk factor measurement will in this case act as the magnet that attracts the subjects to come for education. It can involve larger strata of the population who will not attend more targeted individualized education efforts.

Reimbursement for Preventive Services

One of the impediments to the provision of preventive services has been the lack of a consistent reimbursement system. The increasing debate over the costs of medical services and attempts to control those costs has made third-party payers in the United States reluctant to become involved in financing new preventive services. Their arguments run from the potential for uncontrolled costs to a lack of demonstrable benefit. In socialized systems with fixed or decreasing total budgets, the debate has focused on the ethics of eliminating old services that have some benefit. The lack of scientific evidence for the benefits of mass strategies is also used as an argument. Fortunately, those attitudes are gradually changing with accumulating scientific evidence and increasing consumer demand for preventive services.

In this changing environment, there may be opportunity for building financial support for preventive services. A well-run community program has involved community leaders, including those from the health care financing portion of the community (e.g., third-party payers, politicians, and administrators) and business leaders. Within these groups rests the decision-making authority for determining health insurance benefits. A third source of influence is legislation or regulation that directs insurers to support certain services. This last source of structural change is extremely slow and difficult to implement, however.

Several trends encourage the support of prevention-oriented care. There are gradually merging federal government and professional organization policies on appropriate preventive practice. This occurs in the form of expert panels and reports. Such activity directs the "standard of care" for the nation and has implications for individual community programs. These reports should be widely disseminated throughout the community and used as a source of discussion with third-party payers. A second trend is also supportive, with more business leaders recognizing the value of preventive services. The individuals who make decisions about health care benefits for their employees have considerable impact on health insurance organizations.

ENHANCING PREVENTIVE PRACTICE

In addition to continuing medical education and the role of institutions in enhancing a community approach, general clinical practice may provide a significant aid to health promotion programs. There is increasing availability of technology and methods for rationalizing preventive practice within a clinical care system. These are frequently taught in modern CME programs. However, even practical workshops may not provide all of the skills to implement such programs in an individual clinic setting. For this, consultation at the specific site may be both helpful and essential. An individual who can work with physicians and office staff to develop a health promotion/disease prevention program for that clinic's patients can be important to the overall community program. The benefit is mutual, as the clinic has the technology and resources to deal with individuals who may be referred by screening programs and other community recommendations found elsewhere within this book.

Supporting this system for prevention-oriented care should be a variety of print and electronic materials that enhance and facilitate the messages given by the health care provider. These materials should be readily understood and delivered by usual office staff, and they should be reasonable in cost. Many programs are under development by health educators, and some are currently available to support various health promotion/disease prevention efforts.

It will often be necessary to be proactive in encouraging these programs. Like pharmaceutical "detail persons," program staff members can be effective at establishing a rational health promotion/disease prevention program for health care providers.

CONCLUSION

The involvement of health professionals and health care institutions in community-based health promotion and disease prevention programs is essential. Their active support facilitates the development of the program, its implementation, and finally its incorporation into the fabric of the community. In developing such a program, close attention to the involvement of health professionals, particularly physicians, at the outset is crucial. With the active support of community health professionals, the program has markedly increased chances for success.

REFERENCES

Angard, E. E., Land, J. M., Lenhan, C. J., Packard, C. J., Percy, M. J., Ritchie, L. D., & Shephard, J. (1986). Prevention of cardiovascular disease in general practice: A proposed model. *British Medical Journal, 293*, 177-180.

Carleton, R., Banspach, S., Block, L., et al. (1987). Physician attitudes and behavior concerning cholesterol: Impact of public education. *CVD Epidemiology Newsletter, 41*, 43.

Garfinkel, L., et al. (1986). Smoking habits among health professionals. *Ca-A Cancer Journal for Clinicians, 36*(1).

Kottke, T. E., Blackburn, H., Brekke, M. L., et al. (1987). The systematic practice of preventive cardiology. *American Journal of Cardiology, 59*, 690-694.

Kottke, T. E., Hill, C., Heitzig, C., Brekke, M., Blake, S., Arneson, S., & Caspersen, C. (1985, January). Smoke-free hospitals: Attitudes of patients, employees, and faculty. *Minnesota Medicine*, pp. 53-55.

Maheux, B., Pineault, R., & Beland, F. (1987). Factors influencing physicians' orientation toward prevention. *American Journal of Preventive Medicine, 3*(1), 12-18.

Murray, D. M., Luepker, R. V., Pirie, P. L., Grimm, R. H., Bloom, E., Davis, M., & Blackburn, H. (1986). Systematic risk factor screening and education: A community-wide approach to prevention of coronary heart disease. *Preventive Medicine, 15*(6), 661-672.

Råstam, L. (1988). Preparing primary care for prevention. *Annals of Clinical Research, 20*, 146-149.

Relman, A. S. (1982). Encouraging the practice of preventive medicine and health promotion. *Public Health Report, 97*, 216-219.

Schucker, B., Bailey, K., Heimbach, J. T., et al. (1987). Change in public perspective on cholesterol and heart disease: Results from two national surveys. *Journal of the American Medical Association, 258*(24), 3527-3531.

Schucker, B., Wittes, J. T., Cutler, J. A., et al. (1987). Change in physician perspective on cholesterol and heart disease: Results from two national surveys. *Journal of the American Medical Association, 258*(24), 3521-3526.

Sobal, J., Valente, C. M., Muncie, H. L., et al. (1985). Physicians' beliefs about the importance of 25 health promoting behaviors. *American Journal of Public Health, 75*(12), 1427-1428.

Taylor, R. (1981). Health promotion: Can it succeed in the office? *Preventive Medicine, 10*, 258-262.

Wechsler, H., Levine, S., Idelson, R. K., Rohman, M., & Taylor, J. O. (1982). The physician's role in health promotion: A survey of primary-care practitioners. *Massachusetts Department of Public Health, 308*(2), 97-98.

Wyshak, G., Lamb, G. A., Lawrence, R. S., et al. (1980). A profile of the health-promoting behaviors of physicians and lawyers. *New England Journal of Medicine, 303*(2), 104-107.

Part IV

PROGRAM EVALUATION,
MAINTENANCE, AND DIFFUSION

Chapter 10

EVALUATING HEALTH PROMOTION PROGRAMS
Basic Questions and Approaches

PHYLLIS L. PIRIE

Community health promotion program planners often find themselves under pressure to evaluate their programs—pressure that may stem from administrative requirements, funding agencies, or boards of directors, or, more subtly, from their professional peers. At the same time, these program planners may view evaluation as something extra, imposed from above, diverting funds and energy away from programmatic uses, with little direct benefit to programs. This chapter is directed to the concerns of these individuals, and attempts to provide them with a framework for thinking about how evaluations can be made directly useful to people and their programs.

What does it mean for an evaluation to be useful? Briefly, it means that evaluation results enter into consideration when decisions are to be made about the future shape and direction of a program. The decisions that an evaluation can affect may be programmatic decisions (for example, whether or not to modify specific aspects of the program, such as the content of the educational materials or the type of publicity used to attract participants) or funding decisions, concerning whether the program is to be continued or discontinued, expanded or reduced.

It is important for everyone concerned with evaluation to realize that evaluation results are not the only inputs into such decisions (Weiss, 1988). Decisions are affected also by budgetary considerations, political considerations (for example, pressures from community members, clients, and other organizations), staffing considerations, and the like. Nevertheless, evaluation results can be useful, either by directly influencing decisions about programs or by influencing the kinds of pressures that are brought to bear. The goal of the evaluation should be to produce maximally useful data and to present that data in such a way that they can readily be put to use.

QUESTIONS FOR HEALTH PROMOTION PROGRAMS

This section presents a list of questions that could potentially be asked about a community health promotion program. The most fundamental decision to be made about any evaluation is the choice of question to be addressed, and this list gives a quick summary of issues found to be important in other programs. This can serve as a kind of checklist to be used while attempting to define the question for an evaluation.

Questions for the Planning Stages

Should this program be developed at all? This is the question underlying needs assessment, as program developers attempt to understand the health needs of the population they are working with and the existing efforts to address those needs. This question is really part of the program planning process, and, as such, is discussed in Chapter 4 of this volume.

Are the educational materials appropriate? Most health promotion programs make use of some sort of materials to convey their message, whether those materials are in print, audio, or video form. Judging the appropriateness of these materials has been labeled "formative evaluation" by media researchers (Cambre, 1981). Issues for formative evaluation include accuracy of content, appropriateness of language and/or reading level, attractiveness of models, interpretability of symbols, and general appeal of the material. Additional issues concerning the roles of media in community health promotion programs are discussed in Chapter 7.

Strategies for formative evaluation of health promotion media have included expert panels, focus groups, and in-depth interviews. Expert panels, for example, may be asked to comment on the accuracy of the information contained in the materials. Individuals drawn from the target audience for the materials may be asked to examine the materials and then to answer questions about them, to measure their comprehension of the information. Focus groups may be asked to describe more qualitative responses, such as their interpretations of drawings and symbols. All of these procedures are carried out while the materials are in production, so that changes can be made before the product is finalized.

Questions About Program Operations

Is the program being implemented as planned? Getting an answer to this question is usually tedious and time-consuming. The question implies that there is a clearly specified plan of what exactly should occur. While such a plan may exist, it is often not written down in any one location, so that the evaluator is forced to extract the plan from the program developers' heads. Merely extracting and documenting the plan is often the first major contribution an evaluator makes to the program. Since every single aspect of the program cannot be evaluated, judgments must be made (by the program planners, usually at the prodding of the evaluator) about what are the important elements of the program. Those are the elements that must be monitored. Documenting program implementation not only helps improve the operation of the program, it can also help interpret the outcome evaluation. If a program achieves good outcomes, those wishing to replicate it will need a clear description of exactly what was done. If a program does not achieve good outcomes, it will be important to differentiate inadequate theory from inadequate implementation.

Monitoring program implementation often includes a review of existing program records but may involve the creation of new types of records or systems of recording, or it may involve interviews with participants or direct observations.

Is the program reaching its target audience? This is a key question for community-based health promotion programs, which frequently must market themselves in a public arena, rather than finding a ready-made audience in a school or hospital setting. The question implies that the characteristics of the target audience are known, in terms of size and other demographic characteristics. Counting and characterizing the audience can be accomplished easily in a program that has a formal sign-up procedure, but is much more difficult in the case of programs such as new smoking policies or placing nutrition information in grocery stores and restaurants. Some information about who is aware of such initiatives and their demographic characteristics can be obtained through on-the-spot interviews, for example, with patrons of the grocery stores and restaurants involved in the programs. More precise information about the numbers of individuals aware of such programs can be gained only from population-based surveys, which constitute an expensive data-collection strategy. Audience characteristics for media programs can sometimes be learned from commercial ratings services such as Nielsen or Arbitron.

Who is the program failing to reach, and why? Sometimes a very useful appraisal of the program's ability to reach its audience can be obtained by assessing people who might have been expected to take part but did not. Were they unaware of the program? Were they aware but found the program unappealing? Did they fail to perceive their own need to take part? Answers to these questions can have direct implications for improving the program.

Obtaining data about nonparticipants can be difficult in many circumstances. One major problem is in defining a population of nonparticipants. Program dropouts are one part of this population and can often be identified and surveyed, but they do not represent those who were unaware of the program or who found it too unappealing even to sign up.

Are the program's participants satisfied with their experience? The need to ask this question is often driven partly by an organization's need to satisfy the "consumers" of a program, in the hopes that they will return for other programs or recommend the organization's programs to others. Another rationale for asking the question is the unstated and unproven premise that satisfied participants will have more positive outcomes. For these reasons, participant ratings of satisfaction are one of the most commonly performed types of evaluation. Unfortunately, the results are less useful than one might think. A major problem underlying these evaluations is a positive ratings bias (Stipak, 1980/ 1982): Program participants generally rate their experience as satisfactory. Various explanations have been advanced to explain this phenomenon: cognitive consistency (participants are reluctant to downgrade a program on which they have spent time, money, or energy), self-selection into programs (participants select only those programs that appear on the surface to meet their particular needs), or possibly a general response style of not wishing to appear critical or ungrateful. This positive bias does not mean that participant ratings are useless, but that such evaluations should be carefully designed and the results carefully interpreted.

Are participants complying with actions requested of them? This question is intended as another indicator of program performance, rather than as an outcome measure. If participants are not performing as expected (e.g., attending classes, reading materials, complying with policy), then changes may need to be made in program methods or delivery. For example, a weight control program with stringent dietary requirements may be unsuccessful because even well-motivated individuals find it difficult to perform as expected and quickly become discouraged. Reducing the dietary requirements may actually result in improved performance.

This list of questions about program operations is lengthy, and obviously no single program will be evaluated on all of these questions. The process of determining which of these questions need to be answered to improve a particular program will depend on the specific program and on concerns voiced by the program staff and relevant stakeholders.

Questions About Program Outcomes

Finally, the evaluator may need to focus on questions regarding the program's outcomes: *Is the program having the effect it is designed to have?* Deciding what is meant by program "outcomes" or "effects" is often more difficult than it would first appear. The effects of any program can be conceptualized as a chain of events leading from the program to the ultimate outcome. For example, a smoking cessation program for pregnant women may have various effects on the participants, including changes in maternal knowledge, maternal smoking, infant birth weight, and infant morbidity. Thus the "outcome" of the program could be evaluated on any of these levels. The choice of which outcome to study is determined by several factors: the soundness of the scientific evidence linking the various events in the chain (e.g., since the relationship of infant birth weight to morbidity is well established, evaluating birth weight alone may be considered sufficient), the feasibility and cost of obtaining the measurement (maternal outcomes may be more feasible to obtain than infant outcomes in some settings), the statistical power to detect effects at various levels (due to considerations of measurement variability, it may be statistically easier to detect differences in infant birth weight than differences in subsequent morbidity), and so on. The choice of which endpoint to measure is also dependent upon the needs of the audience for the evaluation; for example, will the program's directors be satisfied if smoking cessation is demonstrated, or, for political or other reasons, do they need to see evidence pertaining to infant birth weight before they are convinced of the utility of the program? Often, a program is evaluated simultaneously on several levels (e.g., both smoking cessation and birth weight are monitored). In many cases, however, tensions exist regarding the choice of levels to be evaluated; frequently, program directors and boards request information on outcomes that are more distal than the evaluator thinks is practical to measure. These cases require careful negotiation and marshaling of scientific and statistical evidence to support the evaluator's case that more proximal endpoints are satisfactory.

Outcome questions are often the first questions posed to the evaluator, but they should be the last ones to be answered. Only if the program seems to be operating in a satisfactory manner can the answers to outcome questions be meaningful (Rutman, 1980).

SELECTING THE QUESTIONS

From this framework the evaluator will need to select questions to be answered in the current study. One factor entering into the choice of questions is the evaluator's own knowledge of the program's stage of development and its probable evaluation needs. Another is the evaluator's assessment of the type of information desired by relevant stakeholders (boards of directors, management, service providers, client groups, and so on) and the decisions that they will be able to make based on the evaluation. In general, learning what types of information each stakeholder group needs is a difficult task. Most experienced evaluators have learned to their dismay that the direct approach—asking each relevant player what he or she would like to know—is not the most fruitful approach. Few people are able to project their information needs in advance (Mowbray, 1988). A variety of formal and informal techniques may need to be used to determine likely information needs. History often gives important clues as well. Weiss (1983) discusses the usual types of stakeholder groups and the information they are most likely to need. Program managers may be most interested in questions concerning program operations, and they may be able to use the results of such evaluations to make changes that improve the delivery of the program. Boards of directors, on the other hand, are more likely to ask questions pertaining to outcomes.

TECHNICAL CONSIDERATIONS:
CONDUCTING THE EVALUATION

Actually carrying out the evaluation is a major task. The issues are the same as those encountered in social research of all types: What is the design? (Are there comparison groups? How are they chosen? When are measurements taken?) How are data to be collected (questionnaire, interview, observation)? What is the quality of the data collection instrument (reliability, validity)? How are the data to be processed and analyzed? The premise underlying all of these choices is that the evaluation should be carried out in such a way that the results will be convincing even to the skeptic. A large body of knowledge has accumulated regarding the best way to make such choices; the principles are taught in numerous courses and are discussed in many articles and textbooks (e.g., Cook & Campbell, 1979; Windsor, Baranowski, Clark, & Cutter, 1984). If expertise to make these choices and carry out the evaluation is not available within the program, it can usually be obtained by hiring outside consultants. University departments of social and behavioral science are often good sources of advice and consultation on such issues.

REPORTS AND RECOMMENDATIONS

The final step in most evaluations is that of summarizing results in such a way that they can be used in making decisions about the program. Usually this means writing a "final report," although in some cases mini-reports or oral summaries may be requested.

Several principles for making results useful have emerged from experience. The first is timeliness; that is, evaluation results can be made useful only if they are communicated at the time a decision is to be made. The second is to make explicit recommendations based on evaluation results (Roberts-Gray, 1988). The latter point makes some evaluators uncomfortable, either because they feel the recommendations are obvious based on the data or because they are uncomfortable when thrust into the role of program designer. Nevertheless, the experience of many evaluators tends to indicate that actual decisions based on evaluation results are more likely to occur when recommendations are stated clearly. The ability to make clear recommendations that are feasible within the organization is one reason that internal staff are sometimes more effective in the evaluation role than are external evaluators; at the very least, internal and external staff may need to work together to make recommendations that can be acted upon.

SUMMARY

The most important part of designing a useful evaluation is not the technical aspect of collecting and analyzing data; the most important part is asking the right questions and presenting the results in such a way that they can usefully inform important decisions. This requires a clear understanding of the goals and institutional context of the program and an ability to project what kinds of decisions will likely need to be made. Program planners may lack the technical expertise to conduct an evaluation and hence may feel that they cannot contribute in this area; however, their knowledge of the program, the organization, and the stakeholders is invaluable in guiding the evaluator to ask the right questions.

REFERENCES

Cambre, M. (1981). Historical overview of formative evaluation of instructional media products. Education Communications and Technology Journal, 29(1), 3-25.

Cook, T. D., & Campbell, D. T. (1979). Quasi-experimentation: Design and analysis issues for field settings. Chicago: Rand McNally.

Mowbray, C. B. (1988). Getting the system to respond to evaluation findings. In J. A. McLaughlin, L. J. Weber, R. W. Covert, & R. B. Ingle (Eds.), Evaluation utilization: New directions for program evaluation No. 39 (pp. 47-58). San Francisco: Jossey-Bass.

Roberts-Gray, C. (1988). An ambiguous fire alarm at Evaluation '87: On the importance of making recommendations. Evaluation Practice, 9(2), 79-81.

Rutman, L. (1980). Planning useful evaluations: Evaluability assessment. Beverly Hills, CA: Sage.

Stipak, B. (1982). Using clients to evaluate programs. In E. R. House (Ed.), Evaluation studies review annual (pp. 585-602). Beverly Hills, CA: Sage. (Original work published 1980)

Weiss, C. (1983). Toward the future of stakeholder approaches in evaluation. In A S. Bryk (Ed.), Stakeholder-based evaluation (pp. 83-96). San Francisco: Jossey-Bass.

Weiss, C. (1988). If program decisions hinged only on information: A response to Patton. Evaluation Practice, 9(3), 15-28.

Windsor, R. A., Baranowski, T., Clark, N., & Cutter, G. (1984). Evaluation of health promotion and education programs. Palo Alto, CA: Mayfield.

Chapter 11

STRATEGIES TO MAINTAIN AND INSTITUTIONALIZE SUCCESSFUL PROGRAMS
A Marketing Framework

R. CRAIG LEFEBVRE

Successful community interventions are typically conceived of as those programs that effectively disseminate knowledge and alter practices and policies at a variety of levels in the community (i.e., with individuals, groups, and organizations). Previous chapters have described a variety of strategies to accomplish these goals. Other writers have provided theoretical models to describe their own programs (e.g., Farquhar, Maccoby, & Solomon, 1984; Lefebvre, Lasater, Carleton, & Peterson, 1987; Mittelmark et al., 1986) or have attempted to identify the more general social change principles that underlie such efforts (e.g., Zaltman, 1983). However, social change programs are valued according to their outcomes; that is, do the changes have a beneficial, documentable effect on the target audience? (See, e.g., Rich & Zaltman, 1978.) Only recently have social change planners examined more long-term outcomes, such as the continuation of program elements beyond an outside agency's funding period.

Program institutionalization has been a central issue in planning and implementing the three community cardiovascular disease prevention

AUTHOR'S NOTE: Preparation of this chapter was supported by Grant HL23629 from the National Heart, Lung and Blood Institute, U.S. Department of Health and Human Services.

projects funded by the National Heart, Lung and Blood Institute: the Minnesota Heart Health Program, the Pawtucket Heart Health Program, and the Stanford Five City Project. In collaborative meetings, and as individual programs, all three have struggled with the problems of designing community interventions that will outlive the period of federal funding. As a participant in one of these programs, I have found addressing the question of how to maintain and incorporate community health promotion programs a daunting task. There are, for instance, no agreed-upon principles or precedents on which to base strategy or conclusions. If anything, the process of trying to continue these programs has been one of discovery, mutual sharing, frustration, and even some successes. We are all learning how to do it. Yet, some principles do suggest themselves. The following pages outline some of the concepts and strategies that have grown out of work in the Pawtucket Heart Health Program (PHHP). While the experiences of this program may be unique, they illuminate issues and outline a strategic framework that may be useful to others addressing similar problems.

THE PAWTUCKET HEART HEALTH PROGRAM

An overview of the PHHP will provide a context for many of the subsequent observations. The PHHP began in 1980 and is an 11-year research and demonstration study in cardiovascular disease (CVD) prevention with a target population of the approximately 72,000 residents of Pawtucket, Rhode Island. Intervention and evaluation overviews have appeared (Assaf, Banspach, Lasater, McKinlay, & Carleton, 1987; Carleton, Lasater, Assaf, Lefebvre, & McKinlay, 1987; Lefebvre et al., 1987), and those interested in details of the project are encouraged to refer to them. For present purposes, it is important to highlight briefly the major theoretical underpinnings of the intervention:

- Community organization follows a *community activation* approach that uses lay volunteers to help design, implement, and evaluate program elements (Roncarati, Lefebvre, & Carleton, 1989).
- Program development uses a *social learning* theory base that focuses on behavior change as the objective. Programs may use cognitive components, skills training, and environmental changes to accomplish behavior change objectives.

- Principles of *behavioral community psychology* are employed to evaluate these programs and to ensure that they meet the requirements of the community.
- *Social marketing* concepts and strategies form the basis for final message, product, and service design, as well as their promotion and delivery to the various audience segments in the community.

PHHP has developed programs to target each of the five major CVD life-style risk factors (high blood pressure, high blood cholesterol, cigarette smoking, obesity, and sedentary living) in individuals, groups, and organizations as well as the community at large. Examples include self-help kits; screening, counseling, and referral events (SCOREs); group behavior change programs led by trained lay volunteers; work-site-, church-, and school-based programs; restaurant menu-labeling and grocery store shelf-labeling programs; and community risk factor campaigns. This broad array of messages, products, and services not only represents a comprehensive approach to community CVD prevention, but presents a significant challenge for long-term maintenance of PHHP.

INSTITUTIONALIZATION

Institutionalization describes the objective of our long-term program maintenance efforts. As defined in *Webster's Ninth New Collegiate Dictionary*, *institutionalization* derives from the verb *institutionalize*: "to make into or give the character of an institution; especially: to incorporate into a structured and often highly formalized system." Moving one step further, *institution* is defined as "(1) an act of originating and getting established, (2) a significant practice, relationship or organization in a society or culture; an established organization or corporation." In approaching the institutionalization of PHHP, two features of these definitions are important. First, it is an active process that may involve making the entire PHHP an institution, or incorporating PHHP—or program elements—into other structures. Second, institutionalization means more than simply continuing an agency; it also refers to practices, relationships, and values that become permanently entrenched in individuals, groups, organizations, and the community at large.

In conceptualizing the process, one must be aware of the numerous potential outcomes that depend upon what one wishes to institutionalize. Each institutionalization objective must be subject to strategic planning that takes into account prevailing community conditions and the overall program goals. Four major steps are included in the strategic framework. The first is deciding who the audience is for institutionalization objectives. A marketing plan is then produced to orchestrate the program elements. This plan often suggests action strategies. Finally, an analysis of the strengths and weaknesses of the program "portfolio" can help refine the plan.

FOUR MODELS FOR SETTING OBJECTIVES

In our planning, four models of institutionalized community organization for CVD prevention prevail. Their targets are individuals, organizations, networks, and coordinating agencies. The first model, an "individual level of institutionalization," posits that key members of the community will assume leadership roles in the "heart health community" of Pawtucket. These individuals may be political or business leaders, physicians, or informal opinion leaders who, by virtue of their volunteer work with PHHP, develop and sustain a personal commitment to continuing program messages, products, or services. This approach represents a grass-roots orientation in which demonstrated individual efficacy in helping others reduce CVD risk serves both motivational and reinforcement functions that become independent of PHHP. Indeed, a number of key volunteers are already involved in self-guided efforts to help others monitor elevated blood pressure, watch what they eat, and exercise more often. The institutionalization of such individuals is an important element in a comprehensive plan. However, they alone cannot maintain the current program's intensity of effort throughout the community.

A second model of institutionalization targets agencies to enable them either to increase existing CVD risk-reduction programs or to add such programs to their current efforts. These efforts have been particularly successful in schools, work sites, and churches. Fitness and health clubs, restaurants, and grocery stores are other suitable targets. A specific example is Pawtucket's Department of Parks and Recreation, which has launched a program called ExerCity that organizes aerobic exercise, weight loss, and smoking cessation groups on a regular basis throughout the year. PHHP staff have trained leaders and provided consultation for these and other types of groups. Yet, individual organizations have assumed responsibility for maintaining these efforts.

A third model for institutionalization is a networking strategy that recognizes that social support is needed to continue individual and organizational commitment to heart health objectives. Bandura's (1982) notion of "collective efficacy" is salient; that is, it is important to bring together individuals or organizations who singly have proven themselves effective in heart health programming and to provide them with the opportunity to address community CVD risk collectively. PHHP has successfully used this approach for monthly staff meetings for our volunteers, PHHP staff meetings involving volunteers, a Chamber of Commerce Worksite Heart Health Committee, a Church Advisory Board, and an employee Fitness and Health Committee in the local hospital, the area's major employer. Each of these networks supports heart health programming efforts by allowing individuals and organizations to discuss issues of mutual concern, develop coordinated efforts, and reinforce each other. PHHP participates in—but does not lead—each of these networks to assure that professional expertise is available to these groups as they identify issues, develop strategies, and implement programs. As the groups learn more about heart health education efforts and begin to institutionalize themselves, we fully expect them to expand their health agendas, and we completely support these efforts.

In the fourth model of institutionalization, a new structure takes on the role of maintaining PHHP programs. This model uses such strategies as developing community boards and establishing private foundations; in other instances, one organization may make a major shift in resource allocation to incorporate the program (e.g., the local hospital's funding of staff positions and the city's expansion of ExerCity staff and mission). Although often perceived as the most effective way to institutionalize a program such as PHHP because it assures continuity and continued coordination of CVD risk-reduction efforts, it also represents the most resource-intensive approach. Although this is an era of scarce resources, and of stiff competition for those resources, such challenges should not discourage use of this model. However, without the supporting elements outlined earlier, a new agency could become like the emperor who had no clothes—that is, an agency with no means of delivering programs because it lacks affiliations and working relationships with the key players in the community's CVD risk-reduction game.

With four possible institutionalization models—individual, organizational, networks, and a guiding or coordinating agency—the question is which ones to choose. There is no evidence to suggest what mechanisms are most appropriate, or effective, in the institutionalization of a health promotion program. However, we believe all are needed. With an effort as comprehensive as PHHP, it is not reasonable to expect one initiative to sustain all of PHHP's programs and activities. Thus to focus institutionalization strategy on just one or two of these goals may not be pragmatic. As with other challenges we confront in PHHP, we have looked to the marketing arena for some guidance. The remainder of this chapter outlines how to approach institutionalization as a marketing challenge.

THE MARKETING CHALLENGE

Institutionalization represents a challenge uniquely suited to marketing concepts and techniques. On one hand, institutionalization is a social marketing challenge. As such, its goal is to convince people and institutions to make long-term commitments to heart health, a concept not easily reduced to tangible products and services. On the other hand, PHHP offers products and services that are quite tangible and can be adopted by a variety of organizations; the challenge is to provide them with the opportunities to do so.

Marketing involves identifying consumer needs and providing products and services that meet these needs in ways that also satisfy organizational objectives (Kotler & Andreasen, 1987; Lefebvre & Flora, 1988). For example, one of PHHP's organizational objectives is to institutionalize heart health in the community. However, few residents in Pawtucket are aware of *their* need for this to happen. Many of them know about PHHP, many have even been involved with the program, but they are surprised to hear "it's all scheduled to end in 1991." The majority of them believe, for lack of evidence to the contrary, that PHHP will last forever. This points out the social marketing agenda: Create the need. The affected constituency (in this case, Pawtucket residents) needs to know that it will play a critical role in institutionalization. Residents will have to buy (or invest in) PHHP— not a single program, but the *whole thing*. Community ownership must be made tangible to them.

But if we can convince them that they need PHHP after 1991, what products and services will meet their needs? Obviously, we believe they need them all or we would not have developed them. However, these assumptions must be tested before we attempt to institutionalize products. To reduce the costs of buying these programs, we have taken care to develop ones that are easily adaptable, will not pose undue personal or financial costs, and are effective. Thus products and packaging must be developed and refined with institutionalization goals in mind—not just based on what we as professionals believe makes a good, attractive product. We need to seek community input from the beginning to assure that all our programs meet the needs of the community and will be used. Otherwise, programs may evolve to such a "state of the science" that only the professionals can use them. Our emphasis on volunteer delivery systems has provided us with the ongoing market testing to assure that we have few square wheels for institutionalization.

ELEMENTS OF THE MARKETING PLAN

A marketing plan for institutionalization needs to consider the objectives, audiences, channels, messages, products, services, and resources that will guide strategy. Each of these elements will be described below.

Objectives. Objectives of institutionalization, as noted earlier, extend beyond continued existence of the program. Other objectives and examples of them include the following:

- *Practices:* These may take the form of health promotive practices of individuals, physicians' practices, restaurant managers continuing to offer heart healthy menu selections, teachers regularly incorporating heart health into their curricula, clean air policies in work sites.
- *Relationships:* Useful relationships include volunteers regularly communicating with each other, work-site health committees, church health committees, and other networks to promote and support heart health efforts.
- *Values:* Individuals preferring to shop at markets that offer lean meats, and employees and management incorporating more physical activity into their daily routines are examples of institutionalized values.
- *Individuals:* People who are identified by others as interested and involved in heart health promotion, for instance, reporters and business leaders, are important to reach.

- *Organizations:* Examples include agencies that offer a variety of heart health programs to their members or the general public, work sites with active health promotion programs, and hospitals whose marketing positions include health promotion and preventive medicine services.

Audiences. Many different audiences can be identified for health promotion programs, but certain segments of the community are particularly important to institutionalization objectives. Among these are the following:

- *Resource managers:* Located in both nonprofit and for-profit organizations in the community and known by a variety of titles, these are the people responsible for deciding how, when, and where to expend personnel and financial resources. They are key individuals for marketing both the need and opportunities for institutionalization.
- *Groups/organizations:* Local civic groups, school boards, work sites, churches, volunteer agencies, and other groups and organizations can be targeted for opportunities to institutionalize heart health programs and services. Civic and other social groups often take on causes; organizations may modify or expand their mission. It is important to identify these potential adopters and meet their needs with an institutionalization plan tailored for them.
- *General community:* The public also should be made aware of the "institutionalization agenda," or the need to prepare for the next step. If the community as a whole does not perceive the need, does not support and encourage institutionalization efforts, and will not reinforce those individuals, groups, and organizations undertaking the task, then the entire marketing effort will suffer.
- *Key individuals with commitment and visibility:* People in the community with leadership and decision-making roles should also be a prime audience for marketing institutionalization. Preferably, many of these people will be highly visible in the community, or at least well known in certain community segments. Gaining their commitment not only bestows legitimacy to the institutionalization effort, but also brings it individuals who can serve as intermediaries with other groups and organizations.
- *Organizational publics:* This term refers to other publics with whom the institutionalization agency (e.g., PHHP) interacts. These may include community groups and organizations with which there have been long-standing ties and good working relationships. They may also include publics outside the community structure, for instance, funding sources, educational institutions, state or national volunteer associations, private corporations, and federal agencies. Targeting these groups with the insti-

tutionalization agenda may help uncover resources that will facilitate the process.

Channels. There are many methods for reaching target audiences with messages, programs, and services. Some of the more important ones for marketing institutionalization include the following:

- *Personal contact by peers:* People are more receptive to messages they perceive as coming from persons like themselves. They are also more likely to act upon information received through personal contact (Rogers, 1983), which is thus an important channel for institutionalization. This not only underscores the importance of recruiting key individuals from the community for this purpose, but also places a responsibility on the agency to select contacts who will be perceived as similar by the target. Status indicators are particularly important to watch in making these decisions. Some contacts will be quite effective when initiated by field staff; others will require senior-level staff as the target rises in status (e.g., CEOs, presidents, senior editors).

- *Mass media:* Mass media have strength in agenda-setting with much of the population that should be employed for institutionalization. The mass audience needs to be aware of institutionalization goals, to understand their benefits, and to be offered methods for becoming involved in the process. The mass media can also report activities (e.g., a monthly blood pressure screening at a local church), highlight individual and organizational efforts that reflect institutionalization, and reinforce participation in the process.

- *Boards/committees:* Both existing community-based boards and committees and those developed for heart health networking can be used to diffuse the institutionalization process. School boards, city councils, chambers of commerce, PTAs, and church governing bodies can be recruited to stimulate activity further. Presentations to these boards and committees represent a cost-efficient way to reach many key community people and resource managers who are important for the promotion of institutionalization.

- *Volunteers:* Program volunteers are an enormous resource for stimulating the grass-roots community organizing needed to motivate and support the efforts of community leaders. The word-of-mouth network that volunteers can establish will also help support mass media efforts to publicize the institutionalization agenda. Given that agency volunteers already have a strong commitment to the program, educating them about this agenda will support other efforts to have the community participate in program institutionalization.

- *Organizations:* Individual organizations, especially those with large memberships and their own media (e.g., bulletins, newsletters), can also diffuse the institutionalization agenda in a way uniquely suited to their constituencies. By involving management and employees in this process, the organization itself may move toward playing an active role in institutionalizing programs from within. This in turn can serve as a model for other organizations and broaden the scope of the entire process.

Messages. Messages are the basis of social marketing. Designing and transmitting messages are strategic steps, and methods for accomplishing them have been outlined by others (e.g., Lefebvre, Harden, & Zompa, 1988; Manoff, 1985). For now, I will review what these messages should communicate.

- *Self-efficacy:* Social learning theory (Bandura, 1986) tells us that people are more likely to do things when they believe they have the requisite skills. For institutionalization purposes, individuals should know (a) they can change their risk behaviors and maintain these changes; (b) they can help others accomplish the same things; (c) they can be effective in helping to change groups, organizations, and the community through their individual efforts; and (d) they can maintain the program. Mass media can be used to highlight examples of individuals who have done these things and can serve as role models. The reinforcement function of this publicity can also motivate people to bring others into the effort.

- *Collective efficacy:* Similar to self-efficacy, collective efficacy focuses on what groups of people can do to (a) help themselves, (b) help others, (c) create healthier environments in organizations and the community at large, and (d) sustain programming efforts. Again, mass media can help support their efforts. It is also important that program staff work with these groups and maximize their chances of success.

- *Organizational self-sufficiency:* Because a program has not required large expenditures of community resources, many people and organizations may well believe that it will be too expensive, in terms of time, people, space, and money, to take on as their own. This belief may be a major barrier to institutionalization, and it should be addressed directly. Cost-effectiveness studies of program components can help show that resource demands are not overwhelming and may actually be investments. Individuals and organizations need to have experience in implementing programs without staff involvement to learn they *can* do it themselves. At the same time, program staff must recognize that they will have to give up control over the program and, in fact, must work to accomplish this. Some staff may question the wisdom of "working themselves out of jobs," yet that is often what is involved. Program efforts that demonstrate commitment to the staff at this time, as well as to institutionalization, can help overcome this barrier.

- *High outcome expectations:* Nothing works better than success—or at least the expectation of it—when attempting to motivate people to do things. Evaluations of program components and overall program impact, especially when they document success, are effective selling tools. When individuals and organizations take part in evaluations (e.g., by conducting the groups or serving as the evaluation site), the data take on even more meaning to them ("It was my program!"). Documentation of these studies and feedback about them (where the mass media again can play a crucial role) are important strategies for institutionalization.

- *Stakeholders:* Throughout the course of a project some individuals and organizations have been stakeholders (i.e., they believe in the importance of the program and have actively worked toward its objectives). This group needs to be broadened to create the widest possible base from which institutionalization activities can be launched. The stake may be a personal interest in CVD, an organizational commitment to healthy members, a positioning strategy in an agency's marketing plan, or a community view of healthy habits as a desirable norm. Whatever they are, the vested interests of many groups must be addressed through formative research and message design that is responsive both to these unique needs and the institutionalization objectives.

Products. The most tangible, and often most visible, aspect of the program is its various products—self-help kits, SCOREs, group programs, curricula, and so on. In preparing these products for institutionalization, whether through individual organizations or a central agency, five product features should be kept in mind:

- *Utility:* Products must be effective and must meet individual and organizational needs. Formative and outcome evaluations should be employed throughout development and implementation to assure that the product is useful to the community, not just to the program staff.
- *Low cost:* Products must be affordable to various consumer groups. In this instance, cost includes not only the fiscal price, but such considerations as whether the product can be used by nonprofessionals, how long the learning curve lasts, and whether the product has a market (that is, if an organization institutionalizes it, will people still want it?). In some cases, demonstrating a market need for the product may be the only incentive required. In other circumstances, products may need to be revised to reduce the cost side of the equation.
- *Adaptability:* The community is a diffuse marketplace. Existing products may need to be modified for different population segments. Rather than

choosing one of two equally unappealing alternatives—developing a product that meets one group's needs and leaving the rest to find their own, or investing in the very costly production of different products to meet each group's needs—adaptable materials should be developed. That is, provide products that individuals and organizations can use immediately, but build in flexibility so that other components can be added to meet specific audience needs. These components might be supplementary materials developed by the program or health education programs in other agencies. The problem in producing adaptable materials is that quality control can quickly be lost. Thus efforts should be aimed at transmitting the *essential* information in ways that cannot be easily misinterpreted by intermediaries, for example, through audio- and videotapes, slide presentations, and other nonprint media. While such methods may increase production costs, in the longer term they help reduce learning costs and provide some insurance that the product's quality will be consistent when delivered by others.

- *Packaging:* The art and science of product packaging will not be reviewed here. My concern is to point out that for a program to be institutionalized, its products must be more attractive to the community than those of other producers. Some packaging issues to consider are as follows: Is it visually attractive on initial review? Does the design allow easy use? Are instructions clear? Is the information presented in a readable format? (What grade level is it written to?) Is enough information presented, but not so much that it turns people off to the product? Most programs have not spent much time on such issues, but many have never attempted to institutionalize themselves either. Successful programs will package themselves well.

- *Quality:* A product's quality is important in determining its potential for institutionalization and also in shaping individual and organizational perceptions of the program. A program that is viewed as having a variety of mediocre or run-of-the-mill products has a poor chance of institutionalization. A program with imaginative and creative products but poor efficacy or little market share will not have a much better chance. Quality is a subjective phenomenon, and it is important to determine how potential consumers define it. Programs that do not produce, or do not embody, quality as the marketplace defines it will have great difficulty in convincing that marketplace to maintain them.

Services. Many programs facing the issue of institutionalization will have invested heavily in direct service delivery. As they move from delivering services to working toward program institutionalization, they must shift priorities.

- *Consultation/training:* We see program staff moving from the role of delivery agents to that of consultants and trainers. This is not to suggest that these roles are "all or nothing" at any stage of a program's existence, but to point out that strategic decisions must be made to reinforce the evolution of staff responsibilities. Volunteers and staff in other agencies and organizations have to be given more responsibility for service delivery. Boards and other networking bodies must take their destiny into their own hands. Neither of these objectives should be attempted overnight, or even within a year in many cases. Program staff need to work with community groups to assure their early success. Yet, at some point the transition must be made. Individuals, organizations, and boards will vary in their ability and speed in assuming these responsibilities. Making them aware of the institutionalization agenda will help this transfer of responsibility take place.

- *Referral:* As new groups begin to assume responsibility for different product and service delivery elements, it is important for the program to support these efforts. One tangible method is for the program to adopt a referral function and reduce or eliminate its activity in these areas. This strategy will not only reduce competition, which might otherwise lessen participation in "new" programs, but will also begin to position these organizations as sources for heart health products and services. Referral also reinforces to these organizations and the general public that the program recognizes their credibility and ability to deliver quality programs. Such recognition is important until new programs begin to mature and develop a strong market position in the community.

- *Direction:* The institutionalization process is not accomplished all at once. Therefore, we do not expect that all direct services will be transferred to other organizations at the same time. Throughout the process, the program must decide when to begin institutionalizing specific products and services. Two major factors guide our strategy in this area. The first is quality: When products and services have been carefully evaluated and found effective, when they are in a form that is usable by others at a reasonable cost, and when they are appropriately packaged, they are ready for institutionalization. The second consideration is positioning: As long as a product or service is not well positioned (i.e., the target audience does not view it as necessary or beneficial), the program should maintain it. Once a clear position has been established, other organizations will be more able to market it effectively. On the other hand, when program institutionalization entails only one entity, the strategy may be to retain products and services with strong market positions to form the core of the new, institutionalized program.

Resources. A barrier to effective institutionalization is the vacuum created by the withdrawal of existing resources and the concomitant lack of resources appropriated from other sources. As with many other subjects in this discussion, resource generation has its own literature.

Below, some of the salient concerns for institutionalization are reviewed briefly.

- *Indigenous sources:* Communities have their own resources, which can be tapped for institutionalization. The extent of available resources has to be considered in determining the scope of the institutionalization objectives and their anticipated costs. It may be judicious for the program to estimate costs before embarking on resource generation, for it is likely that prospective donors will always want to know the bottom line: How much will it cost?

Indigenous resources include people, messages, services, products, and money. Examples of people resources are diverse: program volunteers, faculty and students of local educational institutions, hospital staff, occupational nurses, physicians, news reporters (especially health reporters and food section editors), volunteer agencies, social and fraternal organizations, and PTAs are among many. How many can become involved in institutionalization efforts and commit time to them? One goal of the marketing plan is to identify such people.

Many areas of the community are involved in message delivery through various media. Can work-site newsletters and church bulletins run "health tips" columns? Is heart health part of mandated health education in the classroom? Do restaurants and grocery stores participate in point-of-purchase labeling programs? Do local print and electronic media have staff with specific interest in heart health and CVD who will continue to "cover the story"? Are health promotion and disease prevention part of standard medical practice and patient education? These are just examples of where to look for institutionalization resources that may be quite affordable.

The service industry accounts for the majority of jobs in the U.S. economy. The health care sector is the most rapidly growing one in the industry (Kotler & Andreasen, 1987). This sector involves more than office-based and hospital-affiliated health professionals. It also includes for-profit health centers, health promotion consultants, fitness and health centers, proprietary weight loss and smoking cessation groups with local franchises, and others. Many nonprofit and volunteer agencies may also offer services that overlap with the program's objectives. Rather than viewing these various groups as competitors, the successfully institutionalized program will see opportunities to explore. Many of these groups are looking for better services to offer; if the program has met the obligations for service development outlined earlier, it may have exactly what these groups need. These groups can adopt existing program services. It may also be useful to explore "endorsement" arrangements whereby some services offered by such groups receive the program's "seal of approval" by meeting program-determined criteria for professional, high-quality programs in risk-reduction techniques. (It should also be noted that such endorsements may form the basis for financial remuneration to support other program activities.)

A variety of existing products in the community may also target CVD risk reduction. As with services, these products might be reviewed according to established criteria and receive program endorsement. Before endorsing either services or products, the program must be certain that its name or image has a documentable market value. Without such value, the endorsement concept becomes meaningless to prospective buyers and, more important, to the consumer. Finally, any endorsements or similar arrangements are best outlined in a contractual agreement between the program and the "endorsed" agency. Such agreements should clearly delineate the extent of the endorsement and assure that neither program quality nor program integrity is compromised.

Financial resources in the community are under constant pressure from every direction. It is important to understand the competitive environment and develop a strategy that is responsive to the particular market. Sources of financial support for institutionalization might include local private foundations, community chests, the United Way, corporate foundations, and various public and private organizations that could appropriate monies through changes in funding priorities or shifts in resource allocation. To achieve such outcomes a program must successfully meet community needs and have personnel skilled in grantsmanship and politics.

- *External sources:* The search for support for institutionalization need not be limited to the community. External sources of services, products, messages, and money are also available to the enterprising program. State and national providers of services (e.g., proprietary smoking cessation and weight loss groups) and products (e.g., American Cancer Society, American Lung Association, American Heart Association) are available to continue some programs. Various groups are also involved in developing national campaigns that can be given a local spotlight through the cooperation of community affiliates, departments of health, and mass media. Such campaigns include the National Cholesterol Education Program, the National High Blood Pressure Program, Heart Month, and the Great

American Smoke-Out. Most important, state government, federal funding agencies, philanthropic foundations, corporate foundations, and private industry can also be approached for continuing support.

External resources should not be viewed as an alternative to continued local support. However, such options can help defray the costs of continued message/product/service development, implementation, and coordination that are necessary for the long-term viability of the program.

MARKET STRATEGY:
TRANSLATING THE PLAN INTO ACTION

Incorporating these and other strategies into the unified undertaking of institutionalization should reflect local needs and resources as well as program features. Generally speaking, the organization of the institutionalization marketing plan should bring these strategies together with the following objectives in mind:

- Identify target audience members (e.g., key leaders, work sites, schools, churches, restaurants, social organizations).
- Segment these audiences by adopter status—innovators, early adopters, late adopters, and laggards (Rogers, 1983).
- Identify the needs of each segment.
- Position institutionalization messages, products, and services to each segment.
- Promote diffusion of institutionalization activity.
- Secure long-term financial support.

This plan should be the basis for all program activity regarding institutionalization, and should guide individual staff in their efforts. Therefore, the more specific and detailed the plan, the more useful it will be in focusing program resources on areas of highest priority.

PORTFOLIO ANALYSIS

The final step in planning institutionalization strategy is to review each existing program product and service to determine how it fits with the organization's institutionalization strategy (i.e., marketing plan).

One way to accomplish this objective is through portfolio analysis. Kotler and Andreasen (1987) outline three steps in portfolio analysis: (a) Partition the organization's existing offerings into groups of similar products or services; (b) assess present market conditions for each group and that group's current performance, or market share; and (c) forecast the future location of the products and services, assuming there are no changes in the marketing strategy. Each group of products or services is typically mapped on a grid such as that shown in Figure 11.1.

At PHHP, the two analytic dimensions we have chosen for institutionalization purposes are *viability* and *market need*. The viability dimension includes the following:

- extent to which the product or services meets PHHP objectives (i.e., CVD risk behavior change)
- current quality of the product or service (e.g., content, layout, packaging)
- effectiveness of the product or service, documented through both formative and process research
- economy of scale offered by the product or service (i.e., broader product or service reach requires proportionally less staff time and other resources)
- reasonableness of the learning curve for other people to adopt and manage the program
- potential for institutionalization given current market conditions
- amount of personnel and fiscal resources necessary to continue service delivery

The market need for products and services is reviewed according to the following criteria:

- existence of a documented need in the market for the product or service
- whether or not PHHP is the sole source for the product or service
- known receptivity of the target market for the offering
- sufficient size of the market to justify resource expenditures
- availability of channels for reaching the target audience and delivering the product or service

Decisions about an offering's viability and market need should be based as much as possible on objective evidence and data. However, some subjectivity is inherent in determining whether an existing product or service rates high, medium, or low on each of the two dimensions. Staff and community input can help prevent the myopic decisions that

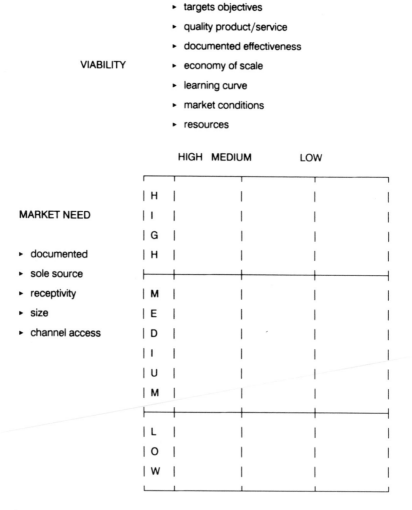

Figure 11.1. Portfolio Analysis Scheme for Program Institutionalization

can ensue when portfolio analysis is left to only a few staff and, worse, has no community input. The outcome of portfolio analysis will be strategic decisions as to how—and, indeed, whether—to institutional-ize program offerings through specific marketing plans and strategy that are developed as outlined earlier. Periodic reviews of the portfolio will allow for the assessment of progress toward institutionalization objectives, and help refine the overall marketing strategy to meet new needs and challenges that may arise.

SUMMARY

The successful institutionalization of community health programs is an outcome in search of a process. This chapter has presented a marketing strategy for maintaining such programs. This strategy involves four steps. The first is to specify individual, organizational, network, and community objectives for institutionalization. The second is to develop a marketing plan that specifics the (a) practices, (b) audiences, (c) channels, (d) messages, (e) products, (f) services, and (g) resources that are available or necessary to reach the objectives. Third, a marketing strategy should translate the marketing plan into a series of steps to reach the objectives. Finally, a portfolio analysis can assess the viability and market need of existing products and services, as well as the program in its entirety, with respect to institutionalization objectives, the marketing plan, and the marketing strategy. It is important to recognize that such strategic planning is an ongoing process in which each step has an impact on the others. It is essential that the community itself be a partner in planning to help define, implement, monitor, and refine the institutionalization strategy.

REFERENCES

Assaf, A. R., Banspach, S. W., Lasater, T. M., McKinlay, S. M., & Carleton, R. A. (1987). The Pawtucket Heart Health Program: II. Evaluation strategies. *Rhode Island Medical Journal, 70,* 541-546.

Bandura, A. (1982). Self-efficacy mechanism in human agency. *American Psychologist, 37,* 122-147.

Bandura, A. (1986). *Social foundations of thought and action.* Englewood Cliffs, NJ: Prentice-Hall.

Carleton, R. A., Lasater, T. M., Assaf, A., Lefebvre, R. C., & McKinlay, S. M. (1987). The Pawtucket Heart Health Program: I. An experiment in population-based disease prevention. *Rhode Island Medical Journal, 70,* 533-538.

Farquhar, J. W., Maccoby, N., & Solomon, D. S. (1984). Community applications of behavioral medicine. In W. D. Doyle (Ed.), *Handbook of behavioral medicine* (pp. 437-478). New York: Guilford.

Kotler, P., & Andreasen, A. R. (1987). *Strategic marketing for non-profit organizations* (3rd ed.). Englewood Cliffs, NJ: Prentice-Hall.

Lefebvre, R. C., & Flora, J. A. (1988). Social marketing and public health intervention. *Health Education Quarterly, 15*, 299-315.

Lefebvre, R. C., Harden, E. A., & Zompa, B. (1988). The Pawtucket Heart Health Program: III. Social marketing to promote community health. *Rhode Island Medical Journal, 71*, 27-30.

Lefebvre, R. C., Lasater, T. M., Carleton, R. A., & Peterson, G. (1987). Theory and delivery of health programming in the community: The Pawtucket Heart Health Program. *Preventive Medicine, 16*(6), 80-95.

Manoff, R. K. (1985). *Social marketing: New imperative for public health.* New York: Praeger.

Mittelmark, M. B., Luepker, R. V., Jacobs, D. R., Bracht, N. F., Carlaw, R. W., Crow, R. S., Finnegan, J., Grimm, R. H., Jeffery, R. W., Kline, F. G., Mullis, R. M., Murray, D. M., Pechacek, T. F., Perry, C. L., Pirie, P. L., & Blackburn, H. (1986). Community-wide prevention of cardiovascular disease: Education strategies of the Minnesota Heart Health Program. *Preventive Medicine, 15*, 1-17.

Rich, R. F., & Zaltman, G. (1978). Toward a theory of planned social change: Alternative perspectives and ideas. *Evaluation* [Special Issue], pp. 41-47.

Rogers, E. M. (1983). *Diffusion of innovations* (3rd ed.). New York: Free Press.

Roncarati, D. D., Lefebvre, R. C., & Carleton, R. A. (1989). Voluntary involvement in community health promotion: The Pawtucket Heart Health Program. *Health Promotion, 4*, 11-18.

Zaltman, G. (1983). Theory in use among change agents. In E. Seidman (Ed.), *Handbook of social intervention* (pp. 289-312). Beverly Hills, CA: Sage.

Chapter 12

BEYOND DEMONSTRATION
Diffusion of Health Promotion Innovations

GUY S. PARCEL
CHERYL L. PERRY
WENDELL C. TAYLOR

Communitywide health promotion involves change. At an individual level, change generally involves adopting new behaviors or modifying old behaviors that will either enhance health or reduce risk factors for disease. At an organizational level, change may mean the availability of new programs and services, new policies, or a modification in roles and practices of personnel. Within a community, change can also involve the mass media channels, as well as the government through the enactment of new laws, ordinances, and regulations. The ultimate success of a health promotion effort is dependent on the extent to which these changes occur within the targeted population, because change at the community level reinforces and supports changes made at the individual and organizational levels. An understanding of how new ideas or social practices spread and are adopted within a community or from community to community is essential to ensuring that health promotion programs will have sufficient impact and time to make a difference in the health outcomes for the targeted population.

Health promotion programs in the United States generally begin with small demonstration research projects to test efficacy and effectiveness. They are then modified and implemented with larger and larger numbers of the targeted population. A program that is powerful in introducing change will have only a minimal impact if it reaches only a small proportion of the population at risk. Thus one of the major challenges for communitywide health promotion is to promote the adoption of innovative programs that show acceptable levels of effectiveness.

This chapter focuses on the process of how health promotion programs are diffused throughout a given population. From a health promotion perspective, these programs or innovations may be viewed as either individual health behavior changes or specific programs designed to influence health behavior. Both types of innovations will be discussed in this chapter, but the emphasis will be placed on the latter, exploring theory and practice in methods to increase impact through greater diffusion.

This chapter is organized into three major sections. The first section provides definitions, reviews theory, and gives examples of how the diffusion process can be applied to health promotion. The second section presents a four-stage model and discusses how social learning theory can be applied to designing intervention to influence the diffusion process. In the third section, a case study is provided to illustrate how a specific health promotion program moved from a demonstration research project to a widely diffused program.

DIFFUSION AS A THEORY AND A PROCESS

Definitions

Rogers (1983) defines an *innovation* as "an idea, practice or object that is perceived as new by an individual or other unit of adoption" (p. 11). Similar definitions of an innovation have been proposed elsewhere (Basch, 1984; Downs & Mohr, 1979; Greer, 1977; Kolbe & Iverson, 1981). A critical component of an innovation is that the idea is perceived as new to the individual, not that the idea is objectively new (i.e., when discovered or first used) (Rogers, 1983). *Diffusion* is defined as "the process by which an innovation is communicated through certain channels over time among the members of a social system" (Rogers, 1983, p. 5).

Examples of Innovations and the Diffusion Process

Three contemporary examples of innovations are presented to illustrate the nature and range of the innovation diffusion process. For example, wearing an automobile safety belt is an innovation because safety belt use is a new behavior for many Americans. The diffusion of this innovation (i.e., more extensive safety belt use) has been studied and analyzed, and the results are disappointing. Despite years of regulations and multimillion-dollar advertising campaigns (mass media communication channel), only a fraction of Americans wear safety belts (Imperato & Mitchell, 1985). National studies based on the observed use of safety belts indicate that only one in eight Americans (approximately 13% of the population) regularly wears automobile safety belts. In contrast to the lack of success for the diffusion of automobile safety belt use, there was a fitness boom in the United States during the 1970s and early 1980s. In fact, some observers contend that a national obsession with jogging developed during this period (Sagon, 1987). For example, during three years in the mid-1970s, the New York Road Runner's Club membership quadrupled in number. In 1963, 100 runners started the 7.8-mile Bay-to-Breakers Run in San Francisco; by 1977, the number of entrants was 8,100 official runners, with another 3,500 running unofficially. Similarly, in 1975 there were 500 runners for the New York City Marathon, and in 1977 more than 5,000 runners started the race (Glover & Shepherd, 1978), a greater than tenfold increase. Jogging or running was an innovation for many Americans that diffused rapidly throughout the country during the 1970s.

Automobile safety belt use and jogging are examples of innovations wherein individuals engage in a particular behavior or practice an activity. On the other hand, an innovation can be an idea to discontinue a practice or habit. For example, smokers are being encouraged by regulations, media promotions, and social pressures to cease cigarette smoking (Schoenborn & Cohen, 1986). The question can be posed, What is the extent to which smoking cessation has been diffused throughout the country? A recent study found that there was a 10% decline in reported national rates of current smoking, from 1977 to 1983, based on the National Health Interview Survey data (Schoenborn & Cohen, 1986). Similarly, the U.S. Department of Health and Human Services (1986) reports a steady decline in smoking prevalence rates.

Programs and Organizational Change as Innovations

The definitions of *innovation* and *diffusion* also encompass the diffusion of programs (in contrast to the diffusion of individual behavior) to larger geographic areas and to a greater number of organizations. Basch (1984) offers a distinction between an individual's decision related to personal change and a decision about organizational change (i.e., acceptance of a program as an innovation). Basch writes that "although organizational change results from individual's decisions, these decisions are made in the context of the individual's organizational role and are not determined by the same factors that influence individual decisions about personal health-related behavior" (p. 59).

Usually, the diffusion of programs as an innovation involves organizational change. The extent of diffusion is determined by the number of organizations or units that implement the new program. For example, during the last decade, for the first time, many businesses and government agencies have implemented health and/or fitness programs. It is estimated that over 31% of the nation's companies with more than 100 employees now provide exercise programs (Patton, Corry, Gettman, & Graf, 1986). Currently, several aspects of the diffusion process are being studied for policies and programs such as smoking policies at the work site, tobacco-use prevention school curriculum, smoking cessation programs at the work site, and health maintenance organizations.

The diffusion of innovations, particularly with programs as innovations, has a significant role for health promotion/disease prevention goals. The diffusion of programs creates organizational change that increases the opportunity for a greater number of individuals to be exposed to the health promotion program. Stone (1984) addresses the importance of the diffusion process as a research area for health education in the school setting:

> Although research has been conducted to evaluate and increase the effectiveness of these interventions [health education], little has been done to evaluate or increase their dissemination or implementation. Consequently, even the most carefully designed and most effective interventions rarely exert even a small fraction of their potential influence since few efforts are made to disseminate them in schools. Thus, research is necessary to understand the variables that influence the successful dissemination of such interventions, their appropriate implementation in schools, and their continued use in the classroom. (p. 80)

Characteristics of the Innovation and the Diffusion Process

Attributes of the innovation, particularly characteristics of program innovations, can influence the speed and extent of the diffusion process. Rogers (1983) identifies relative advantage, compatibility, complexity, trialability, and observability as important characteristics. Relative advantage is simply the superiority (perceived or actual) of an innovation compared to the current practice or existing idea. Superiority can be evaluated or measured in terms of unique benefits, economics, usefulness, convenience, satisfaction, time, prestige factors, and so on. The greater the perceived relative advantage of an innovation, the greater the likelihood of its adoption and subsequent diffusion.

Similarly, the greater the compatibility of the innovation with the existing social system, the greater the probability of the innovation's adoption and diffusion. Compatibility is the perceived or actual congruence of the innovation with the prevalent values and norms as well as with the cultural, psychological, and sociological attributes of the situation. Therefore, a program innovation designed for a given population or specific region is more likely to be adopted and diffused throughout the region than is an incompatible innovation. Further, the less complex, less complicated, and less difficult an innovation is to understand and to use, the greater the likelihood it will be adopted.

Another attribute of an innovation is "trialability," which is the degree to which an innovation may be experimented with on a limited basis or implemented on a limited scale. New ideas that can be tried on a limited basis are more likely to be adopted. The final attribute listed by Rogers (1983) is "observability," which refers to the visibility of the innovation's results to others. Visibility of results stimulates communication about the innovation. The greater number of positive evaluations that may result promote greater adoption and diffusion of the innovation.

Zaltman and Duncan (1977) describe 11 important features of an innovation that will determine its potential for diffusion: relative advantage, impact on social relations, divisibility, reversibility, complexity, compatibility, communicability, time, risk and uncertainty, commitment, and capacity for successive modification. Zaltman and Duncan's descriptions of relative advantage, compatibility, complexity, and divisibility are similar to descriptions of Rogers's first four attributes presented above.

Zaltman and Duncan's (1977) "impact on social relations" refers to the positive or negative influence the innovation may have on social relationships within the target system and social relationships with groups outside the system. Positive social relationships facilitate the diffusion process. Another feature, reversibility, addresses the ease with which an innovation can be discontinued with few and minor lasting consequences. Thus an innovation is more likely to be adopted if it can be discontinued easily without the threat of permanent repercussions, especially in the face of unsuccessful innovation outcomes.

Simple, clear, and easily understood communication about the innovation as well as a short implementation time period, little risk, limited uncertainty, and modest commitment enhance the diffusion process. Finally, "capacity for successive modification" is the capacity of the innovation to be updated and adapted to changing times, in contrast to an innovation that becomes quickly outdated and is not modifiable. An easily updated innovation improves the potential for diffusion (Zaltman & Duncan, 1977).

Overall, the characteristics proposed by Rogers (1983) and Zaltman and Duncan (1977) support the perspective that there are important and critical innovation features that can influence the potential diffusion process, particularly the initial adoption of the innovation. From a practitioner's viewpoint, to improve an innovation's potential for diffusion, it is important to design into the innovation the features described above and to communicate these features to potential users.

Diffusion Theory

Diffusion theory is derived from a body of research that has demonstrated a consistent pattern of ideological or program adoption, over time, by different population groups (Green, Gottlieb, & Parcel, 1987). A consistent pattern of adoption has been described mathematically, and several theoretical constructs have been identified as important variables in influencing the adoption of an innovation.[1]

Individuals and organizations can be classified into adopter categories based on when they first begin using the innovation; the innovation is not adopted at the same time by all adopters. Research from a variety of investigations (e.g., agricultural, consumer, health, technological, and organizational innovations) has demonstrated that the distribution of the adoption of innovations approximates a bell-shaped or normal curve (see Rogers, 1983). A normally distributed frequency distribution permits the classification of adopters by statistical measures such as the mean and standard deviation (Green & Anderson, 1986; Rogers, 1983). Furthermore, the same adopter distribution data plotted on a cumulative basis rather than per unit time represent an S-shaped curve. The sigmoid (S-shaped) growth curve of population growth and the S-shaped diffusion curve of adopter distributions are quite similar. The shape of both follows an exponential curve or accelerating rate of growth/diffusion, reaches maximum inflection point, and thereafter the rate decelerates.

Accordingly, Rogers (1983) identifies five mutually exclusive adopter categories based on the statistical properties of the diffusion curve: innovators, early adopters, early majority, late majority, and laggards. A conceptualization from Rogers of the ideal type of each adopter category is presented below.

Adopter Categories: Innovators to Laggards

Innovators are adventuresome, willing to take risks, and eager to try new ideas; they can accept a high degree of uncertainty and absorb occasional setbacks (e.g., financial loss or loss of other resources). Innovators may not be respected by the other members of a social system, but they have a key role in introducing new ideas to the social system. On the other hand, early adopters are respected members of the social system. Consequently, they command the greatest degree of opinion leadership and serve as role models for members of the social system. Therefore, early adopters can speed the diffusion process by diminishing the uncertainty about the innovation by adopting it and by communicating, via interpersonal networks, positive evaluations about the innovation to other members of the social system. Early adopters are seen as wise and discrete users of new ideas.

Whereas early adopters are leaders, early majority adopters seldom hold leadership positions. Instead, early majority adopters deliberate for some time before reaching an innovation decision. Early majority adopters are just one step ahead of average social system members and thus provide an important link in the diffusion process. Conversely, late majority adopters, usually, are just after or a step behind the average members of a social system. Late majority adopters respond to increasing network pressures, economic necessity, and the persuasiveness of system norms. Late majority adopters are skeptical; before they feel safe about adopting, the utility of the innovation must be clear and the uncertainty about the new idea must be removed.

Finally, laggards, as the name implies, are the last members in a social system to adopt an innovation. Laggards are traditional, suspicious of innovations, and typically are near isolates in the social system. Rogers (1983) writes: "The point of reference for the laggard is the past. Decisions are often made in terms of what has been done in previous generations" (p. 250).

Diffusion Theory Applied to Individual Adoption

Diffusion theory provides a basis for designing programs with interventions timed and targeted to the various stages of the diffusion process, the types of people expected to be adopting at each stage, and the sources of influence to which they are expected to respond. For example, to enhance the adoption and diffusion of an innovation, a cognitively oriented intervention may be most appropriate for early adopters, a motivational emphasis may be effective for the majority adopters, and late adopters may require efforts to dismantle barriers (i.e., environmental, economic, or behavioral) before an innovation is adopted (Green et al., 1987).

Diffusion Theory Applied to Organizations

Organization diffusion theories are particularly important given the growing interest in the adoption, implementation, and long-term viability (i.e., institutionalization) of health promotion programs in order to study the effectiveness of these programs adequately (Goodman & Steckler, 1988).

There are a number of models that provide a distinct perspective on the diffusion process for organizations. For example, the variance approach studies the relationships between characteristics of organizations and organizational innovativeness. A typical variance research finding is that larger organizations are more innovative than smaller organizations. (For a more complete explanation of the variance approach, see Kervasdoue & Kimberly, 1978; Mohr, 1982; Rogers, 1983.)

An example of a process approach is Beyer and Trice's (1978) change process model, which synthesizes the elements of a variety of approaches in the innovation literature (Smith & Kaluzny, 1975; Zaltman, Duncan, & Holbeck, 1973), organizational change literature (Hage & Aiken, 1970; Kast & Rosenzweig, 1974), and policy formulation literature (Dror, 1968). In Beyer and Trice's model, the seven necessary stages in a completed change process are as follows: (a) sensing of unsatisfied demands on the system, (b) searching for possible responses, (c) evaluation of alternatives, (d) decision to adopt course of action, (d) initiation of action with the system, (e) implementation of the change, and (g) institutionalization of the change. These seven stages typically occur in a sequential or time-ordered fashion; Beyer and Trice's time-ordered stages distinguish the process approach from other research approaches to the diffusion process.

In addition to the variance and process approaches, Kaluzny and Hernandez (1987) propose three models of organizational change distinguished by different emphases on the organizational-environmental interface. The first model (rational model) focuses on the internal characteristics of the organization. This model is concerned with the internal functioning of organizations and describes four basic stages in the change process: recognition (of a problem), identification (of possible courses of action), implementation, and adoption (acceptance of implemented change).

The second model is the resource dependency model, which views organizations as part of a larger system that supplies needed resources. In contrast to the rational model, the resource dependency model recognizes the interdependence between the environment and the organization. Therefore, "from this perspective the critical issue is not the utilization of resources within the organization per se but the problems of acquiring these resources from the environment" (Kaluzny & Hernandez, 1987, p. 403). The resource dependency model generates two specific types of organizational responses to the environment: The organization can either respond to changes to fit environmental requirements or, conversely, alter the environment to fit existing organizational capabilities.

Finally, the population ecology model focuses on the long-term transformation of a population of organizations instead of activities of a single organization. Organizations are viewed as "the repository of environmental influences over which the organization and its management have little control" (Kaluzny & Hernandez, 1987, p. 386). The population ecology model is an extension of the natural selection model of biological ecology. Organizational change is explained by examining the distribution of resources in the organization's environment. The preceding three models are useful because each makes different assumptions about the organization-environment relationship. Kaluzny and Hernandez (1987) caution those in managing the change process not to assume that the environment is a constant: Organizations are subject to large changes in the environment.

Thus far different theories, various research findings, and divergent views have been presented on the innovation diffusion process in organizations. The different perspectives provide several models to choose from in investigating and better understanding this process. The next section presents the results of a field study that examined the diffusion process in school settings.

Field Study

Huberman and Miles (1984) studied 12 diffusion efforts for different types of programs to improve schools in 10 states (rural, urban, and suburban settings) from Maine to California. The substantive findings from the Huberman and Miles study point out that high institutionalization of the program was most likely under "mandated, stable use" and "skillful, committed use."

Mandated, stable use was characterized by administrative pressure to implement the program, no serious resistance, and teacher-administrator harmony. Skillful, committed use lacked the element of mandating evident in the earlier approach. Instead, the skillful, committed use scenario involved assistance to increase the user's mastery of the program and to increase commitment. User commitment enhanced community support and resulted in further institutionalization. Conversely, low institutionalization was associated with vulnerability and indifference. Vulnerability was characterized by a lack of organizational structures to protect the innovation from funding problems or departures of advocates.

Finally, the weakest institutionalization was marked by indifference; that is, administrators showed little evidence of concern about the fate of the innovation and there were few or no efforts to assist the users in developing mastery or to stabilize use. Therefore, the innovation was not supported and institutionalization was a remote prospect.

Practical Applications

From a practitioner's viewpoint, the Huberman and Miles (1984) study suggests two significant approaches to improve an innovation's viability and further diffusion. One approach, the "mandated, stable use" strategy, can be viewed as a top-to-bottom process. In this case, top management is committed to the innovation. Therefore, the innovation is used throughout the organization and, eventually, as a result of stable use, it becomes a part of the organization's structure. The top-to-bottom process to develop commitment was effective in a harmonious work environment and when resistance to the innovation's implementation was minimal. This finding supports the practitioner's efforts to establish a firm commitment from management prior to the introduction of an innovation. Management commitment can be a consequential factor for the survival of an innovation.

A second strategy suggested by the Huberman and Miles (1984) study, "skillful, committed use," is to provide support and training for the users of the innovation. In this way, users become more skillful and confident with the use of the innovation. User mastery was associated with increased commitment in the Huberman and Miles study. Therefore, the innovation's chances for institutionalization and diffusion are increased when training programs and supportive resources are provided to enhance the competence and confidence of the innovations users. This perspective is an important one for practitioners to plan for as an innovation is introduced.

In sum, administrative commitment to the innovation and the user's mastery of the innovation are significant factors for the practitioner to prepare for, monitor, and influence. These factors are important determinants of the ultimate viability of an innovation.

MODEL FOR DIFFUSION INTERVENTIONS

Considerable resources go into the development and testing of health promotion demonstration programs. Once a program has been shown to be effective, its potential impact depends on the extent to which the program is diffused throughout the population and the number of people who are eventually exposed to the program. Diffusion research applied to health promotion has lagged behind behavior change research, and we are in the early stages of learning more about how to influence the adoption of health promotion programs and strategies. Most of the research in this area has focused on the adoption of health behavior innovations by individuals, and we know very little about how organizations are influenced to adopt innovative health promotion programs. There is a need for research to determine effective ways of increasing the diffusion of health programs.

The National Cancer Institute has recognized this need, and in 1987 it funded two research projects designed to study the process of influencing the diffusion of smoking prevention programs to schools. This initiative grew out of the awareness that in spite of research and demonstration projects leading to the development of several effective programs to prevent youth smoking, the actual number of schools using these programs was very small. Smoking prevention programs have demonstrated an effectiveness level of preventing up to 60% of students who would have started smoking had they not been exposed to the program (Perry, Murray, & Klepp, 1987). Additional research and development might be able to design ways of influencing a greater percentage of students not to smoke, but clearly the greatest impact could be achieved by increasing the number of students exposed to effective prevention programs.

Intervention Stages

The process framework on which the diffusion intervention model is based is the innovation decision process outlined by Rogers and Shoemaker (1973) and elaborated by Rogers (1983). They describe five distinct stages for the diffusion process: (a) knowledge, (b) persuasion, (c) decision, (d) implementation, and (e) confirmation. The implementation and confirmation stages reflect Rogers's recognition that the use of the innovation is as important as the decision to adopt it. We have combined the first two stages into the "dissemination" stage for the intervention model because intervention strategies can be designed both to inform and to persuade. Rogers's confirmation stage is comparable to the "maintenance" stage in the intervention model.

Dissemination

The intervention strategies in the dissemination stage have two purposes: to provide information about the health promotion program and to increase the motivation of potential users to adopt the program. Intervention strategies are more likely to be effective if they are designed to provide information about an innovative health promotion program and to influence the psychosocial and environmental preconditions for adoption.

In a review of social learning theory as it applies to social diffusion of an innovation, Bandura (1977) suggests that modeling serves as the major vehicle for learning about a new innovation. Modeling is provided by the observation of someone else performing a behavior that involves the innovation and leads to an observable outcome or reinforcement. Observation of reinforcement can provide vicarious reinforcement for the observer. Models can both inform and motivate. Therefore, a diffusion intervention based on modeling can be used to provide information about the relative benefits of an innovative health promotion program as well as to influence expectations and value expectancies for adopting the program. For example, if teachers and administrators from one school district not using a particular tobacco-use prevention program are able to observe teachers in another district successfully using the program, the observers are able to learn information about the program as well as to begin to view in a positive way their potential use of the program. The intervention task is to design methods that will enable the observation of the successful use of the program.

Modeling can be provided through direct observation or through symbolic models, such as those represented in mass media techniques. Thus there are two primary channels for modeling to serve as a determinant of diffusion: media channels and interpersonal channels. The combined effects of both the media and interpersonal channels are referred to as the "dual-link model" (Bandura, 1986). In this approach, modeling influences adoption through a two-step diffusion process that flows from influential persons who learn about innovations from the media and pass them on to others through personal influence.

The implications of learning theory for developing dissemination strategies are not simply that one should use either media or interpersonal channels, but rather that there are ways in which each type of channel can best be applied to achieve the most effective strategies. A school program example can be used to illustrate this principle. It may not be possible or cost-effective to transport school personnel from several school districts to observe the successful use of a tobacco-use prevention program, thus, from district to district, the interpersonal channel would be difficult to use. However, media that could be disseminated to several districts, such as videotape or print materials, could be used to model use of the program by one district. Once these media reach a school district, interpersonal channels such as demonstrations, meetings, and classroom observations can be used to continue dissemination of the program. In both channels, the essential components of the intervention strategies include modeling the benefits, effective use, and positive outcomes of using the program.

Adoption

Interventions applied in the adoption stage are intended to obtain commitment from the organization to adopt and use the health promotion program. Adoption will usually involve a formal decision on the part of organization administrators or key decision makers. The acquisition of knowledge and motivation to use a new health promotion program is necessary but may not be sufficient for adoption of the innovation in practice. According to Bandura (1986), environmental inducements serve as regulators of the adoption of an innovation. The purpose of intervention in the adoption stage is to create favorable environmental conditions to induce and support the decision to adopt.

Adoptive behavior is highly susceptible to the influence of incentives. The innovation itself may provide incentives if it is perceived as having relative benefit and compatibility with existing activities. Vicarious incentives (the creation of expected benefits) can also influence adoption through positive appeals that present social or economic benefits for adoption of the innovation. Thus the two major strategies that can be used in the adoption stage are as follows: (a) Demonstrate how the program will benefit the users and fit effectively into current activities and goals of the organization, and (b) create vicarious incentives that will provide social or economic benefits to individuals or the organization.

For example, if the state department of education requires schools to provide smoking prevention programs, the adoption intervention would be directed at demonstrating how a new program can effectively meet the state mandate and how it can fit into current teaching curriculum. Then, financial incentives (such as free teacher training and low-cost purchase of materials) and social incentives (such as certificates for advanced training and recognition for the school leadership through publicity in public media) are used to encourage adoption of the health promotion program. Strategies need to be used to reach the early adopters and give them visibility so that they will serve as models for the remaining potential users of the program. In the above example, it is important for other school districts to be aware of the incentives provided to the early adopters to help create expectations for the benefits that can be obtained from adoption.

Implementation

The implementation of a health promotion program has two major aspects: completeness and fidelity. Completeness is the extent to which the various components of the program are delivered to the participants. Sometimes programs fail to influence change not because the program was not an effective intervention, but because only part of the program was actually implemented. Fidelity is the extent to which the implementers of a program are true to the intent and methods designed as critical features of the program. For example, if a smoking prevention program based on using peer teachers has been shown to be effective, a lower level of effectiveness might be obtained if new adopters of the program were to modify the program to leave out the peer teaching and substitute teacher lectures. The content would be similar, but the methods would be very different.

Interventions provided during the implementation stage are designed to provide staff with the skills and resource support necessary to conduct the program so that all components are included and there is fidelity to the methods of the program. The primary strategies used in this stage are staff training and technical support. Staff training should make effective use of modeling to demonstrate new skills and skill training that provides the opportunity to practice with feedback and guidance for mastery development. Technical assistance needs to be available when program users have questions or experience some difficulty implementing the program. This assistance is usually provided by a supervisor or staff member who is more experienced or has had additional training to guide program staff through difficult aspects of the program.

Failure to plan for effective implementation is often the major reason new programs fail. It is discouraging to see how often health promotion programs are disseminated and adopted without plans and resources provided for staff training and technical assistance. A major school health education evaluation study showed a clear relationship between staff training and the extent of program implementation as well as student learning outcomes (Connell, Turner, & Mason, 1985). The study of implementation of innovative school programs conducted by Huberman and Miles (1984) also identified teacher skill mastery and availability of technical assistance as key factors influencing program success.

Maintenance

Interventions during the maintenance stage are intended to move the program from being implemented to becoming an institutionalized component of the adopting organization. Maintenance occurs when the program continues to be used beyond the initial trial stage. It is not unusual for the resources made available for a health promotion program to be significantly decreased following initial implementation. The attention given to a new program shifts to other areas of concern as confidence builds in the capability of the program to address problems or identified needs. The challenge for intervention is to provide incentives to the staff to continue program activities and for administrators to provide support for the staff. This usually has to be done without the same level and intensity of effort required to accomplish initial program implementation.

Three types of incentives can be used: (a) feedback on performance, (b) reinforcement through recognition, and (c) the establishment of a monitoring and feedback system. Staff need to know if their efforts are leading to any measurable outcomes. This could include more immediate outcomes such as knowledge change or skill development by program participants as well as longer-range outcomes such as behavior change or risk factor reduction. Success at achieving program objectives helps to provide incentive for continuation of program activities. Failure to achieve objectives that can be linked to incomplete implementation can be used to encourage staff to modify performance or identify the need for additional staff training or technical assistance (return to implementation stage). Thus the monitoring system needs to include both implementation data and outcome data.

Reinforcement through recognition can be accomplished through several techniques, such as certificates of accomplishment, letters of achievement for personnel records, special newsletters to highlight staff accomplishments, articles prepared for local newspapers, special designations (i.e., "smoke-free school," "smoke-free workplace"), special events to give recognition, and opportunities for expanded or new roles to increase interest in work responsibilities. Reinforcement through rewards makes use of material and financial incentives. These rewards may range from simple materials designed to maintain interest and identification with the program (T-shirts, stickers, posters) to financial rewards such as salary increases, fees for advanced training, travel to conferences, or flexible use of work time. A key factor in determining what incentives to use to encourage maintenance of a program is finding out what types of feedback and rewards will be valued by the staff and administrators. This can be done through focus groups and by involving program implementers and key administrators in program planning that includes the provision of incentives for accomplishing program goals and objectives.

DIFFUSION OF THE
MINNESOTA SMOKING PREVENTION PROGRAM

In this section, the natural diffusion of a health promotion program will be described. This innovation, the Minnesota Smoking Prevention Program (MSPP), was developed in 1978 as part of a research and demonstration project for the Interagency Council on Smoking and Health. These projects were funded in order to instigate new approaches to prevent the onset of smoking among adolescents—the onset rates had not declined after the release of the surgeon general's landmark report in 1964. Thus new approaches, beyond knowledge dissemination of smoking's health consequences and fear arousal and values clarification, were sought.

The MSPP was guided, theoretically, by social learning theory, a behavioral model that suggests environmental, personality, and behavioral attributes to modify in order to affect adolescent smoking behavior (Perry & Murray, 1982). Rather than viewing smoking as a health behavior, the program design considered smoking as a social behavior that is meaningful and functional to adolescents. The program emphasizes the acquisition of social skills that enables adolescents to understand why people their age begin to smoke; how advertising, adult role models, and peers may encourage smoking; and what to do to avoid smoking. The program involves six 45-minute classroom sessions, with at least weekly intervals between sessions. MSPP is taught by elected classmates, peer leaders, and the usual classroom teacher. Peer leaders and teachers are both trained prior to program implementation. The peer leaders (4-5 per classroom) are role models for nonsmoking and lead small group discussions in the acceptable language of their classmates. Peer leaders appear to be a critical component of this innovation (Klepp, Halper, & Perry, 1986).

The MSPP was refined further for a series of research studies funded by the National Institutes of Health from 1980. The results of these studies—and others using this social learning approach—point to consistent 40-50% reductions in smoking onset rates that maintain into high school (Flay, 1985; Perry et al., 1987). This innovation, then, appears to be efficacious across multiple studies and sites, and worthy of consideration for larger dissemination.

The transition from a research study to widespread dissemination is not automatic or simple. Although MSPP was being implemented and had been adopted by 6 school districts in Minnesota, reaching all 435 Minnesota districts is quite a different order. One large barrier was financial. The National Institutes of Health research studies were funded for a limited number of schools and for a finite grant period. To begin to "market" the MSPP and the requisite training sessions was not economically feasible for an academic institution. A second barrier was structural. The personnel who developed the MSPP and conducted the research were not trained or suited for the tasks of dissemination, tasks more appropriate for a state agency or a private educational training firm. In order to turn attention from development to dissemination would require the construction of a new team or unit or center. A third barrier was the schools' acceptance of a new program on smoking. Generally, the Minnesota schools included a small unit on smoking as part of the mandated health curriculum. A new program would need to be perceived as a significant improvement in order for a school district to pay for teacher training to replace an existing unit. Smoking, even as a discipline problem, is often not seen to be as grave a problem as alcohol or drug use. Demands from other health topic areas as well as other curriculum areas have made curriculum time precious. In order to attract a substantial number of school districts, then, a strategy was needed that would "free" the program from the researchers, market its efficaciousness, and provide incentives for adoption.

The Omnibus Smoking and Health Legislation

In 1985, the Minnesota Legislature increased the state cigarette tax by 5¢ per pack. A portion of this tax increase was allocated to fund statewide smoking prevention programs administered by the Minnesota Department of Health and the Minnesota Department of Education (Shultz, 1988). Local school districts now receive annual funds to increase and improve their smoking prevention programs at the rate of 54¢ per student. The school districts apply for these funds and must meet the following criteria:

(1) Smoking education is provided at all grades, K-12, based on state guidelines.
(2) In-service training is provided for teachers on smoking prevention to update them on new approaches.
(3) An intensive program is provided for young adolescents, grades 6-8, that is based on a behavioral model and has demonstrated effectiveness in preventing smoking onset.
(4) A schoolwide tobacco-free policy applies to students, teachers, staff, and visitors (Griffin, Loeffler, & Kassell, 1988).

Since the MSPP was one program that met the third criteria, the legislation provided the basis for an ongoing mechanism, with monetary incentives for statewide diffusion.

Before providing a description of this diffusion process, consideration of MSPP as an innovation seems appropriate, particularly as it relates to the theory described in the first section of this chapter. MSPP targets change at the individual and organizational levels. For the individual student, nonsmoking behavior is sought, including nonuse of tobacco, refusal skills, and social skills to help others be nonusers. For the school organization, MSPP requires changes to a behaviorally oriented curriculum, to additional teacher training, to a nondidactic learning approach, and to adolescent peer leaders as classroom instructors. The program has a clear advantage over previous programs in having demonstrated an impact on smoking behavior of young adolescents.

The program fits into typical middle-school classroom sessions and is basically compatible, even if the one-week spacing of the sessions and use of peer leaders are unusual and need careful explanation. MSPP is implemented at individual schools, and so trialability is possible. Previous trials in Minnesota since 1978 have usually been sufficiently compelling, however. The program, because of the extensive training needed, use of peer leaders, and notification of parents, is moderately visible. Some school districts have augmented visibility through newspaper articles, school board meetings, or videotaped sessions. MSPP has been updated annually, based on new research and experiences in the field, and especially on feedback from participating teachers. MSPP was developed so it would be adopted by teachers and then institutionalized by a school district. In Huberman and Miles's (1984) classification, program institutionalization depended on "skillful, committed use," and was limited to a few school districts. The 1985 Minnesota legislation provided the basis for "mandated, stable use" of MSPP and quickly accelerated the process of diffusion throughout the state.

Stages of Diffusion of the MSPP

The four stages of diffusion—dissemination, adoption, implementation, and maintenance—have been utilized to promote statewide adoption of the MSPP. Other curricula are also available in Minnesota that meet the criteria specified in the legislation, but the MSPP had the strongest evidence of effectiveness and so has been promoted by the Minnesota Department of Education.

The promotion of the MSPP occurs as the first stage of dissemination, although information on MSPP is provided prior to the application process. This promotion stresses the program's effectiveness, outcomes in Minnesota, and observations by Minnesota teachers who have participated previously. School districts can receive more information on the MSPP from the university or from the State Department of Education. Teacher training sessions for MSPP are scheduled throughout the school year and throughout the state, so that planning at a local level can proceed even a year prior to implementation. In order to teach the MSPP, a one-day training of teachers is necessary, but funds for this purpose are encouraged by the legislative stipend.

Smoking prevention programs are adopted primarily through the financial mechanism and incentives allocated by the legislature. School districts are informed of the criteria they must meet in order to obtain funding, and then they must complete an application for the funds in which they specify curricula, training, and policy plans and progress. These applications are reviewed by the smoking specialist at the Minnesota State Department of Education and are approved only if they meet the necessary criteria. During the 1986-87 and 1987-88 school years, more than 95% of the 435 Minnesota school districts met these requirements and received funding.

Teacher training is required in order for a district to receive state funding. The purpose of the training is to enhance compliant implementation of programs, including the MSPP. The training materials for the MSPP are user friendly; the training sessions are participatory and enjoyable, conducted in pleasant settings, and involve trainers with extensive classroom experience who have also taught MSPP. At the end of the training, the teachers have all the classroom materials and teaching skills needed for program implementation. They are then required to schedule the sessions and arrange for the election and training of peer leaders.

Implementation of the MSPP occurs throughout the school year. Classroom observations are scheduled to check on compliance and fidelity, but these cannot be afforded for each trained teacher. Annual questionnaires that ask about implementation problems, concerns, and suggestions are sent to all trained teachers in the spring, and year-end school district reports are monitored for actual implementation data. Teachers are invited for follow-up training sessions and retraining at the end of the school year. Maintenance of the MSPP, at this early stage, appears to depend on ongoing categorical funding for antismoking programs, provision of training and retraining as MSPP evolves, formal adoption of MSPP as a mandated curriculum by the school district, and the existence of restrictive smoking policies for students, teachers, and staff that reinforce a nonsmoking norm districtwide. Recognition by the State Department of Education and feedback from ongoing research on adolescent smoking in Minnesota also appear to enhance maintenance. Since only two school years have elapsed since the legislation was passed, only limited data are available on the ultimate effectiveness of this diffusion process.

The Two-State Tobacco Project

The outcomes of legislation such as that passed in Minnesota are difficult to assess, but they are extremely important for future public health promotion efforts. The Two-State Tobacco Project (TSTP) is attempting to assess the impact of the 1985 legislation on the smoking behavior of adolescents in Minnesota (Murray et al., 1988). The research study is funded by the National Cancer Institute and has two parts. The first part is an epidemiological prevalence study of smoking rates among ninth-grade students in 100 randomly selected schools in Minnesota and Wisconsin, and assesses whether trends in smoking differ between the two states over a five-year period. The second part is an intervention study in which 78 randomly selected Minnesota junior high schools were randomly assigned to one of four smoking prevention program conditions—the MSPP, the Smoke Free Generation, the Minnesota State Guidelines for Smoking Prevention K-12, or the school's existing smoking education program. These programs were implemented with seventh-grade students in the 1987-88 school year, and that cohort is being surveyed annually for three years. This second part of the TSTP will provide information on statewide recruitment methods, the necessity and extent of teacher training needed, training methods, teacher compliance to curricula, curriculum adoption, and program effect on adolescent smoking onset rates.

To date, baseline and one-year data have been collected for both the prevalence and intervention studies. Of the schools contacted by letter to participate in the intervention study, 65% agreed to do so. Training sessions for MSPP and the Guidelines were scheduled statewide for all schools in those conditions (the Smoke Free Generation provides training by videotape) by the Minnesota Department of Education in collaboration with the university. Teacher observations were scheduled and completed, monitoring compliance and teacher style, on all teachers in the 78 schools, with MSPP teachers showing the highest rates of compliance to protocol (greater than 90%). Behavioral outcomes and school district adoption data are forthcoming.

The MSPP was not originally conceived as an innovation to be disseminated widely. The original purpose was to create a smoking prevention program that could have an impact on adolescent smoking onset rates. As outcomes from research affirmed the efficacy of this approach, the need to disseminate became a paramount issue. The

Minnesota Legislature provided the appropriate basis and impetus and structure for diffusion, particularly diffusion of an education program for adolescents. The Minnesota experience can therefore be viewed as a natural experiment in diffusion, since the goals and necessary partners changed as more knowledge evolved, but not always in a planned sequence of steps. Still, the experience has many inherent lessons for future health promotion efforts, as each stage of the diffusion process has been actualized. The lessons to date are optimistic ones, and worthy of considerable and more comprehensive study.

NOTE

1. For an extensive discussion of diffusion theory's predictive components, descriptive features, explanatory power, and mathematical and statistical bases, see Rogers (1983), Green and Anderson (1986), Green and Lewis (1986), and Green et al. (1987).

REFERENCES

Bandura, A. (1977). *Social learning theory.* Englewood Cliffs, NJ: Prentice-Hall.

Bandura, A. (1986). *Social foundations of thought and action.* Englewood Cliffs, NJ: Prentice-Hall.

Basch, C. E. (1984). Research on disseminating and implementing health-education programs in schools. *Journal of School Health, 54*, 57-66.

Beyer, J. M., & Trice, H. M. (1978). *Implementing change.* New York: Free Press.

Connell, P. B., Turner, R. R., & Mason, E. F. (1985). Summary of the findings of the school health education evaluation: Health promotion effectiveness, implementation, and costs. *Journal of School Health, 55*(8), 316-323.

Downs, G. W., & Mohr, L. B. (1979). Toward a theory of innovation. *Administration and Society, 10*(4), 379-408.

Dror, Y. (1968). *Public policymaking reexamined.* Scranton, PA: Chandler.

Flay, B. R. (1985). Psychosocial approaches to smoking prevention: A review of findings. *Health Psychology, 4*(5), 449-488.

Glover, B., & Shepherd, J. (1978). *The runner's handbook.* New York: Penguin.

Goodman, R., & Steckler, A. (1988). *A process model for the institutionalization of health promotion programs.* Manuscript submitted for publication.

Green, L. W., & Anderson, C. (1986). *Community health* (5th ed.). St. Louis: C. V. Mosby.

Green, L. W., Gottlieb, N., & Parcel, G. (1987). Diffusion theory extended and applied. In W. B. Ward (Ed.), *Advances in health education and promotion.* Greenwich, CT: JAI.

Green, L. W., & Lewis, F. M. (1986). *Measurement and evaluation in health education and health promotion.* Palo Alto, CA: Mayfield.

Greer, A. L. (1977). Advances in the study of diffusion of innovation in health care organizations. *Milbank Memorial Fund Quarterly, 55*(4), 505-532.

Griffin, G. A., Loeffler, H. J., & Kassell, P. (1988). Tobacco-free schools in Minnesota. *Journal of School Health, 58*(6), 236-239.

Hage, J., & Aiken, M. (1970). Program change and organizational properties. *American Journal of Sociology, 72*, 502-519.

Huberman, A. M., & Miles, M. B. (1984). *Innovation up close.* New York: Plenum.

Imperato, P. J., & Mitchell, G. (1985). *Acceptable risks.* New York: Viking.

Kaluzny, A. D., & Hernandez, S. R. (1987). Organizational change and innovation. In S. Shortall & A. Kaluzny (Eds.), *Health care management* (pp. 378-417). New York: John Wiley.

Kast, F. E., & Rosenzweig, J. E. (1974). *Organization and management: A systems approach.* New York: McGraw-Hill.

Kervasdoue, J., & Kimberly, J. R. (1978). *Hospital innovation in France and the United States: Organizational versus institutional explanations.* Unpublished manuscript, Yale University, School of Organization and Management.

Klepp, K.-I., Halper, A., & Perry, C. L. (1986). The efficacy of peer leaders in drug abuse prevention. *Journal of School Health, 56*(9), 407-411.

Kolbe, L. J., & Iverson, D. C. (1981). Implementing comprehensive health education: Educational innovations and social change. *Health Education Quarterly, 8*(1), 57-81.

Mohr, L. B. (1982). *Explaining organizational behavior.* San Francisco: Jossey-Bass.

Murray, D. M., Jacobs, D. R., Perry, C. L., Pallonen, U., Harty, K. C., Griffin, G., Moen, M. E., & Hanson, G. (1988). A statewide approach to adolescent tobacco-use prevention: The Minnesota-Wisconsin adolescent tobacco-use research project. *Preventive Medicine, 17*, 461-474.

Patton, R. W., Corry, J. M., Gettman, L. R., & Graf, J. S. (1986). *Implementing health/fitness programs.* Champaign, IL: Human Kinetics.

Perry, C. L., & Murray, D. M. (1982). Enhancing the transition years: The challenge of adolescent health promotion. *Journal of School Health, 52*, 307-311.

Perry, C. L., Murray, D. M., & Klepp, K. I. (1987). Predictors of adolescent smoking and implications for prevention. *Morbidity and Mortality Weekly, 36*(45), 41-45.

Rogers, E. M. (1983). *Diffusion of innovations* (3rd ed.). New York: Free Press.

Rogers, E. M., & Shoemaker, F. (1973). *Communication of innovation: A cross-cultural approach.* New York: Free Press.

Sagon, L. A. (1987). *The health of nations.* New York: Basic Books.

Schoenborn, C. A., & Cohen, B. H. (1986). Trends in smoking, alcohol consumption, and other health practices among U.S. adults, 1977 and 1983. *Advance Data, 118*, 1-13.

Shultz, J. M. (1988). *Quantifying the disease impact of cigarette smoking: The development and application of computer software for estimating the health and economic costs of smoking.* Unpublished doctoral dissertation, University of Minnesota.

Smith, D. B., & Kaluzny, A. D. (1975). *The white labyrinth: Understanding the organization of health care.* Berkeley, CA: McCutcheon.

Stone, E. J. (1984). Work group recommendations of the National Conference on School Health Research in the heart, lung and blood areas. *Journal of School Health, 54*(6), 77-82.

U.S. Department of Health and Human Services. (1986). *The 1990 health objectives for the nation: A midcourse review.* Washington, DC: Office of Disease Prevention and Health Promotion.

Zaltman, G., & Duncan, R. (1977). *Strategies for planned change.* New York: John Wiley.

Zaltman, G., Duncan, R., & Holbeck, J. (1973). *Innovations and organizations.* New York: John Wiley.

Part V

APPLICATIONS TO
SPECIAL POPULATIONS:
CASE STUDIES

OVERVIEW

In this section of the book three case studies are presented to illustrate feasible and culturally acceptable approaches to health promotion in minority communities and with special populations such as the elderly. Community-based health promotion programs (especially those involving life-style change) have been criticized for their focus on majority populations and on messages and interventions that seem to appeal to advantaged socioeconomic groups. Ramirez, Mac-Kellar, and Gallion (1988) have noted the paucity of published accounts of public health intervention programming aimed at minorities. Most of the large community health demonstrations of the last decade have occurred primarily but not exclusively with White North American and European populations. Some groups most in need of reducing health risks may be minimally influenced by programs aimed at the dominant culture. This is especially true among recent immigrant and refugee populations, with their varying cultural, dietary, and folk medicine practices.

In discussing minority health issues, Braithwaite and Lythcott (1989) observe: "Because health behaviors are culture-bound, primary prevention efforts that address preventable disease and illness must emerge from a knowledge of and a respect for the culture of the target community to ensure that both the community organization and development effort and any interventions that emerge are culturally sensitive and linguistically appropriate" (p. 283). A few recent published descriptions of health projects (Chng, 1984; Damberg, 1986; Orleans, Strecher, Schoenback, Salmon, & Blackmon, 1989) reflect this sensitivity to the cultural context and to the needs of special groups (Minkler, Frantz, & Wechsler, 1982). The *Report of the Secretary's Task Force on Black and*

Minority Health (U.S. Department of Health and Human Services, 1985) provides additional guides and recommendations for culturally appropriate health programs.

In a recent review of the literature on prevention in minority communities, Ramirez et al. (1988) note a paucity of published accounts and a "lack of attention given to the processes used to develop culturally sensitive public health interventions" (p. 342). The ensuing case studies attempt to begin to remedy this lack of attention by providing accounts of the processes used to engage the community as well as the culture-specific interventions that were developed. In order to provide consistency, each case report follows, in general, the five-stage sequence of organizing health promotion programs described in Chapter 3. The first phase, community analysis, is important in all health promotion programs, but it is especially critical in minority communities. Local history, tradition, natural networks, and related resources must be well understood by program planners before they proceed to the initiation-design phase. The A Su Salud case study in a Mexican-American community provides several illustrations of how accurate community assessment shaped the design of interventions. The authors also discuss some of the practical barriers to effective community organization work.

Information about a community's past experience in implementing health or social change projects is important to understand, as is the history of past racial tensions and/or injustices. Past negative experiences may make some minority community members suspicious of "outsiders" and their "good intentions." During the initiation phase, open and frank discussions of any of these or related issues should be welcomed and seen as natural components of community work. Such early discussions can lay the framework for future ways to resolve differences constructively.

Community residents and leaders must be involved early and have a real, not token, role in decision making for implementing health promotion activities. This early involvement and collaborative decision making are reflected in all three of the case studies presented here. In addition, by building on community self-esteem and civic pride, organizers in the Richmond Black community study were able to root their program deeply into existing social organizations and channels of communication. Employment of minority persons and the use of local minority businesses not only increased project acceptance but increased the potential for community ownership.

The use of lay community volunteers in health promotion dissemination has been reported in many health projects during the last two decades. The case studies presented here provide a rich variety of ways to use local volunteers. Minority persons, like their counterparts in majority populations, are active volunteers and contributors to civic undertakings (Damberg, 1986). In the Zuni Indian Diabetes Project (Leonard, Leonard, & Wilson, 1985), volunteer aerobic instructors were trained and certified to lead classes in the community. Similarly, Hatch, Cunningham, Woods, and Snipes (1986) report on the successful use of church volunteers in a cardiovascular project for Black North Carolinians. Effective use of volunteers, which includes sound management practices, not only enhances overall program diffusion goals but also provides for increased local ownership opportunities.

What general principles, if any, are applicable to work in minority communities? While each community context is unique, several key principles are suggested from the published project experiences cited above as well as from the lessons presented in the case studies in this section. These include the following:

- *The process of actively involving the minority community or group is as important as the interventions implemented.* This process is earmarked by a true partnership (sometimes referred to as a "co-change" approach) with the community that supports local decision making in all phases of the project. Developing a local community board to oversee project planning and implementation is widely used.

- *Community analysis of health conditions and readiness for action should be done in collaboration with the community and local institutions.* This overall assessment reflects sensitivity to local needs, beliefs, and ethnic customs. The importance of family, church, social networks, and related resources must be well understood and used in the community mobilization efforts.

- *It is important to guard against the assumption that all members of a minority group are homogeneous and that one message or one channel of delivery will appeal to the entire group.* There can be considerable diversity among subgroups regarding values and attitudes. Frequent interaction with various target audiences or intermediaries may be required to gain an accurate assessment of acceptable language and/or role models.

- *Readiness of the minority community to work on a particular health issue may depend on the organizer's ability to integrate other community issues (e.g., crime prevention) into the overall project design.* Progress may be slowed until this accommodation takes place. Communities should be approached with "winning" strategies that build on self-esteem and civic pride.

- *In multiracial and ethnic communities more than one group can be involved in and can collaborate on a communitywide project.* This is reflected in the Richmond Stop Smoking case study. Use of community volunteers to support project interventions works well in both minority and nonminority communities.

- *Organizers of life-style change programs need to be sensitive to those members of minority groups whose impoverished basic living situation is far removed from the more affluent life-style images often portrayed in contemporary health promotion campaigns.* Specially designed bilingual and bicultural messages may be required. Those minority members experiencing high negative stress and social isolation may require additional supportive services to make progress in reducing health risks.

- *Conflicts over goals, strategies, personnel, and budgetary control surface in most health projects or demonstrations.* Project organizers and minority community representatives should acknowledge this likelihood early and devise general procedures for conflict resolution.

These seven general principles are, of course, not exhaustive. As more published accounts of successful work with minority communities and groups become available, our knowledge and experience will expand. The phrase *hard to reach* is often used in referring to special groups and minority persons. Perhaps such groups are not that hard to reach; rather, professionals may have found it *hard to hear* what it is that minority groups and others want and expect in a culturally diverse society.

REFERENCES

Braithwaite, R., & Lythcott, N. (1989). Community empowerment as a strategy for health promotion for black and other minority populations. *Journal of American Medical Association, 261*(2), 283-284.

Chng, C. (1984). Vietnamese in America: A case study in cross-cultural health education. *Health Values, 8*(3), 16-29.

Damberg, C. (1986). Strategies for promoting the health of minorities: The school-age population. *Health Values, 10*(3), 29.

Hatch, J., Cunningham, A., Woods, W., & Snipes, F. (1986). The Fitness Through Churches Project. *Hygie, 5*(3), 26-29.

Leonard, B., Leonard C., & Wilson, R. (1985). Zuni Diabetes Project. *Public Health Reports, 5*(3), 26-29.

Minkler, M., Frantz, S., & Wechsler, R. (1982). Social support and social action organizing in a "grey ghetto": The Tenderloin experience. *International Quarterly of Community Health Education, 3*, 3-14.

Orleans, C., Strecher, V., Schoenback, U., Salmon, M., & Blackmon, C. (1989). Smoking cessation initiatives for black Americans: Recommendations for research and intervention. *Health Education Research, 4*(1), 13-25.

Ramirez, A., MacKellar, D., & Gallion, K. (1988). Reaching minority audiences: A major challenge in cancer reduction. *Cancer Bulletin, 40*(6), 334-343.

U.S. Department of Health and Human Services. (1985). *Report of the Secretary's Task Force on Black and Minority Health* (Vol. 1). Washington, DC: Government Printing Office.

Chapter 13

A SU SALUD
Health Promotion in a
Mexican-American Border Community

CESAREO AMEZCUA
ALFRED McALISTER
AMELIE RAMIREZ
RENATO ESPINOZA

A broad program of community health promotion has been implemented in the low-income community of Eagle Pass, on the Mexican-
American border. The community intervention program described here
is a part of a larger study, known collectively as Programa A Su Salud
(To Your Health). Programa A Su Salud has been designed to demonstrate and study the effectiveness of mass media health messages using
culturally relevant role models selected from the local community.
Attention to the media messages and imitation of the role models
of positive behavior, such as quitting smoking, are reinforced when
printed materials are distributed by a cadre of volunteers recruited from
the community. Randomly selected members of the communities are
also offered one-to-one counseling and support to deal with specific
health risks. This chapter reports on several aspects of organizing the
project, including community analysis, design and initiation, implementation, barriers, program impact, and follow-up. The theoretical
base for intervention is also described.

The objectives of the program are to promote health behavior and
reduce risks among low-income persons in southwest Texas. Specific
aims are (a) to reduce the prevalence and prevent the onset of cigarette

smoking, (b) to modify eating habits related to cancer risk, (c) to reduce alcohol abuse, (d) to increase use of appropriate preventive services and practices, (e) to increase physical activity, and (f) to promote use of automobile seat belts.

The baseline prevalence of several risk behaviors was assessed at the onset of the program. Among adult males in the community, 38.1% were smokers and 38.1% reported heavy drinking, defined as more than six drinks on a single occasion. Among women over 30 years old, 55% reported no Pap smear within the last year, and 47.5% reported no breast self-examination within the last year. Among the population 50 years and older, 79.2% reported no colorectal exam within the last year. Finally, among the general population, 41% reported not having had their blood pressure taken within the last year, 56.5% reported no regular physical activity, 85.1% reported no fat avoidance in their regular diets, and 81.6% did not always use seat belts.

The conceptual approach guiding the organization of work within the community is the "lead agency" model, in which a single powerful organization is given responsibility for action, including whatever coalition building or coordination of others' work is needed to meet objectives. This may also be termed an "inside" approach in that the work in the community requires that the selected lead organization change from within—that is, by adopting new job descriptions. We have chosen this approach because it is, for the broadly supported objectives of our work, the least time-consuming way to create durable social change. Other organizing structures are, of course, possible, and are described in Chapters 4 and 6 of this book.

The Eagle Pass Programa A Su Salud was organized as a supporting unit for local public health services, which do not have staff for significant efforts beyond their primary mandates to serve clients in need of clinic-based services. The Texas Department of Health provides an authorizing and administrative oversight, viewing the Programa A Su Salud as an opportunity to test new approaches to community outreach and as a way to help deliver needed education to the study community. The establishment of regional and local health education officers is being considered by the Health Department and the Texas Legislature, with the Programa A Su Salud field staff serving as a model of what the duties of such a person might be.

THE SPECIAL NATURE OF EAGLE PASS:
COMMUNITY ANALYSIS

Eagle Pass, the county seat of Maverick County and the principal gateway to the Mexican state of Cohahuila, is located in southwest Texas, at the intersection of U.S. Highway 277 and U.S. Highway 57, about 140 miles west of San Antonio. According to the U.S. Census, the estimated population of the city and county in 1984 were 23,100 and 34,500, respectively. Over 93% of the population is classified as Mexican-American, with about 7% Anglo and less than 1% Black. The two main sources of economic activity are light industry and commerce. Two additional sources of economic support are various forms of public assistance, including social security, and the income generated by seasonal work that numerous migrant families perform in various states to the north, east, and west. In general, the economic situation in Eagle Pass is very depressed because of a strong dependence on the Mexican economy. The Mexican economy started to decline in 1982 when the dollar-peso exchange rate was $1 to 25 pesos, compared with the present rate of $1 to 2,300 pesos. As a consequence, the unemployment rate in Eagle Pass for 1987 was 28.4%, compared with 8.4% for the state of Texas and 6.2% for the nation as a whole.

Eagle Pass, as a border community with Mexico, combines the American way of politics and management with a Mexican cultural-behavioral background. Some of the main features of Eagle Pass culture include (a) a predominantly Roman Catholic population that respects the Virgin of Guadalupe as both a religious and an ethnic symbol; (b) a strong family orientation, with an average family size of 5.4 members; (3) frequent use of and reliance on home remedies (folk medicine); (4) eating habits that rely heavily on fat for cooking and fatty foods; and (5) heavy drinking (predominantly beer) that is strongly associated with a sense of celebration and escape.

The program staff participated in the identification of the key health concerns of the community. A series of seven focus groups were organized to obtain community input regarding health concerns, knowledge, and attitudes. Five of the groups were composed of members from the community at large and two were formed of opinion leaders, that is, public health providers and prominent political, commercial, and cultural figures.

THEORETICAL BASIS
FOR THE INTERVENTION PROGRAM

Theoretical frameworks for community health change and promotion programs are discussed in several chapters in this volume. In this case study several theoretical considerations guide the application of the concept of social reinforcement in community education. The fundamental principle is derived from Bandura's (1977) distinction between factors influencing acquisition and performance of new behaviors. Mediated communications can model new behaviors so that they are learned (acquired) on a cognitive level (i.e., the person knows how to perform the behavior). But cueing and feedback—direct social reinforcement—are usually needed for behavioral learning, that is, for actually performing the new behavior. Numerous studies of learning via mediated communication show that, when a complex behavior is being taught, effectiveness is sharply enhanced if supplementary interpersonal communication is provided for encouragement, feedback, and reinforcement (Bandura, 1965, 1977; Rogers, 1973; Sheffield, 1961).

In terms of the process model of behavior change, interpersonal communications may perform particular functions at each stage of the behavior change process. Therefore, the most unique and necessary function in the present intervention plan is the provision of cueing, feedback, and reinforcement to encourage acquisition and performance of the attitudes and behaviors that are modeled in the mediated communications.

Simple forms of verbal cueing and reinforcement that can be widely communicated through brief, direct contacts by volunteers were selected. Volunteers make a direct recommendation to their target audience to imitate role models in the A Su Salud television broadcasts and newspaper stories. For example, a volunteer might say, "Mrs. Perez, this coming Tuesday the television program listed here in the calendar will feature Mr. Carrillo. He has just quit smoking, and now that you too have decided to quit smoking, I'm sure that you will be interested in knowing how he is doing it." Volunteers also provide expressions of confidence, praise, and other positive feedback for any achievements, and encourage participants to continue their health-related efforts. These forms of social reinforcement are factors that have been found to be associated with successful cessation of smoking and with maintenance of behavior change (DiClemente & Prochaska, 1982; Mermelstein, Cohen, & Lichtenstein, 1983; Shiffman, 1982). In previous work by the principal investigator, the feasibility of this work was demonstrated when approximately 1,000 volunteers were trained to provide social reinforcement to facilitate the effectiveness of a television course in Finland (McAlister, Puska, Salonen, Tuomilehto, & Koskela, 1982; Puska et al., 1979). Many of the trained volunteers reported success in implementing the program, and significantly higher rates of maintenance of smoking cessation and weight loss were observed in the trained region compared with a region where only the media were provided. Similar programs have been described by others (e.g., Artz, Cooke, Meyers, & Stalgaitis, 1981; Flay, Hansen, Johnson, & Sobel, 1983; Kasl, 1978; Morisky, 1983; Worden, 1983).

PROGRAM DESIGN AND INITIATION

To encourage the concept of social reinforcement for paying attention to and imitating positive role models featured in the mass media messages, a community organization and training program was implemented. We followed the "lay leader" concept illustrated in the North Karelia Project (McAlister et al., 1982; Puska et al., 1979). The basic idea is for the change agent, in our case the staff of Programa A Su Salud, to recruit volunteers and train them in simple skills they can use to encourage and reinforce positive health behaviors of persons in the volunteers' natural social networks. This harnesses the "helper principle" and multiplies the efforts of the paid staff by extending direct social contacts to many more individuals in the community.

The project's printed and televised materials were designed to convey all the "technical" content for learning, that is, to contain the explanations and model behavior changes that promote health. Community volunteers can refer to those materials as needed. They need no expertise other than enthusiasm and good nature to encourage others to look at television programs or read newspaper feature stories and the ability to suggest and reinforce imitation of models tactfully.

Because of the close interdependence between the mass media campaigns and the community organization and training effort, these two components were developed and implemented simultaneously. In order to gain acceptance in the community, the staff hired to implement the community reinforcement component also made contact with various organizations, agencies, and services that affect the health and welfare of the community. These public relations activities formed a foundation for the expansion of the community reinforcement component during the program's second and third years.

To introduce the program activities in the Eagle Pass community, a press conference was held with the mayor and other individuals from the community who are involved in the study. The Sunday immediately following the press conference, a one-page printed flyer titled "Seis Asesinos Importantes Andan Sueltos en el Condado de Maverick" ("Six Important Assassins are Loose in Maverick County") was circulated. The flyer described the "six killers" as avoidable risk factors associated with premature death in the county. These were alcohol abuse, cigarette smoking, obesity and diet, lack of medical checkups, lack of seat belt usage, and pollution. Also described were the health problems caused by or associated with these six risk factors. The flyer promoted the times the television programs were to air and provided a checklist of preventive steps readers could take. The flyer was placed in the local newspaper, the *Eagle Pass News Guide*, and distributed to 5,000 homes. The flyer was also included in the *Zocalo*, the Spanish-language newspaper distributed from Piedras Negras, the Mexican community just across the border from Eagle Pass, with a circulation of 5,000 among Eagle Pass residents (see Figure 13.1).

DEVELOPMENT AND IMPLEMENTATION
OF THE MASS MEDIA COMPONENT

Media development, along with the efforts needed to enlist the cooperation of local broadcasters, will be described first. Two sets of television programs were developed and produced. The first consisted of 15 programs ranging in length from 5 to 10 minutes. In these programs the role models and health information were presented in a news format, with well-known community physicians serving as spokespersons for the program. The second television series consisted of four 30-minute programs presented in a minidocumentary format. In both sets of programs a health education specialist from the community served as narrator, with the role models being the central topic of interest.

For the 30-minute programs, role models who had recently made health changes were recruited from the community. The rationale for selecting individuals from the community rather than hiring professional actors had three bases. First, researchers have demonstrated that an audience is more likely to be persuaded by a communicator if they perceive the communicator to be similar to themselves. Role models recruited from the community were expected to be perceived as much

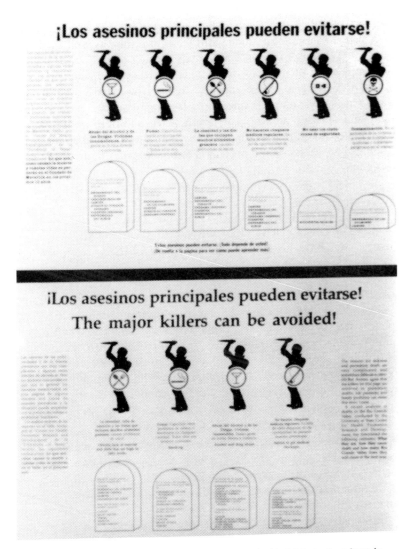

NOTE: Alerting the Community. Six important "assassins" (health risk factors) are loose in Maverick County.

Figure 13.1. The "Six Killers" Flyer

more similar to viewers than would professional actors. Second, it was naturally less expensive to recruit volunteers to participate in our program than to hire actors. Finally, the recruitment of locals had proven successful in the Finnish studies, and there was no reason to suspect that it would not be successful in our program as well.

In the television programs, individuals serving as role models discussed what made them decide to change, how they changed, and how they felt now because of the change. Changes included going in for medical checkups, stopping smoking, efforts and successes in losing weight, and starting an exercise program. In addition, nonsmoking teenagers were recruited to discuss why they do not smoke and how they avoid and/or overcome pressures to smoke from their peers and advertising.

IMPLEMENTATION OF THE COMMUNITY REINFORCEMENT COMPONENT: ROLES AND RESPONSIBILITIES

Since the program strategy is for paid community workers to identify, recruit, train, and supervise volunteers from diverse organizations and networks, volunteers were expected to perform simple skills: (a) Contact other persons and tell them about the television and other programs including role models for behavior change, (b) encourage attention to the role models, and (c) encourage and reinforce imitative behaviors. These simple skills are modeled by the community workers and learned through brief role-play events conducted during the program staff's regular contact with volunteers.

The Role of the Community Workers

The two community workers are very well-known and highly respected women with high school-level educational backgrounds. One of them is a very involved and committed volunteer in different areas of this community and has a strong leadership background. These persons were selected as community workers because they are very aware of the differences between professional values and local cultural values.

Their primary duties consist of making contacts (phone/home visits) to recruit volunteers, keeping in touch with these volunteers, distributing calendars and other printed materials, and conducting other activities at least once a month to encourage attention to the Programa

A Su Salud role model messages and to reinforce positive responses, such as attempts to stop smoking. In addition, the community workers provided individualized referral, counseling, and social support for a randomly selected sample of individuals as part of another component of the program.

The Role of the Volunteers

The role of volunteers is at the core of this work, with people being asked to offer their assistance in the "fight" against the "six killers," a program theme developed out of the focus groups conducted in Eagle Pass in 1985. The volunteers represent both sides: the project guidelines and the community reaction/response to the project guidelines.

Among the basic characteristics sought in volunteers we include being respected within their neighborhoods or other natural social networks, willingness to serve their community, leadership personality to some degree, and organization and discipline.

Each month the volunteers attend a meeting along with the community workers and the community program director. During this meeting they evaluate their work, identify the main barriers to development of the project, and identify the main positive aspects of their work. During these meetings, the next month's programs are previewed so that the volunteers can become more familiar with next topic. Volunteers also receive additional coaching in social reinforcement skills.

The volunteers are taught some basic cultural guidelines to help them be more successful in their community work. Among the suggestions are to respect people's schedules, to maintain confidentiality in their contacts, and never to approach a person of the opposite sex who is alone in the house. Basic training techniques included role playing, the proper use of positive social reinforcement, and how to avoid prejudice, criticism, and conflict. To monitor implementation of community action, an administrative system has been established to record progress.

In the first year of the project, the volunteers were recruited from randomly selected blocks from throughout the community. This strategy was dictated by the need to maintain the research design. The volunteers were then trained to interact with their immediate neighbors, distributing to them materials that described the project and alerted them to the upcoming mass media messages. In the second and third years, volunteers were recruited not only to reach their neighbors, but also to operate through social contacts in other settings, such as schools, businesses, social agencies, health clinics, religious organizations, food stores, and various other work sites.

The volunteers' work is centered on the distribution of printed guides that contain the schedules of television programs and newspaper articles containing health information and featuring role models who have made behavioral changes toward healthier life-styles (see Figure 13.2). These calendars include information on the reverse page in English and Spanish focusing on a specific topic related to the health risk behaviors being featured in the media campaign. The volunteers' approach to their neighbors, co-workers, customers, clients, or companions at church is made formal and given a focus by this viewing guide, which is issued at six-week intervals to allow opportunities for recontacting persons specifically to discuss role modeling and possible imitation of role models (see Figure 13.3).

NETWORKS, ORGANIZATIONS, AND
SOCIAL REINFORCEMENT

The recruitment of additional volunteers for the second year of the project began in September 1986. With one full-time and four half-time community workers putting in long hours, one year later the total number of volunteers had reached 874 individuals. Both individual and group presentations were made in the recruitment effort, which featured the concept of "fighting the six killers" and emphasized the simplicity of the volunteers' role. All available natural social systems that could be used for social reinforcement were tapped, including voluntary and neighborhood organizations such as civic groups and sports clubs. The volunteer block leader approach of the first year was expanded to make training available throughout the city of Eagle Pass. Shopkeepers and persons in other key locations were also recruited for instruction in how they could contribute to the program by distributing printed materials and providing social reinforcement for imitation of role models.

The volunteers enroll formally by completing or assisting in the completion of a "volunteer's sheet," which asks for some personal and background data, information about the volunteer's interests, and the number of persons the volunteer feels he or she can reach to encourage and reinforce.

In addition to their formal social reinforcement role, the volunteers also serve the program by identifying potential role models in their own

NOTE: Volunteers' main activity is the distribution of the monthly calendars. While doing this, they provide social reinforcement.

Figure 13.2. The Volunteers

267

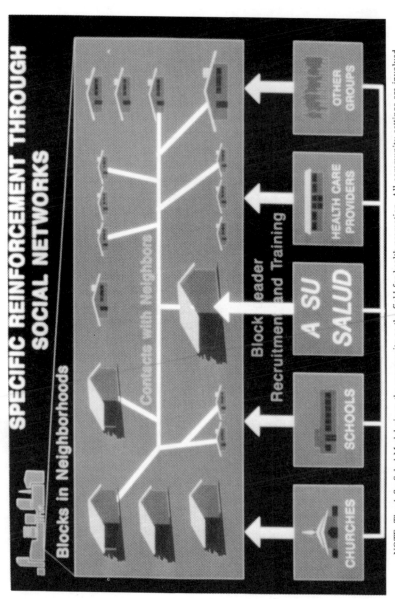

NOTE: The A Su Salud Model views the community as the field for health promotion. All community settings are involved.

Figure 13.3. The Community

social networks. These are individuals from the community who have made recent positive changes in one of more of the health-related behaviors that will be featured in the media campaigns. The need for role models averages about five different people per week in the October to March media campaign period.

The social reinforcement work is distributed across seven categories of networks or organizations, as shown in Figure 13.4. Each of these categories is discussed in turn below.

(1) Neighborhoods. Based at the city's neighborhood centers, we are recruiting volunteers to represent the program in the areas of their residences, usually only their own blocks or nearby houses on their streets.

(2) Business settings. Places of business where large numbers of customers are served and recruited to support A Su Salud as part of their service to customers. These include grocery stores, restaurants, and various shops and stores. Under this category we include work sites with more than 50 employees.

(3) Government. All federal, state, and local government units are being involved so as to reach their employees and the persons for whom they provide service.

(4) Social clubs. Various community service organizations, such as the Lions Club, are being asked to help serve their members in association with the A Su Salud community work.

(5) Health care providers. Because most smokers in Eagle Pass, the great majority of them Mexican-American men, are reluctant to attend group sessions, health care staff are taught simple interaction skills for brief cueing and reinforcement as part of the natural handling of patients who smoke. Health care providers are also potentially powerful sources of reinforcement for new eating habits.

Health care providers are asked to join the A Su Salud program by alerting, encouraging, and reinforcing their patients/clients about the "six killers" and the need to fight them. Emphasis is put on smoking cessation. The key strategy is for health care providers to perform this type of help/counseling as part of their daily professional routines. The main content of their message to their patients/clients is alerting, encouraging, reinforcing, and asking their patients/clients to observe and imitate the media role models. An example of a health care provider's intervention would be a doctor who, while prescribing medication to a hypertensive patient, says, "At the same time, it would be a good idea to watch these TV programs, because they can help you in taking care of yourself by quitting smoking and changing your eating

NOTE: These are persons from within the community who tell about their own experiences in changing from unhealthy life-styles to healthier ones.

Figure 13.4 The Role Models

habits." A TV, radio, and newspaper guide to A Su Salud programming is distributed at appropriate times to each health care professional.

The health care providers approached by A Su Salud include physicians, nurses (RNs, LVNs), pharmacists, lab technicians, mental health counselors, dietitians, and community health educators. Virtually all of the medical care providers are cooperating in this work, as are all pharmacists. The medical care providers typically designate their staff to "volunteer," but we have found them to be reasonably enthusiastic in carrying out the work. A Su Salud community workers opened their involvement for 1986 through participation with other health-related organizations in Eagle Pass in a "health fair."

(6) Education settings. With appropriate administrative approval and support, school principals, school nurses, counselors, health teachers, and other teachers are involved with the A Su Salud social reinforcement program. Two levels of intervention have been applied to the school system: one at the elementary school level and one at the junior high and high school level.

The key volunteers at the elementary level are the school principals, contacted at the beginning of the school year, and the school nurses, who are asked to serve as the bridge between A Su Salud and the teachers. Nurses are asked to deliver the monthly calendars to all teachers, requesting that they make positive statements about A Su Salud to the students, that they post the calendar, and in general convey simple general messages to the children. These include alerting students to A Su Salud and telling them not to nag parents about smoking but to encourage them to use the calendar to pay attention to the media messages and to imitate those behaviors. The school libraries received a copy of a teacher's manual and a videocassette-based role-play activity to teach children how to resist peer pressure to smoke and use drugs. The refusal skills training is designed to prevent the onset of cigarette smoking and drug use. Most teachers have conducted at least one training session on peer pressure resistance.

A similar procedure has been followed with the two junior highs and the high school. However, in addition to the materials for the libraries for use by the teachers, school nurses are asked to encourage students to come visit them during school hours regarding smoking and drug issues. The peer pressure training is delivered by teachers with assistance from A Su Salud staff. Also, radio spot and TV skit contests on refusing smoking and drugs have been conducted in each of the three schools. Winners received small cash prizes provided by A Su Salud, and their entries were aired by the local FM radio station and television channels.

(7) Religious organizations. Roman Catholic churches and a Seventh Day Adventist Church are very involved in the A Su Salud project. The Seventh Day Adventist Church provides significant help to the project because this denomination emphasizes within its beliefs the fight against cigarette smoking, promotes good nutritional habits, and combats alcohol and drug abuse. The majority of the city's population is Roman Catholic, and consequently the social influence of this religious denomination over the whole community is very strong. There are 24 different churches that are cooperating with the community project. These have provided a large number of especially active and enthusiastic volunteers.

PROMOTING ENVIRONMENTAL CHANGE
AND LONG-TERM MAINTENANCE

The concept of environmental change may be considered to be particularly relevant to the modification of behavior in communities. Smoking restrictions can alter social norms. Families prepare and eat together what is commonly available in grocery stores, people eat together in restaurants that serve the community, and children are presented with nearly identical selections in school cafeterias. The model of environmental change for this project is derived from the successful experiences of the North Karelia Project in Finland (McAlister et al., 1982).

The basic notion is to promote and organize voter or consumer demand to increase decision makers' or producers' and sellers' perception of the relative profitability of recommended (e.g., produce) and discouraged (e.g., lard) goods. In practice this is often a difficult and incremental process that may be opposed by natural supply and price factors—for example, the fact that lard is one of the cheapest sources of calories available. The process has three distinct elements: (a) consumer and voter education/awareness to influence the population's expressed desire for products, (b) mobilization of consumers and voters to focus and intensify pressure, and (c) consultation with political officeholders, administrators, and producers and sellers to shape their response to consumers and voters by selecting new policies, altering emphasis of promotion, and so on.

These actions have been carried out by different
community system that have been activated. The mass
the consumer education/awareness and present role __
related to environmental change. A communitywide campaign was
launched to get the city council to pass a smoking ordinance. Following
a presentation of the issue to a regular session of the council, letters of
support were secured from opinion leaders, in particular from those in
health-related organizations and agencies. Businessmen and other civic
leaders were approached for support; merchants were encouraged to
cease or restrict their sale of tobacco voluntarily, resulting in some
restrictions on smoking areas at a large discount store, an insurance
agency, and three popular restaurants and cafeterias. At least three
businesses discontinued selling tobacco products. Program volunteers
were encouraged to write letters to their council members and petitions
were circulated. After about a year of effort, a smoking restriction
ordinance has been approved, patterned after a model ordinance approved by the City Council of Austin two years before.

BARRIERS TO COMMUNITY ORGANIZATION

In its efforts to reach the community, the program has had to deal
with a number of barriers that make it difficult to contact people and
maintain communication. Some of these barriers can be characterized
as social-environmental in nature. One problem encountered by community workers and volunteers alike is having to compete for people's
attention with a variety of door-to-door salespeople, religious outreach
workers, and other organizations that regularly canvas neighborhoods,
including our own project's independent research and evaluation survey workers. A second difficulty is the large number of households from
which many or all of the members migrate for extended periods to
harvest the fields in other states. A third difficulty stems from prejudice
against the health professions, which are seen both as too academic and
too business oriented, rather than as oriented to human service. Finally,
strained relations among neighbors, in part due to the overall economic
depression, make it hard to reach people. Rather than survey questions
or life-style advice, what many say they want is concrete help in the
form of jobs and money.

A second category of barriers reported by the Programa A Su Salud
outreach community workers and volunteers can be described as having

to do with individual or personal factors. The first is what community workers perceive as a high level of personal stress, created by the economic conditions of many families who suffer chronic unemployment and hopelessness. A second difficulty comes from extreme forms of shyness that interfere with the kind of social interactions required for the social reinforcement component to operate. A third difficulty, especially for the neighborhood work, is related to the small-town dynamics of social control, gossip, and suspicion of one's neighbor's motives. Husbands do not like to see their wives interacting with other women, attending meetings, or participating in social gatherings that they do not control. Finally, there is a great deal of justified fear and distrust of "official-looking" people who come around asking questions. A large number of individuals and families in the community are recipients of various forms of public assistance and fear having their eligibility questioned. The fear of mistreatment by immigration officials, drug investigators, and other types of authorities is always present.

STRATEGIES USED TO OVERCOME BARRIERS

In order to break the relative social isolation of some of these families, community workers and volunteers were encouraged to organize and host block parties to help neighbors get to know each other, as a first step toward providing health-related information and reinforcing positive changes in life-styles. Another strategy used to maintain the morale and commitment of the volunteers is that of holding periodic family-oriented picnics in nearby parks. All the modest expenses incurred have been covered by the participants themselves in the form of potluck meals and sharing of food and beverages at the outings. Volunteers also attend monthly meetings with the community workers. They make informal reports of their activities, consult about problems they have encountered, and get positive reinforcement from the staff about their peers. They are also provided with the opportunity to learn and practice social skills that they in turn can use in their outreach efforts.

As a regular part of the operation of A Su Salud, the site director maintains close relations with community leaders and local authorities. Special attention is paid to relations with the local health care community, including private practitioners and public health officials. Regular contacts with mass media representatives are critical for the maintenance and expansion of the work of A Su Salud. The site director and central staff have established close working relationships with various television, radio, and print media outlets in Eagle Pass and Piedras Negras, the Mexican border city across the Rio Grande. In addition to traditional media, A Su Salud messages have been presented through several local newsletters, in electronic displays in banks and stores, and through buttons and T-shirts. Therefore, the name recognition of the program in the city is very high.

Finally, once a year a formal banquet is held, with the participation of civic leaders and local authorities, to recognize outstanding volunteers and to give awards and certificates of recognition to all the major participants in A Su Salud activities. The banquet and awards are financed through fund-raisers and solicitations from organizations and businesses in the community, and the certificates are provided by the sponsor of the program, the University of Texas Health Science Center at Houston.

PRELIMINARY RESULTS

As part of the process evaluation of the program, volunteers were interviewed systematically by the community workers during the summer of 1987. The 399 volunteers who completed those interviews represented the major categories of organizations and networks in the community: 37% operated within commercial/work-site networks, 30% in neighborhoods, and 21% in religious organizations. The rest included educators, health care providers, government agency employees, and social/fraternal club officers.

These volunteers reported a total of 7,860 contacts, or an average of almost 20 each. These included 6,098 adults and 1,762 young people. The interviewed volunteers reported that they had viewed an average of approximately 10 programs featuring role models. Among the interviewed volunteers, 17 reported cessation of smoking, 5 reported changes in drinking, and 196 reported obtaining preventive care from physicians or clinics. Changes in eating habits were reported by 269 volunteers, and 226 said they had increased exercise.

A more extensive interview was completed by 166 of the 399 most active volunteers. These were selected because they had information about changes among people they contacted. Of these volunteers, 120 were neighborhood-based and 27 were involved through their work sites or commercial locations. These volunteers contacted an average of more than 20 persons each. They reported that the people they contacted had viewed an average of approximately 9 programs featuring role models. Among the contacted persons, 21 were reported to have quit smoking. These most active volunteers reported 10 persons changing alcohol use, 328 receiving needed preventive health care, 368 changing diet, and 353 increasing exercise.

SUMMARY AND CONCLUSION

A broad program of community health promotion has been implemented in a low-income community on the U.S.-Mexico border. The efforts include an intensive media campaign featuring role models of positive behavior (i.e., smoking cessation), recruitment of several hundred volunteers to promote imitation of the role models, and community organization to stimulate changes in policies that could influence health behavior (i.e., a city ordinance to restrict smoking). The work in Eagle Pass is being conducted as part of a long-term, partly randomized study of health promotion in which effects on behavior are assessed by surveys and, in the case of smoking cessation, biochemical validation of self-reports. Although the results of the experimental evaluation are not yet available, the present findings clearly demonstrate the feasibility and community acceptance of the theory-based model of change that is being tested.

REFERENCES

Artz, L., Cooke, C., Meyers, A., & Stalgaitis, P. (1981). Community change agents and health interventions: Hypertension screening. *American Journal of Community Psychology, 9*, 361-367.

Bandura, A. (1965). Vicarious processes: A case of no-trial learning. In L. Berkowitz (Ed.), *Advances in experimental social psychology* (Vol. 3). New York: Academic Press.

Bandura, A. (1977). *Social learning theory.* Englewood Cliffs, NJ: Prentice-Hall.

DiClemente, C. C., & Prochaska, J. O. (1982). Self-change and therapy change of smoking behavior: A comparison of processes of change in cessation and maintenance. *Addictive Behaviors, 7*, 133-142.

Flay, B. R., Hansen, W. B., Johnson, C. A., & Sobel, J. L. (1983, July). *Involvement of children in motivating smoking parents to quit smoking with a television program.* Paper prepared for the Health Behavior Research Institute, University of Southern California, and presented at the Fifth World Conference on Smoking and Health, Winnipeg, Manitoba, Canada.

Kasl, S. V. (1978). A social-psychological perspective on successful community control of high blood pressure: A review. *Journal of Behavioral Medicine, 1*, 347-381.

McAlister, A., Puska, P., Salonen, J. T., Tuomilehto, J., & Koskela, K. (1982). Theory and action for health promotion; Illustrations from the North Karelia Project. *American Journal of Public Health, 72(1)*, 43-50.

Mermelstein, R., Cohen, S., & Lichtenstein, E. (1983, August). *Psychosocial stress, social support and smoking cessation and maintenance.* Paper presented at the annual meeting of the American Psychological Association, Anaheim, CA.

Morisky, D. D. (1983). Five-year blood-pressure control and mortality following health education for hypertensive patients. *American Journal of Public Health, 73*, 153-161.

Puska, P., Tuomilehto, T., Salonen, J., Neittaanmaki, L., Maki, J., Virtamo, J., Nissinen, A., Koskela, K., & Takalo, T. (1979). Changes in community risk factors during comprehensive five-year community programme to control cardiovascular diseases (North Karelia Project). *British Medical Journal, 2(6198)*, 1173-1178.

Rogers, E. (1973). *Communication strategies for family planning.* New York: Free Press.

Sheffield, F. D. (1961). Theoretical considerations in the learning of complex sequential tasks from demonstration and practice. In A. A. Lumsdaine (Ed), *Student response in programmed instruction.* Washington, DC: National Academy of Sciences, National Research Council.

Shiffman, F. (1982). Relapse from smoking cessation: A situational analysis. *Journal of Counseling and Clinical Psychology, 50*, 71-86.

Worden, J. K. (1983, November). *Adult communication skills training to prevent adolescent smoking.* Paper presented at the annual meeting of the American Public Health Association, Dallas, TX.

Chapter 14

RICHMOND QUITS SMOKING
A Minority Community Fights for Health

ENID FALLICK HUNKELER
EDITH M. DAVIS
BESSANDERSON McNEIL
JAMES W. POWELL
MICHAEL R. POLEN

Richmond, California, a proud city known for its fierce autonomy and strong community bonding, was chosen as the site of a communitywide campaign to reduce high rates of cigarette smoking in a predominantly African-American community. A partnership of the Kaiser Permanente Medical Care Program (KPMCP), the community of Richmond, and research institutes at the nearby University of California, Berkeley, was formed to launch this project. The guiding assumption of the project was that changing the health norms and beliefs of an entire community will change the health habits of individuals.

A community-based approach to the problem of high smoking rates among African-Americans seemed appropriate for two reasons: first,

AUTHORS' NOTE: We would like to thank the following people for reviewing and commenting on the manuscript: S. Leonard Syme, Ph.D.; Troy Duster, Ph.D.; Edmund E. Van Brunt, M.D.; Bruce H. Fireman, M.A.; Nancy Krieger, Ph.D.; Elaine Stone, Ph.D., M.P.H.; R. Eric Weston, Ph.D.; Marc Rivo, M.D., M.P.H.; Charles L. Curry, M.D.; Jessie Gruman, Ph.D.; and Michael Pertschuk, J.D. We also thank our coinvestigators: J. Ronald Powell, M.D.; Thomas Vogt, M.D., M.P.H.; and Donald P. Fischer, M.D. For their consulting services, we thank Mario A. Orlandi, Ph.D., M.P.H.; John Hatch, Ph.D.; and Nicholas Jewell, Ph.D. Finally, we thank Patricia I. Davis, M.P.H.; Karen Young-Ervin, M.P.H.; Kay Gordon, M.P.H.; Larry D. Hill, M.P.A.; Tamara Baltar; Diana W. Holt; the Richmond Quits Smoking Community Advisory Board; and the people of Richmond, California, for their contributions to the project. Support for this research was provided by National Cancer Institute Grant No. SRC 5 R18 CA39262.

because Blacks have a long history of using community organization to attain social and political goals (Danigelis, 1982; Hessler & Beavert, 1982), and second, because smoking occurs in a social and cultural context (Breslow, 1982; Dekker, 1976; Syme & Alcalay, 1982). Although the prevalence of smoking among Blacks has decreased since 1965 (Fiore et al., 1989), a larger proportion of Blacks than Whites are current smokers (U.S. Department of Health and Human Services, 1983). However, most Black smokers want to quit (Moss, 1979). We believed fewer people would smoke if the social and cultural context could be modified in specific ways to be more conducive to non-smoking.

The particular targets of this community intervention were diverse. We attempted to remove the obvious stimuli in the community that promote smoking and to encourage formal and informal norms against smoking. We promoted smoking as "unhip," "uncool," and socially undesirable behavior. The program encouraged no-smoke policies in the workplace and nonsmoking in public places as well as in private homes. We wanted to increase the active support that people trying to quit received from those close to them, as well as to provide to the public-at-large accessible and relevant information about effective smoking cessation techniques. The key element in all these efforts was making the public aware that smoking is a health problem worthy of action at the community level. We believed that a program of this type could weaken the effect of the powerful, widely prevalent, and continuous forces that now encourage and sustain smoking. If this view is correct, community intervention offers the possibility of significant long-term success in reducing cigarette smoking.

The program attempted to raise consciousness about smoking by integrating program components into existing communication channels and social structures to draw attention to the issue and to promote nonsmoking. The program was tailored for a predominantly African-American community by framing the smoking issue in ways relevant to Black experiences. We used a model of community organization that viewed members of the community as potentially powerful allies; the project's role was to assist them in mobilizing their power against smoking.

The overall goal was to create an environment of community support in which smokers can be helped to quit the habit. A specific goal was to reduce smoking by 20% among Richmond's Black population. This case study is a chronology of the project through completion of three of the five phases of community organization for health promotion described in Chapter 3: community analysis, design and initiation, and implementation. We also describe the beginnings of the fourth phase, maintenance and consolidation, and the fifth phase, dissemination and reassessment. The project is currently in its fifth year.

COMMUNITY ANALYSIS

In March 1984, a group of health service researchers from the KPMCP in Northern California began designing a program to reduce cigarette smoking among Blacks in response to a request for applications for such programs from the National Cancer Institute (NCI). The KPMCP, a large prepayment group practice health maintenance organization, was an appropriate organization to develop the project because it had a medical center in Richmond providing services to about 34% of the city's population. Richmond was ideal because it had a large Black population and many resources that could be recruited for the effort.

Richmond is located in Contra Costa County, in the San Francisco Bay Area. According to the 1980 U.S. Census, the population was 74,676, including 35,799 Blacks (47.9%) and 29,664 Whites (39.7%) (U.S. Department of Commerce, 1983). About 53% of Richmond residents were female. Among Blacks, the median ages of men and women were 23.9 and 26.9 years, respectively; among Whites, the median ages of men and women were 35.6 and 40.6 years, respectively. The median family income for Blacks in 1979 was $14,435, compared with a median family income for Whites of $21,265. Once the site of major shipyards during and after World War II, the city saw economic decline during the 1970s and early 1980s, but has been on the upswing in the past several years, with plans for revived downtown and waterfront-port areas.

The KPMCP has more than 40 years' experience as a health care provider in Richmond and is accountable to that community because membership in the health plan is voluntary. The organization also has a wide array of resources that it is willing to donate to the project and that could potentially be used to help maintain the effort after federal funding ended.

Background information on Richmond was gathered by a planning team that included a Black health professional and longtime Richmond resident, a Black smoking cessation counselor who had extensive experience with Black smokers, a White smoking cessation counselor from the Multiple Risk Factor Intervention Trial (Ockene, Hymowitz, Sexton, & Broste, 1982), and a White research investigator with extensive experience in community organizing and in evaluating health education programs. The members of the planning team all had strong personal as well as professional commitment to the project.

Background data were gathered from the 1980 U.S. census, city and state planning agencies, and a multiphasic examination data bank of KPMCP health plan members in Richmond. Extensive interviews and discussions with a broad array of Richmond leaders and community organizers were conducted to solicit ideas and support; at the same time, a population-based survey of 200 people in Richmond suggested that a majority of Black smokers wanted to quit. Special efforts were made to seek out community leaders who might be critical of the project. Everyone on the planning team participated in discussions with people from Richmond.

The first interviews and discussions were set up with Richmond's Black leaders to obtain both their initial reactions to the idea of the project and information about previous local community-organizing efforts. At that point, we planned to target only Blacks. Black leaders suggested a change: They thought the program should maintain a focus on Blacks but should involve and offer services to all racial groups. They reasoned that it would be inappropriate, as well as politically awkward, to organize a communitywide project for a single racial group in a multiracial city of this relatively small size.

Richmond had two features that are traditional sources of strength in African-American communities: strong kinship ties (Billingsley, 1974; Stack, 1974) and a strong and influential church presence (Childs, 1980; Frazier, 1964). Community mobilization efforts that fail to take these features into account may run a high risk of failure. The community also had a number of other characteristics that offered opportunities for a community-based approach:

- a long history of community mobilization and organization (Richmond was part of the federal Model Cities Program in the 1960s and had well-developed neighborhood councils and crime-watch groups.)
- many separate voluntary organizations, including a separate Black Chamber of Commerce
- a strong sense of community pride
- a high regard for families and children
- an investment in the city's maintaining a positive public image

Richmond also had certain features that could be seen as barriers to a program of this type:

- absence of local newspaper, radio, or television with a primary focus on Richmond
- the fact that only one-third of the African-Americans who lived in Richmond worked there
- a suspicion of outsiders, particularly those who proposed to come in and "help the community"
- more public concern over the problems of crime and drug abuse than over cigarette smoking
- billboards and magazines promoting smoking, particularly among Blacks

Community leaders were sophisticated in their knowledge of federal programs and many were suspicious of those programs from past experience. Before lending their support to the project, these leaders wanted specific information about what the project would really do, where the money would go, who would get the jobs, who would control the project, and what the community would be left with when it was over.

Community leaders expressed concern over the role smoking might have in the high cancer rate in the area noted by the County Health Department (Contra Costa County Health Services Department, 1986). However, although smoking was seen as a serious health problem, people tended to view the solution as requiring individual actions by smokers rather than action at the community level. Issues such as abuse of illegal drugs were seen as more susceptible to community intervention, although tobacco is addictive and a gateway drug. Thus we expected that mobilizing the community around smoking would be difficult. However, we persisted, because smoking is still a major health hazard affecting great numbers of people.

DESIGN AND INITIATION

During the community analysis phase conducted by KPMCP when the project was first being conceptualized, an informal, predominantly Black working group of 20 Richmond community leaders, organizers, and medical providers was organized. This group helped formulate project activities, suggested resources that could be mobilized, provided and gathered letters of support for the final proposal, and publicly supported the project at an NCI site visit.

The project finally funded by NCI was titled Community Mobilization for Smoking Cessation and was referred to in the community as the Richmond Quits Smoking Project (RQSP). It was designed as a five-year study to develop and evaluate an intensive communitywide mobilization to reduce the prevalence of cigarette smoking in a predominantly African-American community. The project had three phases: (a) a baseline household prevalence survey; (b) a programmatic phase, which included continuous field observations by sociologists with previous experience in the ethnography of Black communities and systematic collection of data on the number and type of campaign activities conducted and who participated in them; and (c) a follow-up household prevalence survey.

Success was to be determined in two ways. First, the success of the smoking cessation campaign would be determined by comparing change in prevalence of cigarette smoking among Blacks in Richmond, estimated via independent household surveys of randomly selected adult residents before and after the cessation campaign, to change in prevalence among Blacks elsewhere in the San Francisco Bay Area and throughout the nation in the same time period. An estimate of the net reduction in prevalence of smoking in Richmond would be made by subtracting the change in local or national comparison groups, respectively, from the change in Richmond. Local comparison data are being obtained from a study of cancer awareness among Blacks in Oakland and San Francisco; national comparison data will come from the National Health Interview Survey conducted by the National Center for Health Statistics.

Second, the field observation component would document community reaction to project activities. It would chronicle and assess changes in smoking norms, values, and practices in Richmond during the course of the project. If the prevalence of smoking did not decline immediately but changes in smoking norms and etiquette did occur, we could still predict a reduction in smoking prevalence over time.

The Survey Research Center of the University of California at Berkeley conducted the first of our two surveys in Richmond in the spring of 1986. Interviews were completed with 1,832 Richmond residents aged 20 years and older, including 1,324 Blacks and 508 non-Blacks living in the 21 census-designated neighborhoods in which Blacks made up at least 25% of the population.

Among Blacks in the baseline survey, 46% of the men and 38% of the women were current cigarette smokers. At all ages, men and women with lower incomes and lower educational levels were more likely to be current smokers. Some 64% of the unemployed smoked, and they were twice as likely as employed smokers to smoke heavily (25 cigarettes per day or more). Awareness of the health risks associated with smoking was widespread, even among smokers. For example, over 90% of both smokers and nonsmokers agreed that smoking was harmful to the smoker's health. Even 70% of the smokers agreed that smoking was harmful to the health of nonsmokers, although smokers were more likely than nonsmokers to think that cigarette smoke was not at all harmful to nonsmokers (13% versus 6%). More than one-third of the smokers perceived at least some pressure to quit from people around them; family and household members were the most frequently cited influences, followed by physicians, friends, and co-workers. A total of 60% of smokers agreed with the statement, "Nonsmokers shouldn't make such a fuss about other people smoking," compared with 43% of nonsmokers.

Much of this information directly influenced aspects of the smoking cessation campaign. Perhaps most important, the knowledge that a majority of smokers thought that nonsmokers were making too much of a fuss about smoking reaffirmed our desire to emphasize the benefits of nonsmoking instead of portraying negative images of smokers. Smoking's harmful health effects were already well known in this community, and smokers were already perceiving some pressures to quit from individuals around them. The challenge for the intervention was to convert this knowledge and those pressures into a community-wide campaign.

The RQSP integrated elements suggested by previous research into one comprehensive and tailored campaign. The project drew on government guidelines for creating minority health education programs, community-based programs among Blacks (Cooke & Meyers, 1983; Eng, Hatch, & Callan, 1985; Hatch, 1981; Hatch & Lovelace, 1980), and communitywide health promotion efforts developed at North Karelia, Stanford University, Minnesota, and Rhode Island, referenced elsewhere in this book, and on the results of the community analysis. Some of the recommended elements included the following:

- basing the smoking cessation campaign in deeply rooted and respected community groups and organizations, such as churches, schools, and neighborhood councils
- adapting techniques to fit both the cultural values and time constraints of community members

- being comprehensive, by placing nonsmoking behavior within the total context of health, sex, school, parents, authority figures, and personal growth and development
- conveying a positive image for nonsmoking, emphasizing such attractive elements as freedom, emancipation, independence, and nonconformity
- emphasizing acceptability by peers
- encouraging support from respected leaders and celebrities
- involving the medical community in the campaign so that the message is reinforced not only by friends, neighbors, media, and celebrities, but also by doctors and nurses
- using community volunteers who are already serving as counselors and advisers in times of crisis and need
- using films and videotape productions to involve people directly, increase their status in the community, draw on their expertise, and enhance their self-esteem and community pride
- capturing the interest and enthusiasm of children and teenagers in the campaign by using celebrities, a music video, training in media skills, and secondarily eliciting interest of parents and families in the campaign

Based on the results of these prior community-based efforts and the specific community analysis of Richmond, the designers of the program thought that it would be necessary (a) to mobilize both smokers and nonsmokers, (b) to create different messages and activities for different segments of the Black population, (c) to mobilize resources outside the geographical boundaries of Richmond that affected the community significantly (e.g., hospitals in surrounding areas), and (d) to develop specific plans for maintenance of the effort after federal funding ended. The program included eight principal activities, each of which was designed to relate to and maximize the impact of the others:

(1) Establish and maintain a Community Advisory Board to provide a formal structure to assure significant community input to the project.
(2) Train physicians and other medical providers, the respected authorities on health, to counsel quitters.
(3) Create media campaigns (e.g., videos, bus posters, billboards, television spots) to focus attention on the smoking issue and promote nonsmoking in a noticeable, ongoing manner.
(4) Develop and offer specially tailored stop-smoking materials and services.
(5) Recruit and mobilize community organizations, churches, and work sites to conduct campaign activities, placing special emphasis on

organizations indigenous to African-American communities that could reach the unemployed and those who had dropped out of school.

(6) Hold communitywide events with a smoking focus, for example, "quit nights."

(7) Establish and maintain programs in the schools.

(8) Recruit and train volunteers to support individual smokers' efforts to quit and sustain the campaign after federal funding ends.

The strategy was to identify communication channels by focusing on organizations that influenced Blacks, health, or both and convincing these organizations to initiate activities to reduce smoking among Blacks. For example, organizations that were already working to reduce smoking, such as the American Cancer Society (ACS), were urged to focus on smoking among Blacks, and organizations that focused on Blacks, such as the Black Chamber of Commerce, were encouraged to reduce smoking. Although the project mainly targeted African-Americans, members of all ethnic and racial groups were encouraged to participate. White smokers made use of the project's stop-smoking workshops and counseling services. Specific outreach efforts were made to distribute materials in Spanish to Hispanics and to have a presence at their community events.

The project was based at an office in a central Richmond location rented from a Black Richmond businessman. Whenever possible, project funds, such as for printers, artists, and caterers, were spent in Richmond.

IMPLEMENTATION

In the remainder of this section, the project's eight main activities are reviewed in more detail.

(1) Community Advisory Board. Even before the baseline survey was completed, seven Black members of the informal planning group served as a hiring board for the key position of project coordinator. They recommended a candidate who grew up in Richmond, who was hired. Although the rest of the field staff of seven (including three part-time employees and a full-time secretary) were not selected by the hiring board, the board members often expressed approval of them. The intervention staff were African-American and lived in, grew up in, or knew Richmond well. Most had graduate degrees in public health.

1. American Cancer Society.
2. American Heart Association.
3. American Lung Association.

Hunkeler EF: unpublished data
Illustration by B. Andrews.

SOURCE: Hunkeler, unpublished data. Illustration by B. Andrews.

NOTE: Chart describes sectors of the community coordinated by the Richmond Community Advisory Board.

Figure 14.1. The Community Partnership

After the baseline community survey was conducted, a formalized body, the Community Advisory Board, was created to oversee and coordinate the project, which would be a community partnership of local government, neighborhood organizations, religious organizations, local businesses, schools, local media, voluntary health agencies, and the health care community (see Figure 14.1). The Community

Advisory Board had 30 original members, 19 of them Black, including representatives from each of these sectors of the community. Board membership and leadership were stable, and an average of 13 members attended each meeting. The Board met monthly for three years and was still meeting at the time of this publication. Board meetings often included lively debates, during which community leaders expressed widely divergent points of view, particularly regarding the amount of public opposition the project should initiate directly against tobacco companies.

The Board gave the project legitimacy and assured community ownership and relevance; recruited key resources, leaders, and organizations; reviewed policies, procedures, activities, and materials usually prepared by project staff; and provided overall leadership. There were several attempts to organize the Board into regular standing task forces, but, with the exception of an ongoing media task force, the Board preferred to have small working groups with very specific assignments that met once or twice, such as the Quit Night Committee.

The organization and maintenance of an active advisory board of community leaders with diverse interests and agendas was a serious challenge, especially because smoking was not a high priority for community action. Community pride, increased job opportunities, and a positive public image for Richmond were higher priorities. Active participation and support of community leaders was obtained by organizing campaign activities to promote nonsmoking so that these and other related goals were accomplished. For example, commitments were made to hire Richmond residents, to spend project funds in Richmond, and to publicize, if appropriate, the success of the campaign across the nation.

(2) Physician and other medical provider training. Training was developed to increase the number of physicians and other medical providers trained to counsel smokers to quit, to remind providers of their important role in helping patients quit (Russell, Wilson, Taylor, & Baker, 1979; Wilson, Wood, Johnston, & Sicurella, 1982), to increase the number of patients receiving counseling, and to increase awareness of stop-smoking activities in the community. A respected local pathologist conducted the training sessions at grand rounds or in-service education sessions at health and medical facilities in and around Richmond. Project staff arranged the training, consisting of an introductory and a booster session, and provided materials. More than 200 physicians (of about 230 serving Richmond) and 60 other health providers were trained. A system for ongoing distribution of stop-smoking mate-

rials was developed for physicians and patients at seven of the nine health care facilities serving Richmond.

(3) Media. The media component was designed to establish a noticeable community presence for the campaign, to raise consciousness about smoking as a public health issue, to promote a "you can do it" attitude about quitting smoking, and to publicize specific activities and events. From the first press release, and in all other media releases, Richmond was portrayed as a progressive city that had decided to attack smoking because it was concerned about the health of its citizens. Placing emphasis on the community going on the attack against smoking appealed to many segments of the Black and non-Black communities.

Media activities included two campaigns involving billboards, bus posters, and direct mail, as well as two videos, television coverage, a segment on national television, and numerous press conferences and press releases. Some campaigns and activities specifically targeted Blacks; others specifically targeted smokers and young people, and still others were aimed at mobilizing the entire community. These activities generated excitement in the community at crucial points. An ad hoc media task force composed of Community Advisory Board members and staff reviewed and participated in creating all media campaigns and activities. Media campaigns were tested in the community using supermarket surveys, focus groups, and interviews, and all were reviewed by the Board before implementation.

A video to introduce the project, titled *Breakaway*, was created by a respected Black filmmaker; the video starred well-known community leaders, most of them Black, and a popular Black television news anchor. The video gave the impression that everyone in the community was participating in this project. It also had an element of the unexpected. For example, in it, hip-looking (rather than clean-cut-looking) young people talked about quitting smoking because they cared about their health. They encouraged others to do the same.

The first public advertising campaign was developed in conjunction with a Black advertising agency, using focus groups and supermarket surveys. The theme, "Quitters Are Winners" (see Figure 14.2), targeted smokers, associating quitting smoking with positive values. This campaign used billboards, bus posters, and direct mail.

About the time the Quitters Are Winners campaign was launched, the Board began discussing the issue of targeting minorities, women, and young people in the advertisements of the tobacco companies. At that time, the Board was sharply divided over whether this was simply the usual market segmentation used by advertising agencies or whether such targeting was outrageous. Some members expressed concern that the tobacco industry was one of the few funders of special activities and events in the Black community and they did not want to jeopardize this funding. The Board took no formal position on the subject at the time; however, the topic remained alive.

About a year later, a second public advertising campaign was discussed. This time, both the staff and the Board wanted something more provocative done—something that would generate a more visceral response from the community. The theme *Kick Their Butts Out of Richmond* (see Figure 14.2) was recommended by the staff. The board and staff organized a hearing before the City Council that was to be covered by national television. At that hearing, Board members suggested, among other things, that billboards advertising cigarettes be banned from the vicinities of schools, churches, and homes. The campaign included bus posters, direct mail, and television. Specific legislation to ban billboards advertising cigarettes and alcohol within one mile of any Richmond school has since been proposed by the city's Anti-Drug Task Force, which has taken over leadership on the issue. In a preliminary vote, the City Council passed an ordinance prohibiting billboards advertising cigarettes and alcohol within 1000 feet of the schools.

A direct outgrowth of the board's participation in the project was its willingness of the Community Advisory Board to go on record against the tobacco companies. The Board members saw firsthand how difficult it was to make the environment supportive of nonsmoking when billboards and media everywhere encouraged smoking, particularly among young people. The campaign activity that generated the most excitement in the community was the production of a rap music video, *Stop Before You Drop*. The video, which took more than a year to produce, was used as a mobilizing effort. Substantial resources were committed to making this production exciting and highly professional. Over 300 youngsters (280 of them Black) of all ages, from 14 Richmond schools, several youth groups, parents, teachers, community organizations, and local merchants directly participated in and donated resources to the production. The script is a rap created by Richmond youths. The video portrays smoking as undesirable, "uncool," and "unhip," encourages parents to stop smoking for the sake of their children, shows the environmental influences that encourage smoking,

MEDIA CAMPAIGN THEMES

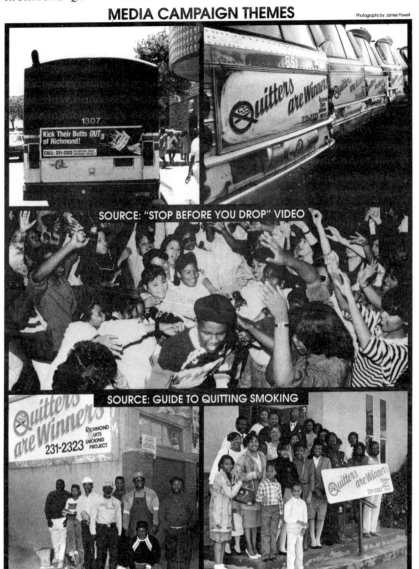

SOURCE: Photographs by James Powell; developed by VWDG.

NOTE: Collage of billboards, posters, and guides to quitting smoking used in the public advertising campaign.

Figure 14.2. Media Campaign Themes

and gives specific information on how to quit. The video production focused the community's attention on smoking by involving its youth in an exciting event that enhanced their self-esteem. News that an MTV-type video was being produced spread quickly once it was clear that the production would actually occur, and numerous newspaper articles appeared about it. The cast rehearsed for months while improving their skills in classes at the local performing arts center. The video was premiered at a gala community event attended by 600 people that included an original live show also written and performed by Richmond youths. The show promoted nonsmoking and discouraged use of illegal drugs. The video is a first-rate production by industry standards and has received national attention and acclaim. It has become a source of great pride and accomplishment throughout the community.

In September 1988, Dan Rather did a five-minute segment on his CBS program *48 Hours* focusing on the production of the video and the *Kick Their Butts Out of Richmond* campaign. In that segment, Richmond was presented as a city truly concerned about health and actively doing things to promote it. In November and December 1989, a prime-time national television special on youth featured a segment on the making of *Stop Before You Drop*.

(4) Stop-smoking materials and services. As is the case with White smokers, Black smokers wanted a variety of services to help them quit. They wanted the services to be relevant to their own experiences and to be easily accessible. Some Black smokers wanted workshops, others wanted individual counseling and self-help materials, while others wanted to quit on their own with encouragement from family and friends. A survey of existing stop-smoking materials and workshops indicated that hardly any were geared to Blacks. To remedy the situation quickly and inexpensively, program staff, with the help of Black smokers, created new stop-smoking self-help materials by reworking existing materials from the NCI. The revisions included changing the tone and making the language more straightforward and the advice more relevant. Pictures of Blacks and some Hispanics and Whites in recognizable locations in Richmond were added. Over 50,000 of these specially developed materials were distributed throughout the course of the project. They included a booklet guide to quitting smoking, a pocket guide with tips for quitting, a resource guide, and a direct-mail piece. The self-help guides were requested by many smokers in the Black community.

Attempts were made in stop-smoking workshops to frame the smoking issue in ways relevant to the concerns of Blacks, particularly regarding family life. The economic burden that smoking-related illness places on Black families and the hazardous effects of secondary smoke on children were stressed. Efforts included conducting workshops at community sites, making them part of regularly scheduled community meetings, and holding them with nonsmokers present. One-session, three-session, and six-session versions were developed and pretested among Black smokers. Two Blacks, one public health nurse and one community relations representative from the project, were trained by the ACS to lead stop-smoking workshops. They tried to make their workshops relevant to the experiences of Blacks. Individual and telephone counseling was available at the project office every day.

Stop-smoking materials were distributed regularly at more than 100 community sites, including restaurants, barber shops, beauty salons, senior centers, grocery stores, churches, recreational centers, youth organizations, the unemployment office, physicians' offices, the police and fire departments, the public library, and the civic center. During the course of the project, more than 100,000 pieces of literature and promotional materials were distributed. Special stop-smoking promotional days were held at selected community sites, and the project participated in the ACS's Great American Smoke-Out. The varied community outreach strategy spread the message to all segments of the Black community, recruited many organizations to the effort, and publicized smoking as a public health problem.

In general, an extremely low-key approach was adopted toward individual smokers because they felt beleaguered already. Services and materials were offered, but often with the proviso "when you're ready."

(5) Mobilization of community organizations. Richmond is a well-organized community with many neighborhood, business, and professional organizations and many youth and church groups. By involving these varied groups in activities related to reducing smoking, all segments of the Black community could be reached. Because the results of our prevalence survey indicated that smoking in the Black population was concentrated among those with lower education, working with organizations that reached these Blacks was a high priority. It was also necessary to reach professional and more affluent Blacks, although fewer of them smoked. They had control of many resources that could assist the effort, and they could also serve as positive role models.

Project staff and volunteers attended all major community events, giving presentations to a wide variety of groups and organizations, including churches, work sites, the neighborhood rescue mission, senior centers, neighborhood councils, and crime-watch groups. These presentations got the antismoking message into Black communication networks. Numerous small events that encouraged nonsmoking, such as no-smoke Sundays at Black churches, no-smoke social events sponsored by the Chamber of Commerce, and a no-smoke open house, were also held. Community volunteers created a play that was presented at schools called "Lungs at Work." Promotional materials with nonsmoking messages printed on them, including church fans, key fobs, and T-shirts, were distributed throughout the community. Ministers promoted nonsmoking in their sermons. Artwork of local artists was displayed prominently in the project office and community groups were encouraged to hold meetings there to enhance the project's presence in the community further. The *Breakaway* video garnered support for the project whenever it was shown to community groups. The priorities of specific community groups and organizations were always integrated into the smoking issue when presentations were made at their meetings. Because some Blacks in Richmond lived in areas where old factories were located, air pollution was a major concern, and the increased health risks of smoking and air pollution combined were often described during presentations. Also, speakers from the project described how smoking had reduced the ability of Black communities to reach their fullest potential because a large number of Blacks were afflicted with smoking-related illnesses.

Throughout the course of the project, several national and statewide events took place that affected people's consciousness about smoking. The Surgeon General declared that nicotine was as addictive as heroin and cocaine. Smoking was banned on airline flights of two hours or less. California voters passed Proposition 99, which added a 25¢ surtax to each package of cigarettes sold. The funds were to be allocated for health education campaigns, physician and hospital services, research, and increased public resources to reduce smoking. After these events, people were much more interested in talking about smoking as a public health problem, and project staff and volunteers increased their community outreach efforts to raise consciousness about smoking and involved more people directly in activities that promoted nonsmoking.

(6) Communitywide events. The project held two main events and had a presence at each of three successive annual "Juneteenth" celebrations, a festival commemorating the abolition of slavery. Juneteenth was attended each of the three years by more than 15,000 Black people. The first event, Quit Night, held early in the project, was attended by about 400 people. Entertainment was provided by a nationally known gospel singer from Richmond, Tremaine Hawkins, as well as by com-

munity youth groups. A city council member made a public pledge to quit smoking. A well-known Black minister asked the audience to quit for at least one day. Over 300 people signed pledge cards saying they would either quit or help a friend quit. The second event was the premiere of the *Stop Before You Drop* video described above. At the Juneteenth celebrations, the project had a booth staffed by Advisory Board members, volunteers distributed stop-smoking materials throughout the crowd, and floats and skits with a nonsmoking theme were developed and performed by Richmond youths.

(7) Schools. Schools were chosen as sites for program activities because smoking generally begins in adolescence (McGinnis, Shopland, & Brown, 1987) and schoolchildren who receive education about the hazards of smoking and the benefits of quitting are more likely to talk to their parents about quitting (Wilcox, Engel, & Reid, 1978; Wilcox, Gillies, Wilcox, & Reid, 1981). Children have been shown to have an impact on the smoking behavior of their parents, other family members, and peers (Rabinowitz & Zimmerli, 1974). Activities in the schools that promoted nonsmoking included poster contests and a newspaper advertisement design contest, building floats for Juneteenth, and producing *Stop Before You Drop*.

The Richmond Unified School District (RUSD) worked closely with program staff and volunteers to remove barriers to implementing the program. Release time was given for the students who participated in the video. Teachers accompanied them on the buses and at the videotaping sessions. In some cases, school credit was given to those who participated. Program staff joined the school's health education task force and worked successfully to have a smoking component for seventh graders included in the mandatory health curriculum. Fifteen teachers were trained to use this component. Teachers from 44 of the 50 RUSD schools were trained to use the video with their classes. During the training sessions they received copies of the video, a discussion guide, and various stop-smoking self-help materials. Focus groups of RUSD teachers helped develop the discussion guide. Plans for widespread and long-term use of the video will be discussed in the section on maintenance.

(8) Volunteer program. At the end of the third year, we developed a volunteer program to increase the social support individuals had for quitting or not starting to smoke. The volunteers were seen as a key element in any plan to sustain the effort in order to promote nonsmoking after federal funding ended.

Volunteers were trained (a) to talk to family members, friends, co-workers, and neighbors about smoking; (b) to offer encouragement and support to young people and ex-smokers trying to stay away from cigarettes and to smokers trying to quit; (c) to identify smokers, determine their readiness to quit smoking, and provide them with appropriate stop-smoking self-help materials; (d) to maintain lists of smoking cessation services and resources and to make appropriate referrals; and (e) to make the social and physical environment more supportive of nonsmoking by establishing support groups, organizing stop-smoking workshops and distribution centers for stop-smoking materials, and promoting communitywide education campaigns.

Volunteers were recruited by project staff through churches, neighborhood councils, and community organizations. All volunteers attended a training session, where they received information about the hazards of smoking, the most effective ways to help smokers quit, stop-smoking materials, and information about available community resources. The training was designed to strengthen leadership and interpersonal skills that volunteers could use in other areas of their lives, such as job interviews or dealing with community issues other than smoking. Unfortunately we trained only 16 volunteers in our program. We had difficulty recruiting volunteers.

INTERIM EVALUATION

A random-digit-dial telephone survey of 400 Richmond residents conducted in August 1989 to determine general awareness of the campaign indicated that over 70% of the respondents knew about one or more of the project's media campaign efforts. The awareness levels were higher among Blacks (76%) and similar for different age groups, educational levels, and smoking statuses (see Table 14.1), indicating that the message was reaching the target population.

Maintenance and Consolidation

As of September 1989, the project was still in the programmatic stage. However, several local organizations, most of them represented on the Community Advisory Board, had already agreed to use their own resources to maintain the effort after NCI funding ended. Activities selected for continuation by the program staff and the Board were chosen because they would keep the issue of smoking in people's minds

Table 14.1

Awareness of Project by Race, Age, Education, and Smoking Status

Strata	N	Percentage
All respondents	400	71
Race		
Black	163	76
Non-Black	229	68
Age (years)		
20-34	136	72
35-54	117	71
≥55	134	73
Education (years)		
<12	67	69
12	114	66
13-15	131	76
≥16	84	74
Smoking status		
current	116	75
former	98	66
never	186	71

SOURCE: Telephone survey of Richmond residents, August 1988, unpublished data.

and provide them with concrete help in their efforts to quit. These activities included the volunteer program, the physician and other health provider training program, the specially tailored stop-smoking services and materials, the videos and discussion guide, and the Board. The organizations targeted to assume responsibility for maintaining these activities were those that had already worked extensively with the project, had resources, and had health improvement as a high priority.

In preparation for direct negotiations with these organizations, program staff drafted a written proposal demonstrating the way in which these groups could help in continuation of the project and how their effort would coincide with their own priorities. Table 14.2 shows each activity and the organization or agency that agreed to continue that part of the project.

While no organization proposed for assuming responsibility for specific program activities was primarily Black, many leaders of organizations described here were. Black organizations planned to continue to participate by distributing materials, showing the rap video, and supporting specific nonsmoking events. Members of the City Council who were on the Board helped project staff prepare a proposal to the

Table 14.2

Organizations and Agencies to Assume Responsibility for Maintenance of the
Richmond Quits Smoking Project

Activity	Personnel/Agency/Organization
Coordination of the volunteer program	Kaiser Permanente Medical Care Program, Richmond
Coordination of physician and other medical provider training	American Cancer Society
Training of physicians and other medical providers	local pathologist
Telephone counseling and free stop smoking workshops	public health nurses Contra Costa County Health Department
Campaign to limit billboards advertising cigarettes and alcohol near schools	City of Richmond Drug Task Force
Coordination of video showings	American Lung Association and Richmond Unified School District
Showing of videos	schools, churches, YMCA and YWCA, Boys' Clubs, Girls' Clubs; Richmond Library; County Health Department; voluntary health associations
Distribution of materials	churches, neighborhood councils; voluntary health associations; schools; health facilities, medical and dental offices; County Health Department; stores, barber shops, beauty parlors, grocery stores, restaurants, other locations
Resources for Campaign Advisory Board	Kaiser Permanente Medical Care Program; Chamber of Commerce, Richmond

city for funds to support part-time staff to oversee the continuation effort, and a volunteer administrative assistant funded by the American Association of Retired Persons was recruited.

The *Stop Before You Drop* video and accompanying discussion guide are being distributed nationally by Durrin Productions, Inc. of Washington, D.C., a commercial distributor. Proceeds generated from distribution of the video will be placed in a special fund, managed by the Kaiser Foundation Research Institute, to support health education activities, health promotion services, and related research and evaluation projects involving the people of the community of Richmond. An advisory committee, including representatives from the Board and other members of the Richmond community, will participate in reviewing and recommending ideas for projects to be supported with these funds.

Dissemination and Reassessment

Data for evaluating the project will come primarily from three sources: the baseline and follow-up household surveys, the observations of the field team, and the data on campaign activities collected by the program staff. The follow-up prevalence survey is scheduled to begin in January 1990. The field observers have been interviewing ministers, school personnel, and participants in the program and observing all project activities. They will continue their observations throughout the maintenance phase.

Several products will be available for use by other communities, including *Stop Before You Drop* and *Breakaway*, a handbook on building health promotion campaigns in Black communities, a volunteer training guide, and a handbook on how to implement a volunteer program similar to the one developed in Richmond.

SUMMARY AND CONCLUSION

A communitywide campaign was developed to reduce the prevalence of cigarette smoking based on the premise that fewer people would smoke if the social and cultural context that surrounds smoking could be made more conducive to nonsmoking. The project was conducted in a predominantly Black community using community organizing strategies tailored to Blacks. The strategies were varied so as to be relevant to the experiences and cultural practices of the different segments of the smoking and nonsmoking population.

The project gained wide community support and participation. It drew much attention to smoking as a public health issue and recruited many organizations to work actively toward reducing smoking among Blacks. Smoking did not achieve the level of community priority of, for example, drug abuse, but it was made enough of an issue that legislation placed before the City Council—to ban billboards advertising cigarettes and alcohol near schools—has a strong chance of being passed. Also, local organizations and agencies plan to continue the effort using their own resources after federal funding ends. It will be another year before results of the follow-up prevalence surveys are available and those of the field observations are analyzed.

As the project progressed, several conclusions about its conduct were reached. First, by involving the community in the earliest planning, the project was able to gain widespread and continuing community support. In conducting the project, we took into account the priorities of the community, even those unrelated to smoking and health. Creating activities that involved young people, such as the video production, resulted in widespread community participation because families and youth and a positive image for Richmond were high priorities for that community. However, when working with youth, it was important to relate to them on their own terms and to allow them to choose the form, style, and content of the health messages directed at them. Establishing credibility by becoming a part of the community's network of organizations helped increase community support and participation, although it meant attending many functions unrelated to smoking or health. Hiring local Black staff and making every effort to spend project funds in the target community gave the project a positive reputation. It was easier to recruit organizations that already had a commitment to improving health to work on reducing smoking among Blacks than it was to add smoking to the agenda of Black organizations that involved or served Blacks in other ways. On the other hand, a number of Black-owned businesses and voluntary associations were willing to distribute project literature and to support project events.

Before this project began, efforts devoted to reducing smoking among Blacks in Richmond were probably similar to those of many other communities. Organizations with resources committed to reducing smoking in the general population did not know how to tailor their efforts to the experiences of Blacks. Black organizations, on the other hand, knew how to reach the different segments of the African-American community but often had few resources to devote to smoking; they were addressing problems they considered to be of higher priority. Time and energy during the course of the project was spent on bringing these two types of organizations together. The effort proved worthwhile. Organizations committed to health expanded their efforts in the Black community. They eventually agreed to be the mainstay of the continuation effort, but with an understanding that their methods had to be tailored to Blacks; Black organizations began to promote non-smoking.

A successful community organizing effort requires maintaining an alliance of diverse groups for a long period. In the course of this project, several successful tactics were devised to assist this effort, including ways to resolve conflicts and divisions. The special interests and agendas of the participating organizations were served whenever possible. Conflicts that arose could usually be defused by emphasizing the common interest in combating smoking. Critics of the program were encouraged to provide feedback and to participate; however, they were asked to offer specific solutions to the problems they identified.

Successful community organizing efforts also require an awareness of local and national events that may affect public sentiment around issues related to the effort. They need built-in flexibility so activities can be initiated to take advantage of unforeseen opportunities to promote the goals of the effort. The main strength of an organized, community-oriented approach is that it can escalate, accelerate, and maintain community trends in positive directions.

In summing up the experience of the project to date, 14 strategies for organizing a community emerged as important for attempts to mobilize an African-American community to promote health. The order of priority will of course vary in different communities and among different segments of the Black population in those communities. Their relative importance depends on the characteristics of the subject populations. The strategies are as follows:

- Involve the community in a meaningful way from the very beginning.
- Use methods tailored to the specific characteristics of that community. Adapt these methods to the values and practices of different segments of the specifically targeted African-American community.
- Embed the program deeply into the existing social organizations and communication channels that reach the smoking and nonsmoking Black population.
- Frame the health issue(s) in ways that unite the entire community in a single cause, as well as in ways that appeal to specifically targeted groups.
- Consider ways to involve other racial and ethnic groups in the program if the target community is multiracial.
- Include activities that increase self-esteem and community pride among Blacks.
- Emphasize winning strategies instead of the magnitude of the problem.

- Channel the influence of families, friends, and co-workers toward promoting nonsmoking.
- Integrate the health issue(s) with the other priorities of the specifically targeted Black community, such as public safety, crime prevention, employment, and drug abuse prevention and control.
- Hire Black staff from the target community and spend project funds in that community.
- Encourage organizations already committed to health improvement to increase the resources they allocate to improving the health of Blacks.
- Mix solid cessation services (e.g., workshops) with exciting and possibly controversial activities that capture the attention and enthusiasm of the entire community, give the campaign real presence, and attract large numbers of participants.
- Enhance the community's existing resources for the effort by bringing in outside funds and support.
- Make plans early to leave a manageable program in the community after outside funding ends.

The preliminary results of our study support the usefulness of targeted interventions. When the final data are in, we will know what was particularly effective with Blacks in Richmond and will have a good sense of how to reduce smoking and other risk factors among Blacks in other communities.

REFERENCES

Billingsley, A. (1974). *Black families and the struggle for survival: Teaching our children to walk tall* (study questions and guide by R. O. Dulin, Jr., & E. L. Foggs). New York: Friendship.

Breslow L. (1982). Control of cigarette smoking from a public policy perspective. *Annual Review of Public Health, 3*, 129-151.

Childs, J. B. (1980). The political Black minister: A study in Afro-American politics and religion. *Reference publications in Afro-American studies*. Boston: G. K. Hall.

Contra Costa County Health Services Department. (1986). *Lung cancer incidence in industrial and non-industrial areas of Contra Costa County from 1970-1984*. Martinez, CA: Author.

Cooke, C. J., & Meyers, A. (1983). The role of community volunteers in health interventions: A hypertension screening and follow-up program. *American Journal of Public Health, 73*, 193-194.

Danigelis, N. L. (1982). Race, class, and political involvement in the U.S. *Social Forces, 61*, 532-550.

Dekker, E. (1976). Youth culture and influences on the smoking behavior of young people. In U.S. Department of Health, Education and Welfare, *Smoking and health: II. Health* consequences, education, cessation activities, and governmental action (proceedings of the Third World Conference on Smoking and Health, New York, June 2-5, 1975; DHEW Publication No. NIH 77-1413). Washington, DC: Government Printing Office.

Eng, E., Hatch, J., & Callan, A. (1985). Institutionalizing social support through the church and into the community. Health Education Quarterly, 12, 81-92.

Fiore, M. C., Novotny, T. E., Pierce, J. P., Hatziandreu, E. J., Patel, K. M., & Davis, R. M. (1989). Trends in cigarette smoking in the United States: The changing influence of gender and race. Journal of the American Medical Association, 261, 49-55.

Frazier, E. F. (1963). The Negro church in America. Liverpool: Liverpool University Press.

Hatch, J. W. (1981). North Carolina Baptist Church program. Urban Health, 10, 70-71.

Hatch, J. W., & Lovelace, K. A. (1980). Involving the southern rural church and students of the health professions in health education. Public Health Report, 95, 23-25.

Hessler, R. M., & Beavert, C. S. (1982). Citizen participation in neighborhood health centers for the poor: The politics of reform and organizational change, 1965-77. Human Organization, 41, 245-255.

McGinnis, J. M., Shopland, D., & Brown, C. (1987). Tobacco and health: Trends in smoking and smokeless tobacco consumption in the United States. Annual Review of Public Health, 8, 441-467.

Moss, A. (1979). Changes in cigarette smoking and current smoking practices among adults. Advance Data, 52, 1-16.

Ockene, J. K., Hymowitz, N., Sexton, M., & Broste, S. K. (1982). Comparison of patterns of smoking behavior change among smokers in the Multiple Risk Factor Intervention Trial (MRFIT). Preventive Medicine, 11, 621-638.

Rabinowitz, H. S., & Zimmerli, W. H. (1974). Effects of a health education program on junior high school students' knowledge, attitudes and behavior concerning tobacco use. Journal of School Health, 44, 324-326.

Russell, M. A. H., Wilson, C., Taylor, C., & Baker, C. D. (1979). Effect of general practitioner's advice against smoking. British Medical Journal, 2, 231-235.

Stack, C. B. (1974). All our kin: Strategies for survival in a black community. New York: Harper & Row.

Syme, S. L., & Alcalay, R. (1982). Control of cigarette smoking from a social perspective. Annual Review of Public Health, 3, 179-199.

U.S. Department of Commerce, Bureau of the Census. (1983). 1980 census of population and housing: Neighborhood statistics program. Washington, DC: Government Printing Office.

U.S. Department of Health and Human Services. (1983). The health consequences of smoking: Cardiovascular disease: A report of the surgeon general. Washington, DC: Government Printing Office.

Wilcox, B., Engel, E., & Reid, D. (1978). Smoking education in children: UK trials of an international project. International Journal of Health Education, 21, 236-244.

Wilcox, B., Gillies, P., Wilcox, S., & Reid, D. (1981). Do children influence their parents' smoking? An investigation of parental smoking behaviour and attitudes to health education. Health Education Journal, 40(1), 5-10.

Wilson, D., Wood, G., Johnston, N., & Sicurella, J. (1982). Randomized clinical trial of supportive follow-up for cigarette smokers in a family practice. Canadian Medical Association Journal, 126, 127-129.

Chapter 15

BUILDING A POSITIVE IMAGE OF AGING
The Experience of a Small American City

DONALD W. KEMPER
MOLLY METTLER

This case study is about the efforts made in one American city to recognize aging as a positive experience for its citizens. In 1979, Healthwise, Inc., a not-for-profit health promotion research center, worked with a coalition of government, community, and business people in Boise, Idaho, to launch a long-term and continuing effort to improve the lives of its "60 and better" population. Through a combination of grass-roots organizing and public and private sector funding, more than 20% of the city's older adults have participated in a series of health-enhancing activities.

This case study describes the activities, the issues surrounding their development, and the impact they have had on healthy public policy at local, state, national, and international levels. A brief discussion of the aging experience is presented, followed by aspects of the project's design, initiation, implementation, and maintenance.

AGING: POSITIVE OR NEGATIVE?

Charlotte, at age 68, is concerned about her future. Widowed, separated from her adult children, and retired from a job she enjoyed, Charlotte feels her world is closing in on her. Her options seem to be disappearing. Her friends talk constantly about forgetfulness and mental decline. Her own memory seems to be slipping. Charlotte is concerned that she is "getting senile."

Marge, at 68, is convinced that life is filled with opportunities—all she needs to do is reach out for them. She reads a lot, is active in several community groups, and fully enjoys her life. Marge jokes about her "slow memory," but she is the first to point out that getting older has brought its gifts.

The differences in the lives of Charlotte and Marge lie in the competing and contradictory visions of senility or wisdom as the foundation of old age. One of the greatest problems of aging is the set of negative beliefs that society associates with growing older. Popularly held misconceptions that old age inevitably brings senility, memory failure, feebleness, and loss of productivity have a major impact on the quality of life for older adults. In the United States and other "graying" countries, this problem must be vigorously addressed. Housing, employment, and health care options for seniors are often narrowly defined in light of ageist assumptions.

Perhaps the most destructive aspect of the negative image of aging is its effect on the expectations of the older individual. People who are constantly exposed to a societal image of the older person as slow, senile, useless, and uninteresting will think of themselves as slower, less mentally sharp, less useful, and less interesting as they grow older. As self-esteem drops, the older person becomes less motivated to stay involved with friends, neighbors, and community groups. This disengagement is worsened by the belief that other "old" people are also frail and feebleminded.

These negative beliefs are untrue or greatly exaggerated. The great majority of older adults maintain their intelligence, judgment, and interests in life as long as they live. Even so, these myths can become self-fulfilling. Isolation, whether self-imposed or not, can reduce a person's ability to function in society. The citizens in one small American city undertook to confront this negative image of aging and to address the possibilities inherent in a vigorous, healthy, and productive older population.

THE BOISE EXPERIENCE

Boise, Idaho, is a city of 102,000 people in the northwestern United States. Historically supported as a timber, mining, and agricultural center, the city and its economy have broadened to include light manufacturing, high-technology electronics, and tourism. It has also become a regional center for banking, trade, government, and higher education. In 1980, the population of Boise included 8,600 people over 65. This population was served by a single senior citizens' center operated by the city with funding support from county, state, and federal agencies.

Boise is also the location of Healthwise, Inc., a not-for-profit center for health education research and development. Since its founding in 1975, Healthwise has become nationally acclaimed for its efforts to improve the quality of medical self-care for young families and for a wide range of other health promotion publications and programs.

In 1979, at the urging of its volunteer board, Healthwise became interested in educational programs to improve the health of older people. At that time very little research had been conducted in the area of health promotion for older adults. After discussions with a wide variety of health professionals, health agencies, and voluntary health organizations, a rather bleak picture developed. The consensus of this review of professionals can be summed up as follows:

(1) Most older people were not interested in changing health behavior.
(2) Of those who were interested, their habits were too ingrained for them to change.
(3) Even if they did improve their health habits, it was too late to do much good.

Over the last eight years, the health planners and educators, nurses, and social workers who make up the Healthwise team have been able to show in dramatic ways that all three beliefs are part of the myths, not the reality, of aging.

The first step taken toward assessing community interest and readiness came when Healthwise conducted surveys of older adults themselves. In discussions with seniors from the Boise Council on Aging, the program team received encouraging signs for gerontological health promotion. The older adults assured the team that health was one of their greatest interests, that they could take the time necessary to make health improvements, and that it would make an important difference to them. With that expressed need and promise, Healthwise, in partnership with the Boise Council on Aging, set out again to gain support for a health promotion program for older adults.

DEVELOPING A VISION FOR THE FUTURE:
EARLY DESIGN AND INITIATION

At an early meeting between Healthwise and the Boise Council on Aging, a senior brought in the January 1973 issue of *National Geographic* magazine, which had a cover article titled "Every Day Is a Gift When You Are Over 100" (Leaf & Launois, 1973). The article described three regions known for their long-lived peoples: Soviet Georgia; Vilcabamba, Ecuador; and Hunza, Kashmir. In all three regions, people of great age were shown to play active, respected, and vital roles in their communities. The photographs presented a favorable image of aging in which people looked forward to growing old. This article embodied the vision for the project. The team set its long-term goal of creating in Boise an image of aging so vital and positive that by the next time *National Geographic* did an article on long-lived peoples, it would include Boise as a featured city.

Coalition Building

With this vision, Healthwise and the Boise Council on Aging set about building a broad coalition of support for the project. Pairs of project staffers and senior volunteers visited most large employers in the Boise area. While the purpose of the meetings was to ask for help only in getting word out about the project, many employers showed their support more directly by contributing funds or materials to the program. At the community level, the coalition included the Boise School District, the YMCA and YWCA, two local hospitals, Boise State University, and the District Health Department. At the state level, the Idaho State Office on Aging and the Idaho Division of Health provided encouragement and statements of support. The coalition was never formalized, but the interagency connections that it fostered have led to many cooperative projects between the Boise Senior Center and other community organizations.

Most important, a large number of older people committed themselves to working on the project. Where possible, every effort was made to work with senior volunteers who had personal connections with the organizations to be visited (e.g., retirees from corporations or current board members). This extra effort at networking resulted in many more open doors for the project. Also, individuals active at the Boise Senior Center and involved with local senior citizens' groups came forward to serve on three working committees: an overall steering committee, a medical advice committee (consisting primarily of health professionals), and a public support committee.

The committees were directly involved with reviewing the text of the handbooks and the scripts of the workshops. Debates were encouraged over any controversial content areas, and in most cases major revisions followed the committee reviews. The opinions of the seniors were highly regarded by the health professionals involved.

Implementation: State and Federal Coordination

In October 1980, Healthwise was awarded a contract ($137,572) by the state of Idaho to create Growing Younger, "a risk reduction program seeking measurable reductions in health risks among senior citizens" (see Kemper, Guiffré, & Deneen, 1981). It was the first such contract executed in the State of Idaho. Further funding for the project was approved by the U.S. Department of Health and Human Services Centers for Disease Control (CDC) as part of its national health risk-reduction program. The Boise program was the only one approved nationally to focus on the health risks of older adults. Over the next three years, additional funds (exceeding $250,000) from the state of Idaho and the CDC were granted as part of the prevention block grant program to complete program development and evaluation.

GROWING YOUNGER:
A PHYSICAL WELLNESS PROGRAM

The premise behind the development of the Growing Younger program is that everyone has two ages: a chronological age, based on how long one has lived, and a health age, which is determined by how one feels and how healthy one is. One cannot reduce one's chronological age, but all of us can lower our health ages and, in a very real sense, grow younger. (For more on wellness in old age, see Dychtwald, 1986; FallCreek & Mettler, 1984.)

While designed as a risk-reduction program, Growing Younger also undertook to address social and attitudinal changes, specifically quality-of-life issues and community attitudes toward the elderly. The program developers were firmly convinced that if a community raises its general expectations about aging, older adults will find it much easier to pursue and to succeed at health promotion activities.

The Workshop Program: Emphasis on Positive Health

Through a series of four 2-hour workshops, Growing Younger helps older adults lower their health age. These sessions focus on exercise, nutrition, relaxation, and self-care. Participants learn the following:

- how to improve flexibility, strength, and endurance
- how to improve their diet gradually without big sacrifices
- how to relieve muscle tension and stress
- how to improve the quality of care they get both at home and from their physicians

In the workshop series, strong emphasis is put on learn-by-doing activities that build knowledge, skills, and friendships among participants. For example, participants practice a soothing shoulder and neck massage on each other and team up to research the side effects of certain medications.

Growing Younger delivers its educational messages with a light touch. Jokes and skits used to illustrate important health points, such as drinking more water and patient-doctor communication, are well received. Participants also particularly appreciate the opportunity to break away from a traditional lecture format and use a more informal, small group approach to learning.

Maintenance of Program Effort

Activities are generally performed in pairs or small groups. If desired, the groups then practice and discuss the skills and information at informal weekly meetings in participants' homes or in other settings. The addition of the informal groups, in effect, doubles the intensity of the program without adding to the cost. The process also establishes a pattern of continued social support after the workshops are completed. Some of these "neighborhood groups" have been meeting weekly for the past seven years.

To promote further enthusiasm for self-care, participants receive useful health aids at each of the four sessions. The aids (penlight, cryogel cold/hot pack, thermometer and magnifier, sunscreen, and an exercise "stretchie" band) are used as focal points for opening activities in the workshops and then as aids for the continued development of self-care skills at home. All content described in the workshops and additional topics of interest such as sexuality and medical consumerism are covered in the *Growing Younger Handbook*, which each participant receives for both workshop and home use.

Participation and Program Impact on Health Risks

During the first 30 months, 1,658 older adults (12% of Boise's 60 and over population) participated in the program. Since that time, the number has grown to more than 3,500 seniors in Boise. The participants have been mostly women (77.3%) and have had an average age of 70 years.

Funding from the CDC Office on Health Education and Risk Reduction stipulated that Growing Younger test the effect of the program on its Boise participants. The results were encouraging. Questionnaire responses prior to and six months following the program found statistically significant positive changes in fitness, nutrition, stress/social, and medical care behaviors. Biometric results were also positive. Six-month posttests showed that, on the average, Growing Younger participants lost weight, reduced body fat, lowered their blood pressure and cholesterol levels, and improved their flexibility. All measures were statistically significant at the .05 level.

The Community Responds:
Grass-Roots Reaction and Diffusion

In Boise, Growing Younger inspired a number of spin-off activities for older adults. Most visible among these are the Happy Hoofers, a walking group that meets twice a week, rain or shine, to hike three to eight miles. There are 200 older adults on the Happy Hoofer roster, and the group is well known throughout the city. Other spin-offs have included greatly expanded exercise and swim classes at the YMCA, an annual picnic, and an official fun walk.

One of the most significant outgrowths of the program was the development of Growing Wiser, a mental wellness companion program to Growing Younger (see Kemper, Mettler, Guiffré, & Matzek, 1986). As their physical health improved, Growing Younger graduates expressed interest in having a program to enhance their mental health. They followed through with that interest, too; of the first 600 graduates of the Growing Wiser program in Boise, 63% were also Growing Younger graduates.

GROWING WISER:
A MENTAL WELLNESS PROGRAM

In 1985, the Fred Meyer Charitable Trust of Portland, Oregon, awarded Healthwise a two-year grant of $236,920 to develop, demonstrate, and evaluate a communitywide approach to promote the independence and mental wellness of older adults in the Boise area.

The Workshop Program

The new Growing Wiser program follows the same format of four 2-hour sessions as Growing Younger, but focuses on the five content areas of memory, mental alertness, coping with loss and life change, maintaining independence, and self-image. It uses a participant handbook, *Growing Wiser: The Older Person's Guide to Mental Wellness*, which contains detailed information and references to the program topics.

Memory. Growing Wiser participants learn how memory works, how it is organized in the brain, how it is affected by aging, and how to make it work better. Participants learn memory techniques to improve name-face recall. They also learn how to protect memory through medication management and good nutrition. Most important, they learn that with age, a "memory shift" occurs. With this shift comes a greater ability to integrate the memories of a lifetime and to extract meaning from one's experiences. It is the very basis of wisdom.

Mental alertness. One of the most persistent myths of aging is that mental decline is inevitable, often expressed as "You can't teach an old dog new tricks." In Growing Wiser, participants learn that the human brain does not wither with age and that mental vitality can be a lifelong attribute.

Loss and life change. Program participants share examples of life changes they have experienced and the wisdom they may have gained from these changes. By better understanding the stages of grief and how best to help others who are experiencing life changes, Growing Wiser participants also gain perspective on accepting and assimilating their own losses.

Choices for living. In this component of the program, participants learn about the importance of social networks and good communication skills. Participants also learn about community resources that help people maintain independent status.

Self-image. Positive self-esteem and a raised self-image are the foundations of Growing Wiser; they are the glue that holds all of the other topics together. In building self-esteem, the negative myths of aging are confronted and replaced with more positive expectations.

Through a dramatic skit, Growing Wiser personifies the myths of aging and puts them in the character of the Naysayer. The program suggests that many people have a Naysayer within who believes in the myths of aging and who is ready to put limits on opportunities and growth. It is the Naysayer who says "you can't" instead of "you can."

The program also suggests that most people have a Sage inside them, too. The Sage is a wise adviser who puts challenges in perspective and who has positive expectations for the future. Growing Wiser participants learn to recognize their internal Sage and to call it forth to dispel the myths of aging. The Sage almost always wins.

To uncover the Sage within, the Growing Wiser formula was developed. It is a step-by-step approach to recognizing and debunking the myths of aging and replacing them with more positive expectations. Participants have ranked the Growing Wiser formula as one of the most valuable parts of the program and one they continue to use.

Program Participation and Impact

During the 18-month evaluation period, 578 senior citizens participated. Of this group, 77% were female; the average age was 71.1. A pre- and four-month postparticipation administration of a 15-question geriatric depression scale indicated a 24% improvement in risk of depression, a major risk factor for institutionalization and morbidity. Memory performance on a name-face memory test also improved.

The Community Responds

As with Growing Younger and the Happy Hoofers, Growing Wiser generated its own spin-off group. The Meeting of Minds Society is a discussion group that meets weekly at the Boise Senior Center. The group has developed a guide on how to start a society such as theirs and has made it available to other interested seniors. At this writing, six additional groups have begun their own Meeting of Minds in other communities. These activities suggest that long-term maintenance of program effort is likely, and that local "ownership" is growing. Such programs also provide evidence of wider diffusion of health promotion efforts.

OVERALL PROGRAM IMPACT ON PUBLIC POLICY
AND THE IMAGE OF AGING

The impact that Growing Younger and Growing Wiser have had on health risk factors has been relatively easy to quantify. While less directly measurable, the impact that these programs have had on public policy and the community's image of aging is nevertheless readily apparent.

Local Policy

Changes were first noted in policies at the Boise Senior Center. The programs resulted in a shift in center use priorities from general recreation to health promotion and educational activities. Attendance for health promotion functions has increased at three times the rate of increase for other purposes.

Greater awareness of good nutrition by Growing Younger participants also led to changes in the local senior nutrition program. Seniors lobbied the Area Agency on Aging to modify its interpretation of federal and state meal service regulations to allow for salad bars and lighter alternatives to the standard nutritious but higher-calorie meals. Such changes were subsequently adopted at other centers.

Local changes were also evident at St. Luke's Regional Medical Center, which became a cosponsor of the programs beginning in 1983 and took over their local management in 1987. During that time, the hospital has greatly expanded its services to older people and created a Senior Life Center to serve their needs better.

City and State Policy

At the municipal and state levels, both the city of Boise and the state of Idaho have identified health and wellness promotion for seniors as a major budgetary area of support for aging services. In addition, five other states using Growing Younger and/or Growing Wiser as program models have adopted statewide policies to promote good health practices for seniors.

National Implications

On a national scale, Growing Younger and Growing Wiser programs are now sponsored in well over 100 communities in 30 states. In every community, the programs have made inroads into raising the image of aging among both the general population and local policymakers. This work has twice been recognized by the U.S. Department of Health and Human Service's prestigious Secretary's Award of Excellence in Community Health Promotion. In addition, Growing Younger and Growing Wiser have been showcased as model programs by the Centers for Disease Control, the American Society on Aging, and the National Council on Aging.

CONCLUSION

Efforts to create a positive image of aging for one small city have led to the creation of the internationally acclaimed Growing Younger and Growing Wiser programs, which have now been replicated in more than 120 cities and towns on two continents. Issues of project design, initiation, implementation, maintenance, and diffusion have been discussed.

If the original vision of the Growing Younger and Growing Wiser programs is to be accomplished, it will come about through a gradual raising of the image of aging in those communities where the programs are sponsored. It is hoped that once policymakers in business, government, health care, education, and other sectors begin to see older adults in a more positive context, policies that affect their employment, housing, health care, and general social standing will begin to change.

The experience of the city of Boise, Idaho, is a modest one. Improvements have occurred, but far more work is needed to assure that those improvements are maintained and extended. Other cities, states, and nations face similar challenges. The image of aging is a determinant of health for older people. Public policymakers who find ways to rebuild that image will strengthen the lives and the health of the people they serve.

REFERENCES

Dychtwald, K. (1986). *Wellness and health promotion for the elderly.* Rockville, MD: Aspen.

FallCreek, S., & Mettler, M. (1984). *A healthy old age: A sourcebook for health promotion with older adults* (rev. ed.). New York: Haworth.

Kemper, D., Guiffré, J., & Deneen, J. (1981). *Growing Younger.* Boise, ID: Healthwise.

Kemper, D., Mettler, M., Guiffré, J., & Matzek, B. (1986). *Growing Wiser: The older person's guide to mental wellness.* Boise, ID: Healthwise.

Leaf, A., & Launois, J. (1973). Every day is a gift when you are over 100. *National Geographic, 143*(1), 15-27.

ABOUT THE EDITOR

NEIL BRACHT holds faculty positions in both the School of Public Health and the School of Social Work at the University of Minnesota. Previously, he has served as Director of the School of Social Work at Minnesota. Prior to that, he was Assistant Dean for Health Affairs at the University of Washington School of Social Work in Seattle (1971-1978) and Assistant Dean, College of Medicine, Michigan State University (1966-1970). He was a Visiting Professor of Social Medicine at Karolinska University, Stockholm, in 1987 and a Visiting Professor of Community Health Sciences at Lund University in Malmo, Sweden, in 1989. Currently, he is a Visiting Scientist at the Fred Hutchinson Cancer Research Center and in the Department of Health Services at the University of Washington's School of Public Health and Community Medicine, Seattle. He also serves as a consultant to the European Healthy Cities project in the Office of Health Promotion, World Health Organization, Copenhagen.

Professor Bracht's scholarly work and publications contribute to the developing disciplines of behavioral epidemiology and applied community-based health interventions. He is a recognized expert on the application of community organization theory and citizen participation strategies to comprehensive community health promotion programs. For the past 10 years, he has been Director of Community Organization and Coinvestigator for the Minnesota Heart Health Program, a research and demonstration project to reduce heart disease and stroke in three midwestern cities. He is a consultant for the National Cancer Institute's 11-community study on smoking cessation (COMMIT), and has just completed an evaluation of the effectiveness of a standardized community mobilization protocol used in these diverse sites. He is the 1990 recipient of the Swedish Medical Research Council's Visiting Scientist Fellowship.

Professor Bracht received his undergraduate degree in Psychology from Loyola University (Chicago) and his graduate degree in Social Work from the School of Social Service Administration, University of Chicago. His graduate public health degree (Medical Care Administration) was received from the School of Public Health at the University of Michigan (Ann Arbor).

ABOUT THE CONTRIBUTORS

CESAREO AMEZCUA, Ph.D., is Faculty Associate and Director of Community Organization and Training at the University of Texas, Health Science Center at Houston.

DIANA CASSADY is a M.P.H. doctoral candidate at the School of Public Health at the University of California, Berkeley.

KITTY CORBETT, Ph.D., M.P.H., is in the Division of Research at the Kaiser Permanente Medical Care Program, Northern California Region, Oakland.

EDITH M. DAVIS, M.P.H., is Community Relations Specialist in community and governmental relations at the Kaiser Permanente Medical Care Program, Northern California Region, Oakland.

RENATO ESPINOZA, Ph.D., M.P.H., is at the University of Texas, Health Science Center at Houston.

JUNE A. FLORA, Ph.D., is Assistant Professor in the Department of Communication, Stanford University, Stanford, California.

RUSSELL E. GLASGOW, Ph.D., is Research Scientist at the Oregon Research Institute, Eugene, Oregon.

JULIE GLEASON, Ph.D., is Consultant in the Center for Health Promotion at the Michigan Department of Public Health in Lansing.

LAWRENCE W. GREEN, Dr.P.H., is Director, Health Promotion Programs, and Vice President, Henry J. Kaiser Family Foundation in Menlo Park, California.

BO HAGLUND, M.D., is affiliated with the Department of Social Medicine at Karolinska Institute, Sundbyberg, Sweden.

ENID FALLICK HUNKELER is Senior Investigator in the Division of Research, Kaiser Permanente Medical Care Program, Northern California Region, Oakland.

DONALD W. KEMPER, M.S.I.E., M.P.H., is Executive Director of Healthwise, Inc. in Boise, Idaho.

LEE KINGSBURY, R.H.Ed., is Health Education Consultant in the Division of Health Promotion Education, Minnesota Department of Health in Minneapolis.

SUSAN KINNE, Ph.D., is Staff Scientist at the Fred Hutchinson Cancer Research Center in Seattle, Washington.

R. CRAIG LEFEBVRE, Ph.D., is Intervention Coordinator at Pawtucket Heart Health Program, Memorial Hospital and he is an Associate Professor of Community Health at Brown University, Providence, Rhode Island.

RUSSELL V. LUEPKER, M.D., is Professor in the Division of Epidemiology and the Department of Medicine in the School of Public Health, University of Minnesota in Minneapolis.

ALFRED McALISTER, Ph.D., is Associate Director of Administration and Community Health Promotion at the Center for Health Promotion Research and Development, University of Texas Health Science Center at Houston.

BESSANDERSON McNEIL, M.P.H., is Program Director of the Optifast Program at Providence Hospital, Oakland, California.

MOLLY METTLER, M.S.W., is National Program Director at Healthwise, Inc. in Boise, Idaho.

MAURICE B. MITTELMARK, Ph.D., is Associate Professor of Public Health Sciences (Epidemiology) at the Bowman Gray School of Medicine, Wake Forest University, Winston-Salem, North Carolina.

GUY S. PARCEL, Ph.D., is Director of the Center for Health Promotion Research and Development and a Professor at the University of Texas Health Science Center at Houston.

CHERYL L. PERRY, Ph.D., is Associate Professor in the Division of Epidemiology in the School of Public Health, University of Minnesota in Minneapolis.

PHYLLIS L. PIRIE, Ph.D., is Associate Professor in the Division of Epidemiology in the School of Public Health, University of Minnesota in Minneapolis.

MICHAEL R. POLEN, MA, is Senior Research Associate at the Center for Health Research, the Division of Research Kaiser Permanente Medical Care Program Northwest Region, Portland, Oregon.

JAMES W. POWELL, BA, is Community Relations Representative at Kaiser Permanente Medical Care Program, Northern California Region, Oakland.

JOHN RAEBURN, Ph.D., is Associate Professor and the Head of the Department of Behavioral Science in the School of Medicine at the University of Auckland, New Zealand.

AMELIE RAMIREZ, M.P.H., is Faculty Associate and the Director of Media Development at the University of Texas Health Science Center at Houston.

LENNART RÅSTAM, M.D., Ph.D., is Associate Profesor in the Department of Community Health Services at Lund University in Malmo, Sweden.

GLORIAN SORENSEN, Ph.D., M.P.H., is an Assistant Professor of Medicine, Preventive and Behavioral Medicine, at the University of Massachusetts Medical School at Worcester.

WENDELL C. TAYLOR, Ph.D., M.P.H., is Assistant Professor in the Center for Health Promotion at the University of Texas Health Science Center at Houston.

BETI THOMPSON, Ph.D., is Assistant Professor at the University of Washington School of Public Health and Community Medicine and she is an Assistant Member at the Fred Hutchinson Cancer Research Center in Seattle.

RITA R. WEISBROD, Ph.D., is Research Associate in the Division of Epidemiology at the School of Public Health, University of Minnesota in Minneapolis.